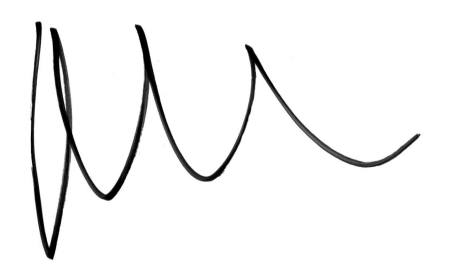

MARK
BITTMAN'S
KITCHEN
MATRIX

MARK
BITTMAN'S
KITCHEN
MATRIX

More Than 700 Simple Recipes and Techniques
to Mix and Match for Endless Possibilities

Pam Krauss Books
New York

Also by Mark Bittman

A Bone to Pick

VB6: Eat Vegan Before 6:00 to Lose Weight and Regain Your Health… for Good

The VB6 Cookbook

How to Cook Everything

How to Cook Everything, the Basics

How to Cook Everything Vegetarian

How to Cook Everything Fast

Kitchen Express

Food Matters

The Food Matters Cookbook

The Minimalist

The Minimalist Entertains

The Minimalist at Home

Copyright © 2015 by Mark Bittman

All rights reserved.
Published in the United States by Pam Krauss Books, an imprint of the Crown Publishing Group, a division of Penguin Random House LLC, New York. www.crownpublishing.com

PAM KRAUSS BOOKS and colophon are trademarks of Penguin Random House LLC.

Library of Congress Cataloging-in-Publication Data
Bittman, Mark, author.
Mark Bittman's kitchen matrix/Mark Bittman—First Edition.
1. Cooking. I. Title.
TX714.B573226 2015
641.5—dc23 2015020733

Selected essays and photographs were previously published in *The New York Times Magazine* column "Eat" between 2011 and 2015.

ISBN 978-0-8041-8801-2
eBook ISBN 978-0-8041-8802-9

Printed in China

Book and cover design by Kelly Doe and Emily Crawford
Cover photographs by Yunhee Kim and (center) Sam Kaplan

10 9 8 7 6 5 4 3 2 1

First Edition

Photograph Credits:

Ian Allen: pages 242–243

Claire Benoist: pages 228–229

William and Susan Brinson: pages 190–191, 212.

Levi Brown: pages 106, 222

Sam Kaplan: pages 16–17, 20–23, 32–33, 36–37, 42–43, 54–57, 74–77, 92–93, 98–103, 112–113, 120–124, 126–127, 130–132, 136–137, 140–143, 150–163, 165, 178–179, 185–189, 210, 216–217, 230–231, 237, 240–241, 244–245, 252–253, 260–265, 267, 278–279, 286–287

Yunhee Kim: pages 12–15, 24–31, 38–41, 44–50, 60–73, 78–83, 88–91, 94–97, 108–111, 116–119, 128–129, 140, 144–149, 166, 168–173, 176–177, 180–184, 192–193, 198, 200–203, 208–209, 214, 218–221, 224–225, 232–235, 248–251, 254–259, 270–271, 272–277, 282–285, 288–291

Brian Klutch: pages 206–207, 236, 238–239

Marcus Nilsson: pages 18–19, 104–105, 196–197, 292–293,

Victor Prado: page 52

Annie Schlechter: pages 84–87

Ralph Smith: pages 280–281

Evan Sung: pages 134–135

ACKNOWLEDGMENTS

The "Eat" column—which began its run in *The New York Times Magazine* in 2011, and continues, though in a different form—had a number of key and consistent influences and sources of energy. Hugo Lindgren not only gave me the job but let me run with it; Matt Willey and Kelly Doe understood the kind of column I wanted to put together and came up with the wonderful design that was then represented in the magazine for more than three years. Gail Bichler further refined it, constantly. Amy Kellner supervised all the photo shoots and, as you can see, some of them were doozies. Bill Ferguson and Claire Gutierrez edited almost all of the stories. The photographs were mostly shot by Yunhee Kim and Sam Kaplan, and much of the cooking and food styling was done by Maggie Ruggiero and my friend Suzanne Lenzer.

Many other people were involved in producing the original pieces: Arem Duplessis, Jason Stefko, Sara Cwynar, Joel Lovell, Lauren Kern, Laura Anderson, Daniel Meyer, Kerri Conan, Meghan Gourley, Eve Turow, Elena Goldblatt, Brian Klutch, Ian Allen, Evan Sung, Claire Benoist, Victor Prado, Marcus Nilsson, Levi Brown, William Brinson, Annie Schlechter, Tom Schierlitz, Ralph Smith, Maggie Ruggiero, Claudia Ficca, Michelle Gatton, Karen Evans, Michaela Hayes, Susan Ottaviano, Jamie Kimm, Chelsea Zimmer, Chris Lanier, Brian Preston-Campbell, Brett Kurzweil, Mariana Velasquez, Paul Grimes, Megan Schlow, Maeve Sheridan, Theo Vamvounakis, Deborah Williams, Raina Kattelson, Angharad Bailey, Kira Corbin, Susan Brinson, Randi Brookman Harris, Kaitlyn Du Ross, Caroline Colston, Bettina Budewig, Leslie Siegel, and Megan Hedgpeth.

Like I said—a lot of people. So when it came time to turn this beautiful mass into a book, we had great material. Here there was a group of people I work closely with, admire, and am indebted to: Daniel Meyer did both grunt and fine work during what I hope is not our last time working together. Kerri Conan provided her usual wisdom and experience. Pam Krauss and Angela Miller ran the show. Kelly Doe, with Emily Crawford, converted the magazine pieces to a book-friendly design and format, which has worked beautifully. Thanks also to Merri Ann Morrell, who did such an incredible and fast job on composition, and also Michael Nagin, Mark McCauslin, Linnea Knollmueller, Stephanie Huntwork, Lauren Monchik, Carly Gorga, Anna Mintz, and Kate Tyler.

None of this would have been possible without Kelly.

CONTENTS

INTRODUCTION

For years I've said, "If you can cook 10 recipes, you can cook 10,000," and while I've always felt it was true, I've never believed it more strongly than I do right now. Writing this book has convinced me all over again that from simple recipes spring nearly endless possibilities.

Real home cooking, to borrow an old but apt cliché, is a marathon, not a sprint. It's something you do day to day, week to week, season to season, year to year, forever. Most of us who cook on a regular basis don't constantly come up with brilliant and innovative dishes—I'd probably be out of ideas in a month—nor do we slavishly following recipes to the letter; I'd be bored in a week. Instead, we stake out a sweet spot somewhere in the middle; we learn how to cook a handful of basic dishes—salad and vinaigrette, tomato sauce, or soup, for instance—and what to do with everyday ingredients, like chicken breasts, shrimp, or potatoes. As soon as we're comfortable with core recipes and techniques we begin to improvise, swapping cilantro for parsley, say, or braising in coconut milk instead of wine, or grilling instead of broiling. We embrace the small but meaningful variations that can transform the identity of a dish, make an old favorite taste like a new creation, and turn a modest repertoire of recipes into a lifetime of wonderful meals.

This book showcases and encourages the kind of creativity and flexibility that make daily cooking not just doable but also pleasurable. And it takes little more than a glance at the chapters here— "Apples, 12 Ways," "Slaw, 8 Ways," "Leg of Lamb, 3 Ways"—you get the idea: to figure out my fundamental approach, pick an ingredient or a dish and see just how many things you can do with it. The result is a collection that looks quite different from anything I've done before, and thanks to the stunning photography, more beautiful. The recipes come in multiple guises: some are conventional with ingredient lists and steps; others are more radical with directions scarcely longer than a tweet. Many are meant to facilitate improvisation in the kitchen, catering to all sorts of cooking styles and preferences.

Whether you like to stick to the script or cook off the cuff, undertake all-day projects or bang out fast weeknight meals, plan a detailed menu or shop first and ask questions later, there is something here for you. With this combination of recipes, art, and text I hope to depict as richly and inventively as I can just how infinitely gratifying cooking can be.

GROUND RULES

1. **All recipes** serve four unless otherwise noted.

2. **Salt and pepper** is assumed for every recipe (except desserts) where it's not mentioned explicitly. Use your judgment, but do use salt.

3. When **neutral oil** is specified you can use grapeseed or corn oil (safflower and sunflower are fine too).

4. **Olive oil** means extra-virgin.

5. All **lemon and lime juice** should be fresh.

6. All **butter** is unsalted.

7. All **cream** is heavy (whipping) cream.

8. **Flour** is all-purpose unless otherwise specified.

9. For **scallions**, use both white and green parts unless specified.

10. For **ingredients** that don't have specific quantities listed, use your judgment and taste, taste, taste.

APPETIZERS AND ENTERTAINING

Even for seasoned home cooks, the idea of entertaining can be daunting. But it doesn't have to be. For the most part, any dish that's good enough to cook for yourself is good enough to serve to a crowd (and there's not a recipe in this chapter or any other that I'd hesitate to make for guests). What you'll find here ranges from simple snack foods, like dips and chicken wings, to "fancy" fare, like tartare. None of it is particularly onerous to prepare, which helps eliminate needless panic and lets you pay as much (or more) attention to your guests as to the food you're serving them. There are also plenty of other apps, hors d'oeuvre, and dinner party showstoppers scattered throughout the book—deviled eggs (page 179) and Cassoulet (page 198), to name just a few.

To take the stress out of entertaining, look no further than the finger-food recipe generator, a fairly effortless and nearly endless roster of canapés that you can whip up from simple ingredients in no time. Or, consult the pièce de résistance, a behemoth dinner-party matrix featuring 48 recipes (drinks, starters, mains, and desserts) grouped into cohesive menus based on region.

And, if it all still feels a little overwhelming, spend some time with the cocktail spread and everything will be just fine.

COCKTAILS
+12 WAYS

Those bottles of premade mixers that line the beverage aisles of supermarkets are the Hamburger Helpers of the cocktail industry: you don't need 'em. Mixing a good drink requires a bit of care, but anyone can do it. Most real cocktails contain little more than fresh citrus and a few other accompaniments like bitters or simple syrup (made by boiling equal parts water and sugar just until the sugar melts; store in the fridge, forever).

Oh, and enough booze so that you can taste it. Most of these use a stiff pour of alcohol, about ¼ cup, nearly a third more than the average jigger. (Most drinks made with the average jigger taste weak, at least to me.) Use the recipes as guidelines and customize according to your preference. Each recipe serves one.

If you stock a bar with a few of your favorite bottles of liquor, along with bitters, sweet vermouth, Triple Sec, simple syrup, and sodas, you only need buy the occasional citrus and mint to provide superior drinks upon the arrival of any guest—or the stroke of 5.

GIN

Tom Collins

Combine lots of ice, ¼ **cup gin**, 1½ **table-spoons lemon juice**, and **1 tablespoon simple syrup** in a mixing glass and shake. Strain into a glass of ice and top with **club soda**. Garnish: **lemon wedge**.

French 75

Shake the same ingredients as above, only this time with slightly less **gin** and **lemon juice**; strain into an empty glass. Instead of club soda, top with *Brut* **Champagne**. Garnish: **lemon twist**.

Southside Fizz

Muddle **mint leaves** and 1½ **tablespoons simple syrup** in the mixing glass; add the **gin** and **lemon juice**; shake. Strain into a glass of ice and finish with **club soda**. Garnish: more **mint**.

VODKA	TEQUILA	BOURBON

Vodka Soda

Fill a glass with ice. Add ¼ cup vodka and top with ½ cup club soda; stir. If you like, add **fresh lime juice**. Garnish: **lime wedge**.

Margarita

Combine lots of ice, **¼ cup tequila**, and **1½ tablespoons each Triple Sec and lime juice** in a mixing glass and shake. **Salt** the rim of another glass and strain in the mixture. Garnish: **lime wedge**.

Old-Fashioned

Muddle a **sugar cube** and **2 dashes Angostura bitters**. Add ice and pour in ¼ cup whiskey. Garnish: **lemon twist**.

Moscow Mule

Add **1½ tablespoons lime juice** and **2 tablespoons simple syrup** to the **vodka**. Instead of soda, top with **ginger beer**. Garnish: **crystallized ginger**.

Paloma

Skip the Triple Sec; combine everything else plus **1 tablespoon grapefruit juice** in a glass with a salted rim; don't shake. Top with **club soda**. Garnish: **grapefruit wedge**.

Manhattan

Skip the sugar cube; add **2 tablespoons sweet vermouth** to the ice and whiskey and gently stir; strain into a glass. Garnish: **maraschino cherry**.

Cosmopolitan

Add **1½ tablespoons each lime juice and Triple Sec** plus **1 tablespoon cranberry juice** to the **vodka** and **soda**. Shake and strain into a chilled glass. Garnish: **orange twist**.

El Diablo

Substitute **lemon juice** for lime juice and add **1½ tablespoons crème de cassis**. Shake and strain into a glass with ice and top with **ginger beer**. Garnish: **lemon wedge**.

Mint Julep

Muddle **mint leaves** and **1 tablespoon simple syrup** in a glass, then add the ice and whiskey—slightly more, if you like. Garnish: **lots of fresh mint**.

PARTY DIPS
+3 WAYS

Maybe it will happen during the Super Bowl, or the World Series, or March Madness, or the weekend when you buy that 65-inch TV screen. But at some point, if you're like most Americans, you are likely to have some friends over to watch the Big Game—and your friends are going to show up hungry.

Give them dips. Fatty dips. Caramelized onion dip is a great place to start, but there are many other classic dips to serve with chips and beer— or croutons and wine. Here, potted shrimp is punched up with smoked paprika and cayenne; and then there's the showstopper: pork rillettes. Smooth, fatty, and intensely flavored, it's sometimes called *confiture de cochon*, which means "pig jam." How can you resist that? All of these will serve about 8 sports fans (or others).

Pork Rillettes

SERVES: 8

20 to 25 black peppercorns

4   allspice berries

2   whole cloves

8   coriander seeds

2   pounds fatty, boneless pork shoulder
    (or leg), cut into chunks

    Salt

1   garlic clove, lightly crushed

1   bay leaf

1   fresh rosemary sprig

2   cups unsalted chicken stock

    Freshly ground black pepper

    Crackers, toasted baguette slices,
    or bread, for serving

1. Heat the oven to 275°F. Finely grind the
peppercorns, allspice, cloves, and coriander
seeds in a spice grinder. Put the pork in a
large, deep skillet or Dutch oven and sprinkle
with salt and the spice mixture. Add the garlic,
bay leaf, rosemary, and stock and put the
pot over medium heat. Bring to a simmer,
cover, and put the pot in the oven. Cook until
the pork is falling apart and beginning to
caramelize and the stock has almost entirely
evaporated (remove the cover, if necessary, to
get the liquid to evaporate), 2½ to 3 hours.

2. Strain the mixture; reserve the fat and
discard the garlic, bay leaf, rosemary, and any
gristle. Transfer the pork to a bowl and mash it
into small shreds with the back of a fork. Add
¼ cup of the reserved fat and stir to combine.
Taste and season with salt and pepper if you
like (keep in mind that the colder you serve the
rillettes, the less salty they will taste). Pack the
rillettes into a small bowl, wide-mouth jar, or
another container, top them off with more of
the liquefied fat if there is any, and refrigerate
(covered tightly, they will keep for at least a
week). Serve cold or at room temperature.

Pimentón Potted Shrimp

SERVES: 8

¼   cup extra-virgin olive oil

1   tablespoon minced garlic

    About 1 pound small or medium
    shrimp, peeled and rinsed

1   tablespoon pimentón (smoked paprika)

    Generous pinch of cayenne, if the
    paprika is sweet

    Salt and freshly ground black pepper

12 tablespoons (1½ sticks) unsalted
    butter, softened

1   teaspoon grated lemon zest

2   tablespoons lemon juice, or more to
    taste

    Chopped fresh parsley, for garnish

    Crackers, toasted baguette slices, or
    bread, for serving

1. Put the oil and garlic in a large skillet over
medium heat. When the oil is hot, add the
shrimp and sprinkle with the pimentón,
cayenne, and plenty of salt and some pepper.
Stir to combine and cook, shaking the pan
once or twice and turning the shrimp once or
twice, until they are pink all over and opaque
all the way through, about 5 minutes.

2. Let the shrimp mixture cool slightly, then
transfer it to a food processor and add the
butter, lemon zest, and lemon juice. Pulse
several times, until the shrimp is roughly
chopped (not puréed) and everything is well
combined. Taste and adjust the seasoning
(keep in mind that the colder you serve the
spread, the less salty it will taste). Transfer
the mixture to a serving bowl or several small
ramekins, cover with plastic wrap, and refrigerate until the mixture is firm, about 1 hour.
Garnish with parsley and serve with crackers
or bread.

Caramelized Onion Dip

SERVES: 8

2   pounds yellow onions (6 to 8 medium),
    chopped (5 to 6 cups)

6   tablespoons extra-virgin olive oil, plus
    more as needed

    Salt and freshly ground black pepper

1   tablespoon fresh thyme leaves

1½ cups whole-milk yogurt

1   tablespoon lemon juice, or more to taste

2   leeks, white and light green parts,
    julienned

    Crudités or crackers, for serving

1. Put the onions in a large skillet over medium
heat. Cover and cook, stirring infrequently,
until the onions are dry and almost sticking to
the pan, about 20 minutes. Stir in 2 tablespoons of the oil and a large pinch of salt and
turn the heat down to medium-low. Cook,
stirring occasionally and adding just enough
additional oil to keep them from sticking. The
onions are ready when they're dark, sweet,
and jammy, 40 minutes to 1 hour later.

2. Sprinkle with black pepper, stir in the thyme,
and remove the onions from the heat. When
they're cool, fold them into the yogurt and stir
in the lemon juice. Taste and adjust the seasoning, then transfer the mixture to a serving
bowl. (At this point, you can cover the dip with
plastic wrap and refrigerate for up to 2 days.)

3. Wipe or wash out the skillet and put it over
medium-high heat. When it's hot, add the
remaining 4 tablespoons oil. A few seconds
later, add half the leeks, turn the heat up to
high, and sprinkle with salt and pepper. Cook,
turning the leeks with a spatula, and watching
closely so they don't burn, until browned and
crisp. Drain on paper towels and repeat with
the remaining leeks, adding more oil to the
pan if necessary to keep them from sticking.
Garnish with the crisp leeks and serve immediately with crudités or crackers.

TARTARE
+RECIPE GENERATOR

In the go-go '80s, "tartare" pretty much meant a pile of raw, well-seasoned chopped beef topped with a raw egg yolk. It was seen as food for the carnivorous power-lunch crowd—tartare even had a cameo as a status symbol in *Wall Street*—and for old-fashioned people who ate at old-fashioned restaurants.

I'm not sure what the first nonbeef tartare was, but I do remember getting a chuckle when my friend and co-author Jean-Georges Vongerichten first introduced me to beet tartare. Tuna tartare has far surpassed beef in popularity, lamb tartare is fashionable, and carrot tartare is expensive. In short, it's time for home cooks to forge ahead.

It couldn't be simpler; if you can chop or use a food processor, you can make tartare. The method is mostly an exercise in buying and tasting: first you find meat, fish, or vegetables you'd want to eat raw (quality is essential, of course), and then you find combinations of garnishes that work. A few natural combinations to get you started: salmon with egg, chives, anchovies, and capers; scallops with zucchini, miso, and soy sauce; tuna with mustard and soy.

Bear this in mind: Despite its fancy reputation, tartare is a rustic dish at heart (cavemen probably ate some version of it), so some rough edges might be just the thing.

Lemon zest

Capers

Scallions

Salmon

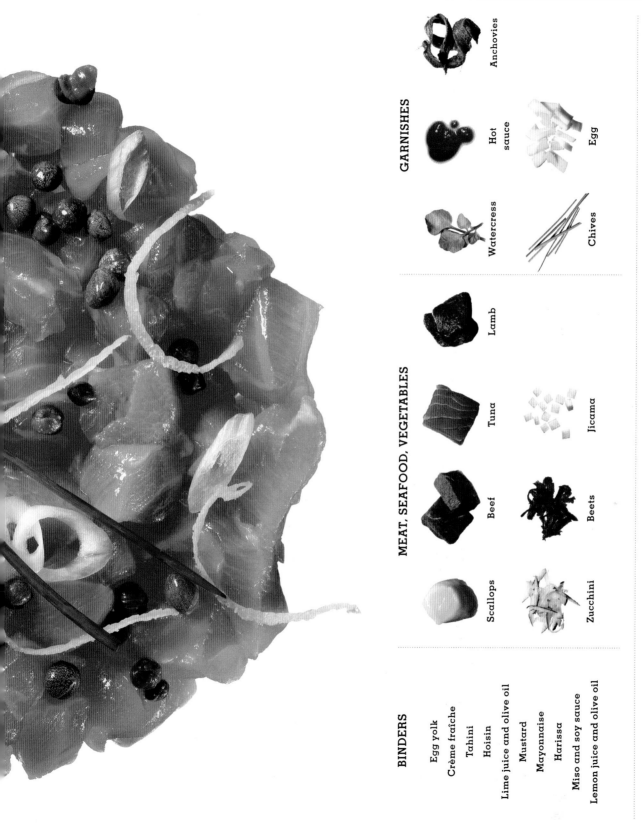

BINDERS

Egg yolk

Crème fraîche

Tahini

Hoisin

Lime juice and olive oil

Mustard

Mayonnaise

Harissa

Miso and soy sauce

Lemon juice and olive oil

MEAT, SEAFOOD, VEGETABLES

Scallops

Beef

Tuna

Lamb

Zucchini

Beets

Jicama

GARNISHES

Watercress

Hot sauce

Anchovies

Chives

Egg

Tartare Universal Instructions

In a large bowl, combine about 1 pound of fresh meat, seafood, or vegetables (chopped well but not minced) with 2 tablespoons of binder (these can be combined; egg yolk and mustard, for example) and 4 tablespoons of garnishes (mix at will). If the tartare seems dry, add extra binder or a tablespoon or two of olive (or other) oil. Serves 6 to 8 as an appetizer.

CHICKEN WINGS
+12 WAYS

Americans are a wing-loving people. The Buffalo variety, by most accounts "invented" at the Anchor Bar in, yes, Buffalo, is the official food of our most sacred event of the year: the Super Bowl.

And though we are also a grilling people, wings seldom make the cut, being passed over for burgers, dogs, steaks, fish, and meatier cuts of chicken. This is a mistake; the grill is the perfect place for the wing.

A grill with one side that's hot and one side that's cool—one side with no or very little fire underneath it—is what you need: put the wings on the cool side, cover the grill, and let the ovenlike heat melt the fat through the grates without any fear of charring flare-ups from below.

Because you're not relying on this part for any browning, it's okay to crowd the wings, even stacking them slightly, if need be. The time it takes to render the fat and cook the wings is more than enough to whip up one of the sauces here, few of which require cooking. Make the sauce in a bowl large enough to accommodate the wings so you can toss them in directly from the grill.

Once the wings have been cooked and are coated in sauce, the final, all-important crisping stage goes quickly. Put the wings on the hot part of the grill, taking care not to crowd them. The sauce will brown quickly, so turn the wings frequently until the outsides are caramelized.

All told, the process is much less of a pain than deep-frying and the results—tender meat, crunchy skin, and a smoky char—are Super Bowl–worthy.

Marinated and Grilled Chicken Wings Universal Instructions

Heat a charcoal or gas grill; the fire should be moderately hot and the rack 4 to 6 inches from the heat. Leave one side of the grill cooler for indirect cooking. Cut 3 pounds of chicken wings into three sections; discard the wing tips or save for stock. Toss the wings with a little neutral oil and place on the cool side of the grill. Cover the grill and cook, checking and turning once or twice, until most of the fat has been rendered and the wings are cooked through, 15 to 20 minutes.

Put the wings in a large bowl with your chosen sauce and toss to coat. Now, put the wings on the hot part of the grill and cook, uncovered, turning as necessary, until they're nicely browned on all sides. SERVES: 6 to 8.

Garam Masala

Combine **4 tablespoons melted butter, 1 tablespoon garam masala, 1 tablespoon minced fresh ginger, 1 teaspoon minced garlic,** and **some salt** to taste. (It should be a thin paste.)

Buffalo

Combine **⅓ cup relatively mild hot sauce, 4 tablespoons melted butter, 1 tablespoon sherry or white vinegar,** and **1 tablespoon minced garlic.**

Lemon-Garlic-Pepper

Combine **⅓ cup olive oil, 3 tablespoons lemon juice, 2 tablespoons minced garlic, salt** to taste, and **lots of freshly ground black pepper.**

Teriyaki

Combine **½ cup soy sauce** and **½ cup mirin** (or **¼ cup honey** mixed with **¼ cup water**) in a small saucepan over medium heat. When it boils, turn off the heat and stir in **1 tablespoon each minced garlic and fresh ginger.** Cool before tossing with the wings.

Miso

Combine **½ cup miso, 2 tablespoons honey, 1 tablespoon rice vinegar,** and **some freshly ground black pepper.** Whisk, adding a splash of hot water to thin it out, until smooth.

Barbecue

Combine **½ cup ketchup,** 2 tablespoons water, **1 tablespoon wine or rice vinegar, 1 teaspoon soy sauce, 1 teaspoon chili powder, 1 teaspoon ground cumin, 2 tablespoons finely chopped onion,** and **1 teaspoon minced garlic.**

Chipotle-Lime

Combine **⅓ cup olive oil, 3 tablespoons chopped chipotles in adobo** (include some of the sauce), **3 tablespoons lime juice,** and **1 tablespoon minced garlic.**

Korean Style

Combine **¼ cup soy sauce, ¼ cup Korean red chile paste or Sriracha, 2 tablespoons rice vinegar, 2 tablespoons honey, 1 tablespoon sesame oil, 2 tablespoons minced garlic,** and **1 tablespoon minced fresh ginger.**

Curry Yogurt

Combine **½ cup yogurt, 2 tablespoons olive oil, 2 tablespoons lime juice, 1 tablespoon curry powder,** and 1 teaspoon ground cumin.

Thai Peanut

Combine **⅓ cup coconut milk, ¼ cup peanut butter, 1 tablespoon soy sauce, 1 tablespoon fish sauce,** and **2 tablespoons lime juice.** Whisk until smooth.

Fish Sauce

Combine **½ cup fish sauce, ½ cup sugar, 2 whole fresh hot red chiles** (like Thai), **2 tablespoons minced garlic,** and **lots of black pepper** in a saucepan. Whisk to incorporate the sugar. Cook over medium heat until it thickens into a thin syrup. Discard the chiles. Baste the wings for just the last minute or two of high-heat cooking.

Jerk

In a blender or food processor, combine **4 roughly chopped scallions, 1 peeled shallot, ½ habanero or Scotch bonnet chile, ½ inch peeled fresh ginger, 2 garlic cloves, 1 tablespoon fresh thyme leaves, 1 tablespoon allspice berries, 1 tablespoon honey, 2 tablespoons lime juice,** and **¼ cup vegetable oil.** Blend or process into a paste.

TINY PANCAKES
+13 WAYS

It started simply enough: One night, I needed to make myself something to eat, and I had a few ounces of leftover scallops from dinner the night before. I remembered something I learned in Madrid called a *tortillita*, which inspired me to produce a kind of eggy pancake—or, if you like, a floury omelet. I beat together an egg and a little flour until smooth, wanting to thicken the mixture just enough so that it wouldn't run in the pan. I chopped the scallops and added them to the batter, along with a bit of onion, some parsley, salt, and chopped fresh chile, then shallow-fried all this by the spoonful in abundant oil. Predictably, the little guys—eight in total—took a couple of minutes per side to become gorgeously golden. I sprinkled them with salt, squeezed a few drops of lemon juice over each, and ate the entire batch by myself in about the same amount of time as they took to cook.

Thus began my season of tiny pancakes. Recognizing that my batter would support whatever I cared to put in it, and that anything that would cook in 5 minutes (or that was already cooked), was fair game, I set out to make them with almost every ingredient I could get my hands on. In short, anything will work, although some vegetables or meats are better when precooked.

Eventually, I moved on from fish or vegetables—plus salt, olive oil, and lemon—to the sophisticated combinations here, some of which can be served after a meal, as dessert, four per person.

Shrimp

Add **1 teaspoon each soy sauce and sesame oil** along with **the chopped shrimp.** Garnish: **chopped fresh cilantro** and **a squeeze of lime juice.**

Roasted Red Pepper

Add **the chopped pepper** and **½ teaspoon ground cumin.** Garnish: **lemon juice.**

Peas

Add **chopped shallots** and **chopped fresh mint** along with **the peas**. Garnish: **more fresh mint**.

Tiny Pancakes Universal Instructions

Beat together 1 egg, 2 teaspoons water or milk, and 2 tablespoons flour. Stir in ⅓ to ½ cup of any of the suggested ingredients, finely chopped; season with salt and pepper (or sugar, if you are making sweet pancakes). Add a not-too-thin layer of olive oil (or butter) to a large skillet over medium heat. When hot, spoon in 8 pancakes, and cook, turning once, until golden on both sides, 2 or 3 minutes per side.

Cooked Chicken

With **the chicken**, add a few tablespoons **chopped spinach or kale**. Garnish: **lemon juice**.

Olives

Add **the olives** and **1 teaspoon chopped fresh rosemary**. Garnish: **more rosemary**.

Peach

Use **1 teaspoon balsamic** in place of the water, plus **chopped fresh tarragon** with **chopped peach**. Garnish: **more chopped peach**.

Tomatoes

Drain the tomatoes before adding; stir in **minced garlic** and **fresh basil**. Garnish: **more basil**.

Squid

Add **a suspicion of garlic** and **lemon zest** along with the **chopped squid**. Garnish: **chopped fresh parsley** and **lemon juice**.

Pear

Add **crumbled blue cheese** along with **the chopped pear**. Garnish: **drizzle of balsamic vinegar**.

Cooked Spinach

Add **½ teaspoon curry powder** when you stir in **the drained and chopped spinach**. Garnish: **yogurt**.

Blueberries

Add **lemon zest** and **millet** with the **blueberries**, and serve with **confectioners' sugar**. Garnish: **maple syrup or honey**.

Cucumber

Add **1 teaspoon any miso** along with the **chopped cucumber**. Garnish: **sprinkle of soy sauce**.

Asparagus

Add **1 teaspoon Dijon mustard** along with **the chopped asparagus**. Garnish: **lemon juice**.

STUFFED GRAPE LEAVES
+RECIPE GENERATOR

Dolmades or dolmas—better known as stuffed grape leaves—have long been a fixture of Mediterranean-style appetizer spreads. We eat them happily, but most of us have never endeavored to make them ourselves.

I first tackled dolmas in a forlorn upstate New York town that had some vineyards, and since then, I've made the project routine, because DIY dolmas are not only doable but also have the significant advantage of allowing you to choose what goes into and around them. Whether they are from the grocery store (not great) or a Mediterranean market (much better), dolmas are typically grape leaves stuffed with soft rice, sometimes lentils, or meat and doused with lemon. At home

you can play around with the flavors of the fillings, and use other grains and leaves.

You can buy jarred grape leaves—just the leaves—that are ready to be stuffed. But things get a little more interesting when you find your own grape leaves or opt for other leafy greens like collards or kale.

Quicker-cooking grains like bulgur, quinoa, and white rice, as well as couscous, can go into the stuffing raw. Brown rice and farro—which provide a chewy texture—should be parboiled in plenty of water for 20 minutes, then drained and cooled before being added to the stuffing mix. Store the finished grape leaves in their cooking liquid for up to a week.

Citrus zest

Capers

Dried tomatoes

Raw bulgur

Fresh herbs

Olives

SEASONINGS

Dried spices

Chilies

Saffron

GRAINS

Raw couscous

Raw quinoa

Raw white rice

Parboiled brown rice

Parboiled farro

FILLINGS

Dried fruit

Peppers

Raisins

Fennel

Edamame

Ground meat

Scallions

Pine nuts

Grape Leaves Universal Instructions

Combine the grains (parboiled or raw; see text above) with 1 cup filling (any combination you like) and seasonings to taste. Drizzle with olive oil, sprinkle with salt and pepper, and let the fillings marinate while you prepare the leaves.

Buy jarred grape leaves, or trim the thick stems and veins from fresh grape leaves, fig leaves, cabbage, collards, or kale; you want about 35 leaves altogether. Blanch the leaves (not the jarred ones) in boiling water until pliable, then blot them dry with paper towels. Line the bottom of a pot with a few (about 5 or so) of the 35 leaves.

Stuff each remaining leaf with about 1 tablespoon filling, then roll and stack them in the pot. Add water or stock to barely cover the rolls, and add a drizzle of olive oil and a squeeze of lemon juice. Bring almost to a boil, then cover and simmer until the filling is tender, 15 to 20 minutes for couscous and bulgur, 25 minutes for quinoa, 30 minutes for parboiled farro and brown rice, and 45 minutes for white rice. Let cool, then remove and serve. Yield: About 30 rolls (6 to 8 appetizer servings).

FINGER FOODS
+RECIPE GENERATOR

Whenver guests are due to drop by, some of us have an inclination toward panic. I get that. But if you lay in a few good-tasting and versatile supplies, you can produce some pretty mean canapés (or canapé-like creations) without much effort and very little stress.

These are not much more complicated than making a tuna-fish sandwich sprinkled with parsley, only better. You begin by providing a base: this might be crackers or croutons (little toast squares, really), hunks of sturdy bread, or vegetables that can serve as containers: celery, endive, hollowed-out cherry tomatoes, those cute little pickled red peppers, tortilla chips, mini-papadums, whatever.

Then you add a spread, perhaps better (if less attractively) described as "the glue": hummus or other bean mashes; soft, creamy cheese; "caviars" of eggplant or olives; pestos of basil or walnut; guacamole; creamed deviled eggs—you get the idea. This is the main flavor, but also serves as a liaison between your platform and your garnish, which also adds flavor: minced bacon or nuts, "real" caviar, chopped cornichons or olives, or capers or anchovies, and so on.

With just the ingredients pictured here, the combinations number 504. (We did the math.) Endive with crème fraîche and salmon roe? Absolutely. Papadums with hummus and pickles? Why not? Start with more or start with less, it still should be enough to quell the panic.

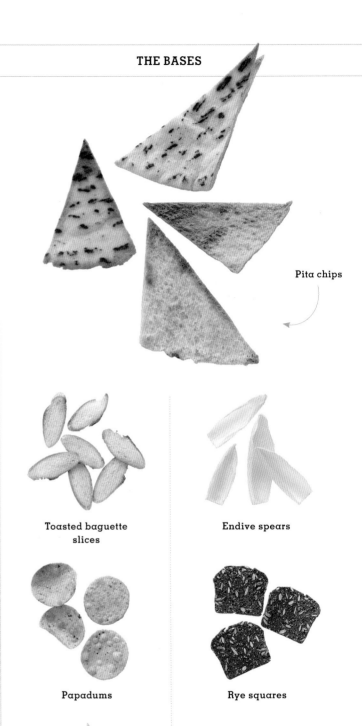

Pita chips

Toasted baguette slices

Endive spears

Papadums

Rye squares

Celery sticks

Roasted
eggplant

Roasted
red
peppers

Pesto

White bean mash

Prosciutto

Pickles

Jalapeños

Cream cheese

Hummus

Smoked salmon

Olives

Sprouts

Goat cheese

Crème fraîche
(seasoned with salt,
pepper, lemon juice,
and fresh herbs)

Cornichons

Dried tomatoes

Capers

Salmon roe

Nuts

THE STRESS-FREE DINNER PARTY

For experienced cooks, seeing what's in your fridge and thinking of a simple way to prepare it make a terrific weeknight strategy. But a dinner party is rarely the time for spontaneity, even for veterans.

Enter the Dinner Party Matrix, a virtual mini-cookbook within a cookbook featuring 48 recipes, from drinks to dessert, with starters and main courses in between. While designing a cohesive menu for entertaining can be as tricky as executing it, the full menus here (grouped vaguely by region) make it virtually foolproof.

These are not "Vietnamese" or "French" menus but, rather, menus that encompass broad geographical areas, drawing on the flavor profiles found in what I think are the most sensual culinary traditions of the world. Rather than singling out specific cuisines, I've opted for regions like "Mediterranean" and "East Asia," which give you a great deal of liberty and avoid the kind of specificity that many people find restrictive.

The premise is that it's easy to adapt a dish to a particular cuisine by changing its seasonings. Using the same technique, you can make butternut-squash soup, for example, taste as if it came from the Mediterranean (or Latin America or Asia) by tweaking a few ingredients. To shift the soup toward South Asia, for instance, substitute curry powder and ginger for the sage.

The primary recipe for each dish is Mediterranean, but there is so much leeway built into this "system" that you can also mix and match among the menus. The matrix is set up so that you can make a "unified" Latin American menu, but it doesn't seem at all strange to me to begin a meal with pork-and-shrimp meatballs, follow those with eggplant curry, and finish with chocolate sorbet. (To drink? I do love the gazpacho Bloody Mary.) It also makes sense to start with fennel-apple salad (a fast, simple fall classic), move on to braised fish with pickled onions and end with the soothing cardamom panna cotta.

The number of courses is also flexible. If you're feeling unambitious, or simply in the mood to eat light, just do a salad and an entrée. If you're feeling energetic, do a soup and a salad and a finger food, followed by a main course and a dessert. The whole idea is to provide options and inspiration, to let you create something that's not insanely difficult but is incredibly impressive.

You should be able to serve four if you choose one recipe from each page, though the meat entrées can serve more. As always, add salt and pepper to taste.

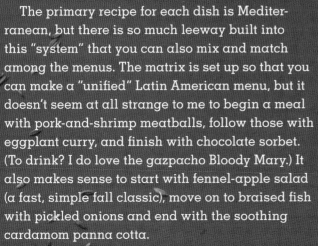

DRINKS

	FRUIT COCKTAILS	MARTINIS	NONALCOHOLIC
MEDITERRANEAN	**Gazpacho Bloody Mary** Purée **2 pounds ripe tomatoes, 1 seeded and peeled cucumber, ½ bell pepper, 1 cup vodka, ¼ cup olive oil, 2 tablespoons lemon juice, 1 teaspoon salt, ½ teaspoon minced garlic,** and **Tabasco and Worcestershire sauces** to taste. Garnish: **cucumber sticks.**	**Rosemary Martini** Combine **1 cup gin, ¼ cup vermouth,** and **1 rosemary sprig;** chill for 1 to 2 hours, then strain. Serve in martini glasses rubbed with a split **garlic clove** (if you like). Garnish: **lemon twists.**	**Basil Lemonade** Squeeze the **juice from 4 lemons;** combine the rinds and pulp with 4 cups water, **½ cup sugar,** and **¼ chopped fresh basil** in a saucepan. Cook over medium-heat until the sugar dissolves; steep for 10 minutes. Strain, combine with the lemon juice, and chill. Garnish: **fresh basil leaves.**
EAST ASIA	 **Soju with Cucumber and Lime** Cook **⅓ cup sugar** and ⅓ cup water in a saucepan until the sugar is dissolved; cool. Purée with **1 pound seeded and peeled cucumbers, 1½ cups soju** (Korean rice liquor), and **⅓ cup lime juice.** Chill. Garnish: **lime twists.**	 **Sake Martini** Combine **1 cup vodka, ¼ cup sake,** and **1 scant teaspoon soy sauce;** chill. Garnish: **crystallized ginger.**	 **Hot Green Tea with Cider** Steep **3 tablespoons green tea** (or 4 tea bags) in 3 cups almost-boiling water for 3 minutes; strain. Meanwhile, bring **1 cup apple cider** and **2 teaspoons honey** to a boil; combine with the tea and serve hot.
SOUTH ASIA	**Dried-Fruit Sangria** Cook **1 cup chopped mixed dried fruit (raisins, apricots, figs, etc.)** and 1 cup water in a saucepan over medium heat; cool. Combine with 1 (750ml) bottle **fruity red wine, ¼ cup lemon juice,** and **3 tablespoons Grand Marnier.** Chill.	 **Salty Lime Martini** Cook **¼ cup sugar,** ¼ cup water, and **¾ teaspoon salt** in a saucepan over medium heat until the sugar and salt dissolve; cool. Combine with **½ cup lime juice** and **1 cup vodka;** chill. Garnish: **lime twists.**	**Mango Lassi** Purée **2 cups yogurt, 1 cup chopped mango,** 1 cup water, 1 cup ice, **2 tablespoons sugar,** and **¼ teaspoon ground cardamom.** Garnish: **sprinkle of cardamom.**
LATIN AMERICA	 **Piña Colada** Cook **⅓ cup sugar** and ⅓ cup water in a saucepan over medium heat until the sugar dissolves; cool. Purée with **2 cups pineapple juice, 1 cup coconut milk, 1 cup white rum,** and 1 cup ice. Garnish: **pineapple slices.**	**Chili Vodka Martini** Cook **¼ cup sugar,** ¼ cup water, and **1 chopped jalapeño** in a saucepan over medium heat until the sugar dissolves; cook and strain. Combine with **1 cup vodka** and **¼ cup vermouth.** Chill. Garnish: **jalapeño slices.**	**Horchata** Soak **1½ cups long-grain rice, 2 cinnamon sticks,** and the **rind and pulp of 1 lime (reserve juice)** in 4 cups water overnight in the refrigerator. Remove and discard cinnamon and lime; purée the rice and liquid with 2 cups extra water and **½ cup sugar.** Strain and stir in the reserved lime juice. Chill.

	SOUPS	SALADS	FINGER FOOD

Sage-Garlic-Squash Soup

Cook **1½ pounds chunked winter squash** and **1 chopped medium onion** in **2 tablespoons olive oil** for 5 minutes. Add **1 tablespoon each minced garlic** and **chopped fresh sage** and **4 cups chicken or vegetable stock**; simmer until the squash is tender, about 15 minutes. Purée. Garnish: **sage leaves** (browned in **olive oil**, if you like).

Fennel-Apple Salad with Olives

For the dressing, whisk or blend **⅓ cup olive oil** and **2 tablespoons lemon juice**. Slice **1 pound fennel** and **½ pound tart apples** (peeled or not). Toss with **½ cup roughly chopped black olives** and the dressing. Garnish: **chopped fresh parsley**.

Parmesan Meatballs

Gently combine **1 pound ground pork or beef** (or a combination), **1 cup grated Parmesan**, **¼ cup bread crumbs**, **¼ cup chopped onion**, **¼ cup chopped fresh basil**, and **1 large egg**. Shape into 1-inch meatballs. Cook in **olive oil**, turning as needed, until done; work in batches, if necessary. Serve with toothpicks.

MEDITERRANEAN

Miso-Squash Soup

Use **neutral oil**. Substitute **2 tablespoons minced fresh ginger** for the sage and water for the stock. When the squash is tender, whisk together 1 cup of its hot liquid with **⅓ cup miso**; stir back into the soup, then purée. Garnish: **drizzle of sesame oil**.

Fennel-Asian-Pear Salad

For the dressing, use **⅓ cup neutral oil**, **2 tablespoons rice vinegar**, **1 teaspoon sesame oil**, and **2 teaspoons soy sauce**. Substitute **Asian pears** for the apples and **1 tablespoon toasted sesame seeds** for the olives. Garnish: **chopped fennel fronds**.

Pork and Shrimp Meatballs

Instead of the ground meat, pulse **½ pound each pork shoulder and shrimp** in a food processor until chopped. Skip the Parmesan and egg; use **chives** instead of the onion and **fresh cilantro** instead of the basil. Add **1 tablespoon fish sauce**. Cook in **neutral oil**.

EAST ASIA

Curried-Squash Soup with Apricots

Use **neutral oil**. Substitute **1 tablespoon each minced fresh ginger and curry powder** for the sage. Add **½ cup chopped dried apricots** along with the stock. Garnish: **toasted pistachios or other nuts**.

Fennel-Carrot Salad with Yogurt Dressing

For the dressing, use **⅓ cup yogurt**, **2 tablespoons lime juice**, and **1 teaspoon minced fresh ginger**. Substitute **carrots** for the apples and **chopped cashews** for the olives. Garnish: **chopped fresh mint**.

Chicken "Tikka Masala" Meatballs

Use **ground chicken**. Substitute **¼ cup chopped almonds** for the Parmesan and fresh **cilantro** for the basil. Skip the egg. Add **1 tablespoon each minced fresh ginger and garlic**, **½ teaspoon each ground cumin and coriander**, and **1 pinch each ground cardamom and turmeric**. Cook in **butter**.

SOUTH ASIA

Chipotle-Squash Soup with Toasted Pepitas

Use **neutral oil**. Substitute **1 or 2 canned chipotle chiles** with some of their adobo for the sage. Garnish: **toasted pepitas** (pumpkin seeds).

Fennel-Jícama Salad with Queso Fresco

For the dressing, use **⅓ cup olive oil**, **2 tablespoons lime juice**, and **1 tablespoon minced jalapeño**. Substitute **jícama** for the apples and **crumbled queso fresco** for the olives. Garnish: **chopped fresh cilantro**.

Spicy Cumin Meatballs

Use **ground pork or beef**. Skip the Parmesan; substitute **1 tablespoon chopped fresh oregano** for the basil. Add **1 tablespoon minced garlic**, **1 tablespoons tomato paste**, **1 teaspoon ground cumin**, and **hot red chile flakes** to taste. Cook in **olive oil**.

LATIN AMERICA

	MEATS	FISH	VEGETABLES

MEDITERRANEAN

Roasted Lamb with Rosemary

Heat the oven to 425°F. Combine **3 tablespoons chopped fresh rosemary, 1 tablespoon minced garlic,** and **1 tablespoon lemon zest.** Cut slits into a leg of lamb; rub all over with the rosemary mixture. Roast until the internal temperature reaches 130°F, 1 to 1½ hours.

Braised Fish with Lemon

Dredge **1½ pounds white fish fillets in flour.** Brown fish on both sides in **¼ cup olive oil,** then remove. Pour off all but 2 tablespoons oil; add **1 chopped onion** and **1 tablespoon minced garlic;** cook 2 minutes. Add **2 cups vegetable or chicken stock, 2 tablespoons lemon juice, 4 thyme sprigs,** and the fish; cook until flaky and opaque, about 5 minutes.

Eggplant Parmesan

Heat the oven to 375°F. Dredge **2 pounds sliced eggplant in flour,** then brown in batches on both sides in **¼ cup olive oil** (add more oil as needed); remove from the pan. Layer in a 9-inch baking pan with **2 cups tomato sauce, 2 cups grated mozzarella, 1 cup grated Parmesan,** and **½ cup fresh basil leaves.** Bake until bubbly, 20 to 30 minutes.

EAST ASIA

Roasted Pork with Cilantro

Heat the oven to 300°F. Substitute a **pork shoulder** for the lamb. Skip the rosemary mixture; purée **1 cup fresh cilantro, 2 tablespoons peanut oil, 1 garlic clove, 1 teaspoon chopped fresh ginger,** and **1 tablespoon lime juice.** Roast, turning and basting every 30 minutes, until the internal temperature reaches 150°F, about 3 hours.

Fish Braised in Chili Sauce

Use **peanut oil** to brown the fish, as above. Purée **2 inches fresh ginger, 3 garlic cloves, 2 shallots,** and **4 small Thai chiles;** substitute this for the onion and garlic. Substitute **fish sauce** for 1 or 2 tablespoons of the stock, **lime juice** for the lemon juice, and **1 tablespoon sugar** for the thyme.

Char Siu Eggplant

Skip the tomato sauce, cheese, and basil; don't brown the eggplant. Marinate the eggplant at least 1 hour in a mixture of **2 tablespoons each honey, hoisin, soy sauce, white wine,** and **oyster sauce,** and **½ teaspoon five-spice powder.** Heat the oven to 400°F; roast eggplant on a baking pan, turning occasionally, until tender, about 30 minutes.

SOUTH ASIA

Roasted Lamb with Yogurt

Heat the oven to 425°F. Skip the rosemary mixture; instead, combine **½ cup whole-milk yogurt, ¼ cup chopped fresh cilantro,** and **1 tablespoon each minced fresh ginger, minced garlic,** and **curry powder.** Roast until the internal temperature reaches 130°F, 1 to 1½ hours.

Fish Braised in Cilantro-Curry Sauce

Use **neutral oil** to brown the fish, as above. Purée **½ cup coconut milk, 1 small bunch cilantro, 2 garlic cloves, 6 scallions,** and **1 tablespoon curry powder;** add this as braising liquid along with 1 cup of the stock. Substitute **lime juice** for the lemon juice and skip the thyme.

Curry Eggplant with Chickpeas

Brown eggplant as for Eggplant Parmesan. Cook **1 tablespoon minced ginger, 1 teaspoon each ground coriander, ground cumin** and **mustard seeds,** and **¼ teaspoon each cayenne** and **turmeric** in neutral oil until fragrant; add **2 cups chopped tomatoes;** cook until thickened (use as the sauce). Use **2 cups cooked chickpeas** for the cheeses and **cilantro** for basil.

LATIN AMERICA

Roasted Pork, Pernil Style

Heat the oven to 300°F. Substitute **pork shoulder** for lamb. Skip the rosemary mixture; purée **1 onion, 3 garlic cloves, 2 tablespoons fresh oregano, 1 jalapeño,** and **2 tablespoons each olive oil** and **orange juice.** Roast, turning and basting every 30 minutes, until the internal temperature is 150°F, about 3 hours.

Braised Fish with Pickled Onions

Toss **1 sliced red onion** with **1 teaspoon salt;** rinse after 30 minutes. Simmer **1 garlic clove** in **¼ cup each white vinegar and water,** 5 minutes; strain over the onion. Stir in juice of **1 lime, 1 lemon,** and **1 orange.** Brown fish in neutral oil. Use **stock** for lemon juice, and **oregano** for thyme. Serve onions on top.

Eggplant Baked with Salsa

Brown eggplant as for Eggplant Parmesan. Cook **1 chopped onion,** and **1 tablespoon each minced garlic** and **jalapeño** in **1 tablespoon olive oil,** 5 minutes. Add **2 cups chopped tomatoes;** cook until saucy. Add the **juice of 1 lime** (use this as the sauce). Use **2 cups cheddar** as the cheese, and **cilantro** instead of basil.

POACHED FRUIT	SORBETS	PANNA COTTAS	
Champagne-Poached Pears Combine 2½ **cups each sugar, Champagne, and water** with a **sprig of thyme** in a saucepan; bring to a boil. Add **4 peeled and cored pears**; simmer over medium-low heat until tender, 10 to 20 minutes. Cool, then remove the pears. Simmer the liquid until reduced by half, then drizzle over the pears.	**Chocolate Sorbet** Combine ¾ **cup each sugar and unsweetened cocoa powder.** Slowly whisk in 2 cups boiling water until the sugar dissolves and the mixture is smooth. Stir in **1 teaspoon vanilla extract.** Chill, then churn in an ice-cream maker (or freeze, stirring every 30 minutes or so, to make a granita).	**Vanilla Panna Cotta** Cook **one package unflavored gelatin** in 1 cup cream over low heat, stirring, until dissolved. Add **2 cups half-and-half, ½ cup sugar,** and **1 split vanilla bean.** Cook, stirring, until steaming; turn off the heat, cover, and steep for 30 minutes. Strain and pour into 4 greased custard cups; chill until set.	**MEDITERRANEAN**
Poached Pears with Star Anise Substitute more water for the Champagne, and add **2 star anise, 3 whole cloves,** and **2 teaspoons black tea** (or 1 tea bag) for the thyme. Strain the poaching liquid before reducing.	**Green-Tea Sorbet** Make tea, using **2 tablespoons green tea** (or 3 tea bags) and 2½ cups almost-boiling water; strain. Stir in ¾ **cup honey** and **1 tablespoon lemon juice.** Chill, then churn in an ice-cream maker (or freeze to make a granita).	 **Lychee Panna Cotta** Substitute **4 roughly chopped fresh lychees** for the vanilla bean.	**EAST ASIA**
Ginger-Poached Pears with Yogurt Sauce Skip the Champagne. Substitute **honey** for the sugar and **5 fresh ginger slices** for the thyme; use 3 cups water. Don't reduce the poaching liquid; instead, combine ¼ cup of the cooled poaching liquid with **1 cup yogurt.** Drizzle over the poached pears.	**Coconut Sorbet** Cook **2 cups coconut milk, 1 cup sugar,** and ½ cup water over medium-low heat until the sugar dissolves. Stir in **1 tablespoon lime juice.** Chill, then churn in an ice-cream maker (or freeze to make a granita).	 **Cardamom Panna Cotta** Substitute **4 cardamom pods** for the vanilla bean.	**SOUTH ASIA**
Poached Pears with Chili-Chocolate Sauce Use more water for the Champagne and **a cinnamon stick** for the thyme. When pears are cool, discard poaching liquid. Cook **2 ounces semisweet chocolate; 2 tablespoons each butter, sugar, and water;** and **1 teaspoon chili powder** over low heat until smooth. Drizzle over pears.	**Cinnamon-Orange Sorbet** Cook **2 cups orange juice, 1 cup sugar, 1 cinnamon stick,** and **1 teaspoon grated orange zest** over medium heat until the sugar dissolves; strain. Chill, then churn in an ice-cream maker (or freeze to make a granita).	 **Honey-Lime Panna Cotta** Substitute **honey** for the sugar and **2 tablespoons lime zest** for the vanilla bean; reduce the half-and-half to 1½ cups.	**LATIN AMERICA**

PICNIC
BASKETS
+3 WAYS

Go to picnic hot spots—parks, beaches, outdoor concerts, and the like—and see what people are carrying. Mostly, it's bags of store-bought food, not coolers of home-cooked provisions. Grab-and-go counters of picnicky food are almost universally mediocre and exasperatingly expensive, but I do understand the temptation to outsource. If the weather is hot, you might not feel like cooking in the first place and you'll also need to pack it, transport it, and ensure that it's still edible by the time it reaches its final destination.

The recipes here can be scaled up or down as needed, and they are built to last, so you don't have to worry about timing. They are hardy enough to hang out in the fridge for a while, and many benefit from that resting time, like the classic French "bathed bread" sandwich and the salads featuring sturdy ingredients such as lentils, green beans, seaweed, and chicken.

If you're going to eat these dishes within a few hours of making them, you can just leave them at room temperature; otherwise, they'll be fine for a day or two in the fridge. Ingredients that tend to go limp, like croutons and fragile fresh herbs, should be packed separately, but I've kept those to a minimum.

Pan Bagnat

Halve **a large loaf of crusty bread** horizontally and remove some of the crumb from each half to make it slightly hollow. Build the sandwich, layering on **sliced ripe tomatoes, roasted red peppers, marinated artichoke hearts, red onion slices, olives, capers, fresh basil leaves,** and **anchovies** (if you like them). **Oil-packed tuna** is classic; **grilled chicken** is also good. Sprinkle with **salt** and **pepper**, drizzle with **red-** or **white-wine vinegar,** and douse with **olive oil.** Close the sandwich, wrap well in aluminum foil, and weight it down with something heavy (a skillet, a brick, whatever). Refrigerate overnight or for up to 24 hours. Cut into pieces, and serve.

Green Beans with Lemon Vinaigrette

Blanch **green beans** in boiling water, then plunge them into an ice bath to stop the cooking. Toss with a vinaigrette made with **olive oil, lemon juice,** and **a tiny bit of minced garlic.** (To turn this into a main dish, sear some tuna until crusty on the outside but still raw in the middle. Cut into thick slices or chunks, and toss with the green beans and dressing.)

Lentil Salad

Cook some **French green lentils.** While they're still warm, combine with **ripe tomatoes, olives, capers,** and **crumbled feta.** Toss with a vinaigrette made with **olive oil, red-wine vinegar, Dijon mustard, minced shallots,** and **chopped tarragon.**

MIDDLE EASTERN PICNIC BASKET

Street-Cart-Style Chicken Salad

Combine **boneless chicken thighs** with **lemon juice, chopped garlic, fresh oregano, ground coriander, turmeric,** and **olive oil;** marinate in the fridge for up to 4 hours. Grill the chicken (or cook it in a skillet), then chop it into chunks. Toss with a dressing made with **equal parts mayonnaise** and **Greek yogurt,** plus **some lemon juice** and **chopped fresh parsley.**

Grated Carrots with Tahini Dressing

Toss **raw grated carrots** with a dressing made with **tahini, olive oil, lemon juice, ground cumin, harissa or other hot sauce, chopped fresh parsley,** and a little water to thin it out. Refrigerate until serving.

Fattoush

Chop up **some pita** (this salad should be at least half bread), and toast in the oven, tossing occasionally, until crisp (you can store these croutons, tightly covered, for up to 2 days). Combine **chopped ripe tomatoes, cucumber, red bell pepper, plenty of chopped fresh parsley and mint, olive oil,** and **lemon juice.** Pack the pita croutons separately, and toss together right before serving.

ASIAN PICNIC BASKET

Cold Seared Steak with Tomatoes and Soy

Cook **some steak** to your liking (on the grill, if possible), let it cool completely, then slice it (you can do this up to 2 days in advance). On the day you're going to eat it, toss with plenty of **halved cherry tomatoes, grated fresh ginger and garlic, soy sauce, a little sesame oil,** and **a squeeze of lime juice.** Scatter with **fresh cilantro, basil, or mint** (or a combination) before serving with **lime wedges.**

Soba Noodles with Chilled Dashi

To make dashi, combine **a piece of dried kelp** (kombu) and 4 cups water in a saucepan over medium heat. Don't let the mixture boil; as soon as it's about to, turn off the heat and discard the kelp. Add **½ cup dried bonito flakes** and stir; let sit for a few minutes, then strain, add **some soy sauce** to taste, and refrigerate for up to 2 days. Cook some **soba noodles,** and rinse under cold water to cool; toss with **a little neutral or sesame oil.** To serve, pour some of the cold dashi into bowls and top with the noodles. Garnish: **chopped scallions.**

Sesame Seaweed Salad

Rinse **dried seaweed** (a mixture is best), then soak it in at least 10 times its volume of water until tender, about 5 minutes. Drain, and gently squeeze to remove excess water. Pick through the seaweed, discard any hard bits (there might not be any), and roughly cut it with scissors if the pieces are large. Toss with **sesame oil, soy sauce,** and **mirin** (or sugar). Garnish: **toasted sesame seeds.**

SOUPS, STEWS, AND SANDWICHES

It all started with soup. The recipe format that appears most frequently in this book (where a certain ingredient or type of dish is broken into four categories based on cooking method) was born with the piece called "Vegetable Soup, 12 Ways." The idea was that once you mastered a small handful of very simple methods for achieving various results (in this case, creamy, brothy, earthy, and hearty), you could cook pretty much any kind of vegetable soup you wanted for the rest of your life without needing a recipe. Nothing lends itself better to kitchen improvisation than soup, and the recipes in this chapter take full advantage of that flexibility. In addition to vegetable soup done twelve ways, there are nine different takes on cold soup, another twelve ways to tilt that summertime staple of gazpacho, and nine simple, speedy stocks that are the basis of a lifetime's worth of satisfying soups. Among the more involved recipes is a mind-blowingly rich tortilla soup and soba noodles in dashi broth that could rival any restaurant's. And there are some great stews, too.

If soup doesn't quite feel like a meal without a sandwich on the side, the sandwich generator and burger matrix have got you covered, inspiring all sorts of out-of-the-box combinations (cumin-chile-lamb burger, anyone?) that, just like soup, you can tweak and customize to your heart's content.

QUICK STOCK
+9 WAYS

For years, I've written about the merits of home-made stock (which to my mind is far superior to canned or boxed stock).

But even if you do make your own stock, you might not have it on hand *all* the time, and it's not usually something you can whip up at a moment's notice. What's needed is something you can produce more or less on the spot. Although water is a suitable proxy in small quantities, when it comes to making the chest-warming soups that we rely on when temperatures drop, water needs some help.

Fortunately, there are almost certainly flavorful ingredients sitting in your fridge or pantry that can transform water into a good stock in a matter of minutes. The process may be as simple as simmering fresh herbs, mushrooms, or even tea in water, or browning aromatics to create richness, or adding staples like crushed tomatoes or coconut milk. To further maximize flavor in minimal time, it pays to reach for ingredients that pack a punch, like miso, anchovies, chipotles, Parmesan rinds, and sometimes even leftovers.

These recipes are meant to be fast, so by "simmer" I mean as little as 5 minutes and no more than 15. In the continuing spirit of speed, convert these into soups using things that also cook quickly: some combination of chopped greens or other tender vegetables, cooked grains or beans, shellfish or thinly sliced meats. The recipes here yield about 6 cups of stock, enough for four servings of soup.

Herb Stock

Combine 6 cups water with **a small handful of rosemary, thyme, or sage sprigs; a large handful of parsley sprigs; a few bay leaves; 1 or 2 crushed garlic cloves;** and **a pinch of black peppercorns.** Bring barely to a simmer, then turn off the heat; steep a few minutes, and strain.

Rustic Tomato Stock

Sauté 1 **tablespoon minced garlic** and **2 teaspoons minced anchovies** in 2 **table-spoons olive oil** until fragrant. Add **3 cups crushed canned tomatoes,** 3 cups water, and a **sprig of thyme, rosemary, or basil** (or a combination), if you like. Bring to a boil, simmer, then fish out the herbs if you used them.

Tempeh Stock

Crumble **1 pound of tempeh** into 6 cups water, bring to a boil, simmer, then strain. This is amazingly well balanced, meaty, and full-flavored, especially for a vegan stock.

Coconut Stock

Combine **4 cups coconut milk**, 2 cups water, **1 tablespoon fish sauce** (or to taste), the **juice of a lime**, some **chunks of fresh ginger** (you can leave the skin on), **1 fresh chile**, **3 or 4 crushed garlic cloves**, and **1 stalk lemongrass** (if you can find it). Bring to a boil, simmer, and strain.

Flavorful Fish Stock

Combine **1½ pounds white fish bones or cleaned heads**; some **roughly chopped carrot, celery, and onion**; **1 bay leaf, 1 crushed garlic clove**, a few slices of lemon, and **4 or 5 black peppercorns**; ½ cup white wine; and 5½ cups water. Bring almost to a boil, simmer, and strain. If you like, substitute crushed tomatoes or cream for some of the water.

Prosciutto-Parmesan Stock

A wonderful broth for white beans and greens, tortellini, or rustic vegetable soup. Combine some **prosciutto rinds or ends** (or 4 ounces sliced prosciutto), **a few pieces of Parmesan rind, 2 crushed garlic cloves, 1 rosemary sprig**, and 6 cups water. Bring to a boil, simmer, then strain.

Smoky Tea Stock

A perfect broth for udon noodles. Drop **a few slices of ginger** into 6 cups water, bring to a boil, then turn off the heat. Let rest for a few minutes, then stir in **¼ cup Lapsang Souchong tea leaves** (green tea is also good). If you can't find loose tea leaves, use 4 tea bags. Steep for 5 or 10 minutes, then strain. Season with **soy sauce** if you like, and add some **black pepper** to taste.

Mushroom Stock

Toss **1 pound trimmed button mushrooms** and **a few dried porcini** into 6 cups water. It need not be more complicated than this, but adding some **onion, carrot, or celery** makes it even better. Bring to a boil and simmer. Strain the mushrooms out if you like, but make sure to use them for something.

Miso Stock

So simple it almost feels like cheating; a great broth for tofu and spinach, shrimp, scallops, squid, or soba noodles. Bring 6 cups water almost to a boil. In a separate bowl, combine ⅓ to ½ cup **miso** with a splash of the simmering water; whisk until smooth, then with the heat at a minimum, whisk the miso mixture into the pot. Do not boil this mixture, but heat added ingredients gently.

COLD SOUP
+9 WAYS

Vichyssoise once seemed the height of sophistication, something served only in French restaurants, and serious ones at that. It turns out, however, that cold leek-and-potato soup (an American invention, by the way) is just cooking-from-the-garden stuff, as simple as it gets.

The same is true for the other eight cold soups here. All of them are about taking the vegetables and fruits of summer—asparagus, avocado, and melon, to name a few—and turning them into soups that are weather-appropriate, namely cold. There are nine recipes here, but you'll see patterns that make them adaptable to whatever is in your fridge or, if you're lucky, your garden. The simplicity really lets the flavor of the featured ingredient shine. Some recipes use stock (most savory soups are better for it), but water works, too. And there is no meat in any of them; in fact, most can be made vegan without much trouble.

The smooth and creamy soups are best made ahead of time, so that they have a chance to chill way down. In fact, you can prepare them even a couple of days in advance. (Just hold off stirring in the cream until you are ready to serve.) And a sweet soup is a simple way to take advantage of an abundance of summer fruit.

Bear in mind that everything tends to taste less salty when it's cold, so just wait until the last minute to salt to taste. Bear this in mind, too: soup is something you can have any time of year, but the same can't be said for good melon, asparagus, or strawberries, so make the most of them when they're available. And don't forget to consider the array of gazpachos, on page 42.

Each recipe serves four.

Puréed Fennel

Sauté **1½ pounds chopped fennel bulb** and **1 chopped medium onion** in **2 tablespoons butter** to soften, about 5 minutes. Add **5 cups stock** or water; boil, cover, lower the heat, and simmer until the fennel is tender, about 15 minutes. Cool slightly, purée, strain, and refrigerate. Garnish: **chopped fresh chervil.**

Puréed Carrot

Substitute **chopped carrots** for the fennel; keep the onion. Don't strain. Garnish: **chopped fresh parsley.**

Puréed Asparagus

Skip the sautéing and the onion. Use **chopped asparagus** (peeled, if it's thick) instead of fennel, and add **1 large peeled and cubed potato.** Garnish: **lemon juice** and **olive oil.**

CREAMY	SWEET

Vichyssoise

Melt **2 tablespoons butter** in a large pot. Add **3 peeled and cubed potatoes** and **3 chopped leeks** (white and light green parts only). Cook for about 3 minutes, stirring, until softened. Add 4 cups stock. Bring to a boil, cover, lower the heat, and simmer until the vegetables are tender, about 20 minutes. Purée, then let cool. Stir in **½ cup or more cream** before serving. Garnish: **chopped fresh chives.**

Melon Soup

In a bowl, whisk together **2 cups yogurt, ¼ cup milk,** and **1 cup chopped fresh mint leaves** until mint is fragrant; strain and discard solids. In another bowl, combine the grated flesh of **a medium melon, 2 tablespoons lime juice,** and **1 teaspoon chili powder;** refrigerate bowls for 2 hours, stirring once. To serve, spoon yogurt mixture onto melon and stir. Garnish: **chopped pistachios.**

Avocado Vichyssoise

Instead of cream, stir in the coarsely chopped flesh of **1 or 2 avocados** before puréeing. Garnish: **chopped fresh cilantro.**

Garden-Greens Vichyssoise

Substitute **2 cups fresh spinach or other greens,** or **1 or 2 peeled and cubed zucchini,** for the leeks. Garnish: **olive oil.**

Sparkling Pineapple Soup

Use **sparkling wine** instead of yogurt (open last); skip the milk and mint leaves. Substitute **3 cups grated pineapple** for the melon and **lemon juice** for the lime juice; skip the chili powder. Combine everything in one bowl, stir gently, and serve immediately; do not refrigerate. Garnish: **toasted coconut.**

Strawberry-Orange Soup

Keep the yogurt; substitute **orange juice** for the milk and add **1 tablespoon sugar** with the mint. Use **2 cups sliced strawberries** instead of the melon; keep the lime juice and chili powder, and add **2 tablespoons sugar.** Garnish: **whipped cream** and **chopped fresh mint.**

GAZPACHO
+12 WAYS

Grilled
Gazpacho

Gazpacho is so easy to prepare that children old enough to manage a blender can make it themselves. Whether you're eight or eighty, a recipe that requires minimal effort is always appreciated.

So, here it is done a few ways that you're probably familiar with and a bunch more that you're probably not. (If Thai Melon Gazpacho is already in your rotation, good for you, and I surrender.) The "recipes" here (a few of which take some artistic license with the term "gazpacho") amount to little more than lists of ingredients and quantities because the method doesn't bear repeating twelve times: combine everything in a blender or food processor, process to your desired texture, chill in the refrigerator if you like, garnish, and eat.

You do need to decide a few things, and texture is one; for a completely smooth soup, turn on the machine and let it run. If you prefer some chunks, pulse the machine—this works best with a food processor; or, if you're a stickler for precision, purée about half of the ingredients, chop the rest by hand, and stir them together. These will each serve four.

GREEN	RED

Avocado and Pea

2 avocados, 2 cups cooked fresh or frozen peas, 2 tablespoons olive oil, 3 tablespoons lemon juice, 2½ cups water, **salt**, and **pepper**. Serve smooth. Garnishes: **chopped fresh mint** and **freshly grated Parmesan**.

Cucumber, Grape, and Hazelnut

2 cucumbers, 1 pound green grapes, 1 thick bread slice, ⅓ cup hazelnuts, 2 to 3 tablespoons olive oil, 2 tablespoons sherry vinegar, 1 small shallot, 1 cup water, **salt**, and **pepper**. Serve smooth. Garnish: drizzle of **olive oil**.

Classic Gazpacho

2 pounds ripe tomatoes; 1 cucumber; ½ yellow bell pepper; 2 thick bread slices; ¼ cup olive oil; 2 tablespoons red-wine vinegar; 1 garlic clove; 1 cup water; **salt** and **pepper**. Garnish: drizzle of **olive oil**.

Tomato and Soy

2 pounds ripe tomatoes, 1 cucumber, ¼ cup fresh cilantro, 2 thick bread slices, 2 tablespoons sesame oil, 2 tablespoons soy sauce, 2 tablespoons rice vinegar, 1 cup water, and **pepper**. Garnishes: **chopped scallions** and **toasted sesame seeds**.

Kale and Olive

Sauté **2 bunches chopped kale** in **olive oil** until soft; cool. Combine with **2 cucumbers**, ¼ cup **green olives**, **2 bread slices**, ¼ cup **olive oil**, 2 tablespoons **red-wine vinegar**, 2 cups water, **a pinch of hot red chile flakes**, and **pepper**. Serve smooth. Garnish: **Parmesan**.

Thai Melon

2 pounds honeydew, peeled, seeded, and cubed; 1 cucumber, 2 thick bread slices, 2 tablespoons olive oil, 1 tablespoon fish sauce, 2 tablespoons lime juice, 1 small shallot, 1 cup water, and **pepper**. Garnishes: **chopped Thai basil, fresh cilantro, and mint**.

Tomato, Strawberry, and Basil

1 pound ripe tomatoes, 1 pound strawberries, 1 cucumber, 2 bread slices, ¼ cup olive oil, 1 tablespoon balsamic vinegar, 1 tablespoon lemon juice, 1 garlic clove, 1 cup water, **salt**, and **pepper**. Garnishes: **chopped basil and Parmesan**.

Romesco Style

1½ pounds ripe tomatoes, ½ pound roasted red peppers, 1 thick bread slice, ⅓ cup roasted almonds, ¼ cup olive oil, 2 tablespoons sherry vinegar, 1 garlic clove, 1 cup water, and **salt** and **pepper**. Serve smooth. Garnishes: **chopped parsley and olive oil**.

Tomatillo, Avocado, and Orange

Grill or broil **1½ pounds tomatillos** until lightly charred. Chop and combine with **2 avocados**, **2 thick bread slices**, 2 tablespoons olive oil, ¼ cup orange juice, 1½ cups water, **salt**, and **pepper**. Garnishes: **corn kernels** and **cayenne**.

Zucchini and Herb

Sauté **2½ pounds chopped zucchini** in **butter** until tender, 15 minutes; cool. Combine with **1 thick bread slice**; ¼ cup each **fresh basil, parsley, and mint**; 2 tablespoons olive oil; 3 tablespoons lemon juice; 1 cup water; and **salt** and **pepper**. Garnish: **pine nuts**.

Grilled Gazpacho

Rub **1½ pounds tomatoes**, **1 red onion**, sliced into rounds, **1 halved zucchini**, and **2 bread slices** with **olive oil**; grill until lightly charred. Combine with 3 tablespoons olive oil, 1 tablespoon red wine vinegar, 1 garlic clove, and 1 cup water. Garnishes: **parsley and olive oil**.

Tomato and Radish

1½ pounds ripe tomatoes, ½ pound radishes, 1 cucumber, 3 corn tortillas (toasted or fried until crisp), ¼ cup neutral oil, 2 tablespoons lime juice, a dash of hot sauce, 1 garlic clove, 1 cup water, **salt**, and **pepper**. Serve chunky. Garnishes: **chopped onion, cilantro, queso fresco**.

VEGETABLE SOUP
+12 WAYS

I'm not anti-recipe (obviously), but some preparations just don't need them—and most vegetable soups fall into that category. Copy the following page, stick it onto your refrigerator, and work your way through it. By the time you're done, you'll never again need a recipe for vegetable soup. Promise.

A few practical notes: Most soups will taste as good or better the next day, so consider making a double batch and refrigerating (or freezing) the leftovers. But never boil a soup after you've added dairy to it; instead, reheat gently.

If you want a super-smooth soup (and just about any of these soups can be puréed if you like), use a standing blender—let the soup cool a bit first—which creates a finer purée than an immersion blender or food processor does; you might even strain the soup after puréeing it.

Garnishes are all optional, though herbs add a dimension that will be lacking otherwise. If you taste as you're cooking, you'll be fine.

These recipes will serve four good appetites.

Creamy Spinach Soup

Put **1 chopped medium onion, 2 peeled garlic cloves,** 3 cups water, and **salt** and **pepper** in a pot over high heat. Boil, cover, lower the heat, and simmer until the onion is tender, about 10 minutes. Add **10 ounces chopped fresh spinach** and ½ **cup fresh parsley;** cook until the spinach is tender, 2 to 3 minutes. Add **1 cup Greek-style yogurt** and purée. Garnish: **spoonful of Greek-style yogurt** and some **more parsley.**

Vegetable Broth with Toast

Put **2 chopped carrots, 2 chopped medium onions, 1 chopped small potato, 2 chopped celery ribs, 2 garlic cloves, 10 sliced fresh mushrooms, 1 cup chopped tomatoes** (canned are fine), **10 parsley sprigs,** ½ **ounce dried porcini,** 8 cups water, and **salt** and **pepper** in a pot over high heat. Boil, lower the heat, and simmer until the vegetables are soft, 30 minutes or longer. Strain and serve over **toasted good bread.** Garnish: **chopped celery leaves.**

Squash and Ginger Soup

Substitute **1 tablespoon minced fresh ginger** for the garlic and **4 cups chopped butternut squash** for the spinach (it will take longer to soften). Skip the parsley and substitute **half-and-half** or **cream** for the yogurt. Garnish: **spoonful of cream.**

Curried Cauliflower Soup

Substitute **1 tablespoon minced fresh ginger** for the garlic, **2 cups cauliflower florets** for the spinach (they will take longer to soften), **1 tablespoon curry powder** for the parsley, and **coconut milk** for the yogurt. Garnish: **chopped fresh cilantro.**

Egg Drop Soup

Beat **4 large eggs.** Boil the strained stock, lower the heat so it simmers, and add the eggs in a steady stream, stirring constantly until they're cooked, 1 to 2 minutes. Stir in ¼ **cup chopped scallions, 1 tablespoon soy sauce,** and **1 tablespoon sesame oil.** Skip the bread. Garnish: **chopped scallions.**

Rice and Pea Soup

Boil the strained stock, lower the heat so it simmers, and add ¾ **cup white rice.** Cook until tender (10 to 15 minutes), then add 2 cups **fresh or frozen peas;** cook for a minute or two. Skip the bread. Garnish: **grated Parmesan.**

Bean Soup

Put **1½ cups dried beans, 1 chopped medium onion, 2 chopped carrots, 2 chopped celery ribs, 2 bay leaves, 1 tablespoon fresh thyme leaves,** and **6 cups water** in a pot over high heat. Bring to a boil, lower the heat, cover, and simmer until the beans are soft, at least 1 hour, adding more water if necessary. Season with **salt** and **pepper**. Garnish: drizzle of **olive oil**.

Minestrone

Sauté **1 chopped medium onion, 1 chopped carrot, 1 chopped celery rib,** and **1 teaspoon minced garlic** in **3 tablespoons olive oil** for 5 minutes. Add **2 cups cubed potatoes** and **salt** and **pepper;** cook for 2 minutes. Add **1 cup chopped tomatoes** (canned are fine) and **5 cups water.** Bring to a boil, lower the heat, and simmer for 15 minutes. Add **1 cup chopped green beans;** simmer for 20 minutes. Garnish: **chopped fresh parsley** and **grated Parmesan.**

Chickpea and Pasta Soup

Substitute **chickpeas** for the beans and **fresh rosemary** for the thyme, and add **1 cup chopped tomatoes** (canned are fine). When the chickpeas are almost tender, add **½ cup small pasta.** Cook until the pasta and chickpeas are tender, 10 to 15 minutes. Garnish: **a few chopped rosemary leaves.**

Spicy Black Bean Soup

Use **black beans** and substitute **fresh oregano** for the thyme. When the beans are done, add **1 tablespoon chili powder, 1 dried or canned chipotle,** and the **juice of 1 lime.** Garnish: **chopped fresh cilantro** and **sour cream.**

Mushroom Soup

Substitute **1½ pounds sliced fresh mushrooms** (preferably an assortment) for the potatoes; sauté until they brown, 10 to 12 minutes. Substitute **½ cup white wine** for the tomatoes, skip the green beans, and add **a fresh thyme sprig** with the water. Garnish: **a few thyme leaves.**

Tomato and Garlic Soup

Use **2 tablespoons minced garlic** and substitute **2 tablespoons tomato paste** for the celery. Skip the potatoes and beans; use **3 cups chopped tomatoes** (canned are fine) and **3 cups water.** Cook the tomatoes for 10 to 15 minutes. Garnish: **lots of chopped or torn fresh basil.**

SOBA NOODLE SOUP

A bowl of soba is a beautiful, exotic, and delicious centerpiece for a Japanese meal: the not-too-soft, nutty buckwheat noodles sit in a mahogany dashi broth that's as clear and glossy as beef consommé, not only salty and umami-complex but sweet as well. My favorite variety, tamago toji, is egg-topped. When it's made right, the egg is almost foamy, soft-scrambled and tender, deliciously flavored by the dashi, a bit of which it absorbs.

To learn how to make it just right, I asked my friend, the estimable Jean-Georges Vongerichten, for help. He hooked me up with a chef named Yoshitaka Nakamura, who explained that my dashi wasn't bad; it was simply the wrong broth for the job. Soba dashi contains bonito flakes (dried and shaved from a fish in the tuna family, and available in every Japanese food market) but no konbu (seaweed, which I've always included in dashi), and it involves soy and mirin in far larger proportions than I ever used. With the right recipe, dashi is a snap.

The egg technique is a bit more complicated. They're beaten and added to the boiling dashi one-third at a time, using a special spout-fitted pot that lets you pour the broth out from under the eggs without it getting cloudy. Most of us don't own that pot.

After a day of experimenting at home, I solved the problem by making extra broth and cooking the egg in that surplus after combining the broth and noodles, then spooning the cooked egg into the bowls. Not as elegant, perhaps, but it works.

Soba Noodle Soup

SERVES: 4

3	cups lightly packed shaved bonito flakes	2	tablespoons sugar
			Salt
¾	cup soy sauce, preferably light (not low-sodium but usukuchi)	1	sheet nori
		4	large eggs
			About 1 pound soba noodles
¼	cup mirin	½	cup chopped scallions

1. Heat the oven (or a toaster oven) to 300°F. Bring a large pot of salted water to a boil. In another large pot, bring 10 cups water to a boil; stir in the bonito flakes, turn off the heat, and steep for 10 minutes—no more. Strain into a large bowl; discard the flakes.

2. Put the soy sauce, mirin, sugar, and a pinch of salt in the pot you used to make the broth; bring to a boil. Let it boil for a minute, then add the bonito stock; bring it back to a boil, and transfer 6 cups to a separate pot and keep hot. (This will be the broth for the soup; what remains is for cooking the eggs.) Toast the nori in the oven until slightly crisp, about 5 minutes. Cut into quarters and set aside. Crack the eggs into a bowl or a large measuring cup with a spout and beat until frothy.

3. Cook the noodles in the boiling salted water until just tender, 3 to 4 minutes, then drain, quickly rinse under cold running water, and drain again. Put a portion of noodles into each of 4 soup bowls. Using a circular pouring motion, slowly stream the eggs, one-third at a time, into the smaller amount of boiling broth; as the first third sets, add the second; as the second sets, add the third, then turn off the heat and let the eggs sit for a minute. In the meantime, ladle the stock (the one without the eggs in it) over the noodles. Use a slotted spoon to scoop a portion of the egg into each bowl, garnish with the nori and scallions, and serve.

MEXICAN SOUPS

There's nothing quite like chile-harvest season in New Mexico. At many farms, supermarkets, farmers' markets, and even random street corners, people buy green chiles by the meshsack— 8 pounds, or 20, or 40—and then pay someone with a gas-powered, hand-cranked, lotto-drum–like steel basket to roast them on the spot. The smell is intoxicating.

During my last visit, the best green-chile dish I had was eaten out of a plastic-foam tray in my rented Jeep. It was dead simple: little strips of pork shoulder stewed just a bit—not until they're fall-apart tender—with big pieces of onion, garlic, chopped roasted green chiles, a little chopped tomato, and enough liquid to keep everything moist enough to justify the use of warm flour tortillas.

Most of these green chiles are called Big Jims, though there are other varieties. They're long, sometimes up to 12 inches, and fairly slender, light green, and pretty mild. Poblanos work just fine for this dish, though they're sweeter and hotter than Big Jims, as do Anaheims or Cubanelles (sometimes called Italian frying peppers).

My favorite red-chile dish was a tortilla soup from a restaurant right across the border in Texas. The original begins with beef stock, but I use chicken legs as the base of the stock, pulling off the meat when it's tender, with a couple of beef bones or ribs thrown into the pot to give the smoky chipotle broth that extra depth.

Pork and Green Chile Stew

(Adapted from the Pepper Pot, Hatch, New Mexico)

SERVES: 4 to 6

1½	pounds pork butt or shoulder, trimmed of excess fat and cut into small strips or chunks
1	medium onion, roughly chopped
	Salt
1	tablespoon minced garlic

1	14-ounce can diced tomatoes, with their liquid
2	cups roughly chopped Roasted or Broiled Green Chiles (see below)
	Garlic powder (optional)
	Warm flour tortillas or rice, for serving

1. Put a large, deep skillet or Dutch oven over medium-high heat. When the skillet is hot, add the pork and cook, stirring occasionally to keep it from sticking, just until the meat juices evaporate, about 8 minutes (you're not looking to brown the pork here). Add the onion and a sprinkle of salt and cook, stirring occasionally, until it softens slightly, 4 to 5 minutes.

2. Add the garlic, tomatoes, and 1 cup water, not quite enough to cover the mixture. Bring to a boil, and let it boil vigorously for 2 to 3 minutes. Add the chiles, a sprinkle of salt, and a sprinkle of garlic powder, if you're using it. Reduce the heat so the mixture bubbles gently but steadily, and cover partly. Cook until most of the liquid evaporates, 6 to 10 minutes (there should be some juices left in the bottom of the pot, but the mixture shouldn't be soupy). Taste, add a little more salt if necessary, and serve with warm flour tortillas or over rice.

ROASTED OR BROILED GREEN CHILIES

MAKES: 2 to 3 cups

8	to 10 large green chiles, like Anaheims or poblanos, or 10 to 12 slightly smaller Cubanelles

1. Heat the oven to 450°F or turn on the broiler and put the rack about 4 inches from the heat source. Put the chiles on a foil-lined baking sheet or roasting pan. Roast or broil, turning the chiles as each side browns, until they have darkened and collapsed, up to 1 hour in the oven or 15 to 20 minutes under the broiler.

2. Wrap the chiles in foil, or put them in a bowl covered tightly with plastic wrap. When they're cool enough to handle, remove the skins, seeds, and stems under running water. Use immediately or store, covered, in the refrigerator for up to a few days.

Tortilla Soup

(Adapted from the Rose Garden restaurant, Anthony, Texas)

SERVES: 4 to 6

2½	pounds bone-in chicken thighs or legs
1	pound beef bones, or a cut of beef with a lot of bone in it, like short ribs (optional)
1	medium onion, quartered (skin on)
1	head garlic, halved across the equator (skin on)
¼	cup vegetable oil, or more as needed
6	corn tortillas

	Salt
2	tablespoons canned chipotle chiles in adobo, or to taste
½	cup chopped fresh cilantro
2	avocados, pitted, peeled, and cubed
4	to 8 ounces plain melting cheese, like mozzarella (not fresh), Oaxaca, or Jack, shredded or cubed
	Lime wedges, for serving (optional)

1. Put the chicken, the beef bones if you're using them, 3 of the onion quarters, and the garlic in a large pot. Add water just to cover (about 10 cups) and bring to a boil. Reduce the heat so the liquid bubbles gently. Cook, skimming the foam off the surface every now and then, until the chicken is very tender, 45 minutes to 1 hour.

2. Meanwhile, put the vegetable oil in a large skillet over medium heat. When the oil is hot but not smoking, fry 2 of the tortillas (one at a time, if necessary), turning once, until crisp and golden, 2 to 3 minutes per tortilla. Drain on paper towels. Cut the 4 remaining tortillas into strips, add them to the skillet, and fry, stirring to separate them, until crisp and golden, another 2 to 3 minutes. Drain on paper towels and sprinkle with salt while they're still warm.

3. When the chicken is tender, transfer it to a plate or cutting board with tongs or a slotted spoon (or put it in the fridge or freezer so it cools faster). When it's cool enough to handle, shred the meat with your fingers, discarding the bones and the skin. (If you used beef, discard it or save it for another use.)

4. While the chicken is cooling, strain the stock and discard the solids. Peel the remaining onion quarter and put it in a blender with the chipotle, ¼ cup of the cilantro, and a sprinkle of salt. Crumble in the 2 whole fried tortillas and add enough stock to fill the blender a little more than half-way. Purée until the mixture is as smooth as possible.

5. Pour the purée and remaining stock back into the pot and bring to a boil. Reduce the heat so the mixture bubbles gently and cook for 5 to 10 minutes. Stir in the shredded chicken, taste, and add more salt, if necessary. Divide the avocados, cheese, and the remaining ¼ cup cilantro among 4 to 6 bowls. Ladle the soup into the bowls and garnish with the fried tortilla strips. Serve immediately with lime wedges, if you like.

MOSTLY VEGETABLE STEWS
+3 WAYS

Curry-Creamed
Spinach and
Tofu Stew with
Potato Crust

Early spring is a transitional season, not only for weather but also for cooking. Light stews with springtime ingredients and satisfying crusts are the perfect dish for that time of year. These are neither the gut-busting braises of winter nor the cold soups of summer, but something in between.

Chicken potpie is a perfect example. This version celebrates spring with the addition of peas (traditional) and asparagus (less so) and the exclusion of cream, and substitutes a cobbler-like biscuit topping (so much easier) for the classic pie crust.

The other crusts here take their cues from the stews they top. Cajun-style shrimps get a layer of cooked grits, which after some time in the oven (and an optional but recommended run under the broiler) turn out nice and crisp. Instead of putting cubes of potato in an Indian-inspired mixture of creamy spinach and tofu (or pork), I put thin slices on top, which become crunchy as they bake.

Lighter stews with more creative toppings—just what's needed for transitional cooking.

Shrimp Stew with Grits Crust

SERVES: 4

½	cup whole milk	2	tablespoons flour
	Salt		Pinch (or more) of cayenne
1	cup stone-ground grits	2	cups shrimp stock, fish stock, clam juice, or water
1	cup grated Cheddar cheese		
	Black pepper	2	tablespoons lemon juice
3	tablespoons olive oil	1	cup chopped scallions
1	large onion, chopped	1	cup chopped fresh parsley
3	celery ribs, chopped	8	ounces peeled shrimp, roughly chopped
2	green bell peppers, chopped		

1. Heat the oven to 375°F. Combine the milk with 2 cups water and ½ teaspoon salt in a medium saucepan over medium heat. Bring nearly to a boil, then whisk in the grits. Reduce heat to low, and simmer, whisking often, until thick, 10 or 15 minutes. Stir in the Cheddar and ½ teaspoon black pepper. Set aside.

2. Put the oil in a large, deep, ovenproof skillet over medium heat. When it is hot, add the onion, celery, bell peppers, ½ teaspoon salt, and ¼ teaspoon pepper; cook, stirring occasionally, until the vegetables soften, 8 to 10 minutes. Sprinkle in the flour, and cook, stirring frequently, until the flour turns a light brown, 2 to 3 minutes.

3. Stir in the cayenne, stock, and lemon juice, scraping up the browned bits, and bring to a simmer; add the scallions and parsley. Taste and adjust the seasoning, then stir in the shrimp.

4. Spread the grits over the top of the stew; bake until the grits are firm and lightly browned, 20 to 25 minutes. To brown the grits even more, run the skillet under the broiler for a minute or two. Scoop the stew and grits into bowls, and serve.

Vegetable and Chicken Stew with Rosemary Biscuits

SERVES: 4

6	tablespoons olive oil	2	cups chopped asparagus
1	leek, washed and chopped	2	tablespoons cornstarch
	Salt and pepper	2	cups flour
2	cups quartered button mushrooms	1½	teaspoons baking powder
2	cups chicken stock	¼	teaspoon baking soda
1	carrot, chopped	1	tablespoon chopped fresh rosemary
8	ounces boneless chicken thighs or breasts, diced		Zest of 1 lemon
		4	tablespoons (½ stick) butter, in bits
1	cup fresh or frozen peas	1	cup buttermilk
		2	large eggs

1. Heat the oven to 400°F. Put 3 tablespoons of the oil in a large ovenproof skillet over medium heat. When the oil is hot, add the leek and a sprinkle of salt and pepper; cook until softened, about 5 minutes. Add the mushrooms, and cook until their liquid has released and evaporated, 8 to 10 minutes.

2. Add the stock and bring to a boil. Reduce to a simmer, and add the carrot and chicken; cook until the chicken is cooked through, 8 to 10 minutes. Stir in the peas and asparagus. In a small bowl, whisk the cornstarch with a few tablespoons of the broth until smooth; add to the pot and stir until the liquid thickens a bit. Taste and adjust the seasoning.

3. Put the flour, baking powder, baking soda, rosemary, lemon zest, ½ teaspoon salt, and ¼ teaspoon pepper in a food processor. Add the butter and remaining 3 tablespoons olive oil, and pulse until the mixture looks like small peas. Add the buttermilk and eggs, and pulse until just combined and sticky.

4. Spread about half of the batter over the stew, leaving a few gaps for steam to escape. Spoon the remaining batter into a baking dish. Bake the stew until golden and bubbly, about 25 minutes, and the extra batter until golden, 20 to 25 minutes. Scoop the stew and crust into bowls, adding in extra pieces of biscuit as desired.

Curry-Creamed Spinach and Tofu (or Pork) Stew with Potato Crust

SERVES: 4

	Salt	1	piece firm or extra-firm tofu, cut into ½-inch cubes, or 12 ounces thinly sliced pork shoulder, cut into ½-inch strips
3	pounds fresh spinach, trimmed		
2	tablespoons butter		
2	teaspoons garam masala or curry powder		
¼	teaspoon grated nutmeg	1	large russet potato, thinly sliced (with a mandoline, if you have one)
2	cups coconut milk	2	tablespoons olive oil
½	cup plain yogurt		Black pepper

1. Heat the oven to 425°F. Bring a large pot of water to a boil, and salt it. When the water is boiling, add the spinach and cook for about a minute. Plunge the spinach into a large bowl of ice water, squeeze the moisture from the leaves, and roughly chop them.

2. Put the butter, garam masala (or curry powder), and nutmeg in a large saucepan over medium heat. When the spices are fragrant, add the coconut milk, yogurt, the spinach, the tofu (or pork), and 1 teaspoon salt. Bring to a boil and cook, stirring occasionally, until the spinach has absorbed much of the liquid; taste and adjust the seasoning, then transfer to an ovenproof dish.

3. Toss the potato slices with the oil, and sprinkle with salt and pepper. Lay them over the top of the spinach and tofu (or pork) without overlapping too much. Bake until the potatoes are golden and crisp, 25 to 35 minutes. Scoop into bowls, and serve.

SANDWICHES
+RECIPE GENERATOR

THE ELEMENTS

Prosciutto with Asparagus
and Red Pepper
on Pumpernickel

Pâté with Cornichon,
Onions, and Mayo
on a Bagel

THE BASE

Pumpernickel bread, toasted

Bagel halves, toasted

Multigrain bread

Baguette slices

Dense German bread (like vollkornbrot,
aktivbrot, vitalbrot)

THE SPREAD

Compound butter

Seedy, good-quality mustard

Cream cheese with scallions

Crème fraîche with chives

Mayonnaise seasoned with horseradish,
red pepper, etc.

Pesto

Duck Breast with Beets
and Cream Cheese
on Multigrain Bread

Pickled Herring with Bacon,
Carrots, and Crème Fraîche
on German Bread

THE CENTERPIECE

Prosciutto or
bresaola

Chopped liver or
pâté

Sliced cheese, like
Emmenthal or
Havarti

Seared scallops,
sliced if they are
very large

Crab or tuna salad

Sliced cooked
fillet of salmon,
smoked or not

Loosely scram-
bled eggs, with
parsley or chives

Watercress,
Belgian endive,
curly endive

Cooled cooked
asparagus with
olive oil and
vinegar, thinly
sliced

Cooked thinly
sliced chicken or
duck breast

Pickled herring

Cooled and sliced
boiled potatoes
tossed in oil,
vinegar, salt,
pepper, and
parsley

THE GARNISH

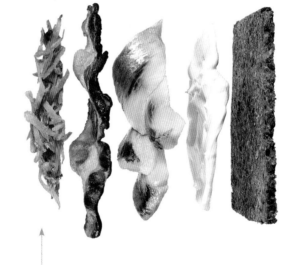

Roasted red
pepper strips

Pickled onions

Sliced cornichons
or cubed beets

Thinly sliced red
onions with dill

Crispy toppings
like bacon and
fried carrots

Thinly sliced
cucumbers
tossed with
olive oil and dill

Caviar or
salmon roe

For something that has almost unlimited potential, the sandwich is too often staid and unimaginative. But not if you use reasonably unusual ingredients (like the ones here). It all starts with good bread, and continues with spreads, which should be seasoned assertively. The "body" of the sandwich—open-faced or not—is the key, of course, and it's here that it pays to open the vault: not tuna but anchovies, not ham but prosciutto, not hamburger but beef tartar. Top-pings can be the difference between a boring sandwich and an inspired one; don't hold back.

BURGERS
+9 WAYS

Standing over a grill full of hamburgers, with a spatula in one hand and a beer in the other, is about as American as it gets. So traditional is this summer ritual that it's easy to forget how far burger culture extends beyond American soil.

Countless cuisines feature their own versions, which in some cases are better, or more interesting, than our default version. So, for the sake of mixing it up—and frankly, because you probably don't need me telling you how to make a classic hamburger—here are nine burgers that move beyond beef.

Doneness is a matter of preference, but in my world, lamb burgers are medium-rare, pork just barely pink in the middle, tuna and salmon practically raw in the center, and shrimp and scallops just barely opaque.

For all of these, begin by starting a charcoal or gas grill; the fire should be moderately hot (very hot for tuna) and the rack about 4 inches from the heat. These cook times are short, so you shouldn't walk away. Just stay at your post; anything else would be un-American.

FISH AND SEAFOOD	PORK	LAMB

Tuna

Cut **1½ pounds tuna** into large chunks; put one-fourth of it in a food processor with **1 teaspoon each Dijon and mayonnaise,** and **1 tablespoon capers.** Process until pasty. Pulse in the remaining tuna until chopped and well combined with the purée. Form 4 burgers, brush with **oil,** and grill over high heat until seared on both sides but rare, 4 to 6 minutes. Topping: **lemony mayo.**

Italian-Sausage Style

Cut **1½ pounds boneless fatty pork** (preferably shoulder) and **1 small fennel bulb** into chunks; pulse in a food processor with **1 tablespoon chopped garlic** and **2 teaspoons fennel seeds** until the meat is ground. Shape into 4 burgers and grill, turning once, 4 to 8 minutes total. Toppings: **sautéed bell peppers** and **onions.**

Greek Style

Cut **1½ pounds boneless lamb shoulder, breast, or neck** and **1 small onion** into chunks; put them in a food processor with **1 tablespoon chopped garlic** and **2 tablespoons each mint and parsley.** Pulse until the meat is ground. Shape into 4 burgers and grill, turning once and melting **slices of feta or smoked mozzarella** on the patties, 4 to 8 minutes total. Topping: **sliced cucumbers.**

Salmon-Avocado

Substitute **skinless, boneless salmon** for the tuna, and **⅓ cup chopped avocado** and **2 teaspoons soy sauce** for the mustard, mayo, and capers. After the fish is chopped, stir **2 chopped sheets toasted nori** into the mixture. Grill 4 to 8 minutes total. Toppings: **sliced cucumber and avocado** (and use a **sesame seed bun**).

Chorizo Style

Omit the fennel. Up the **garlic to 2 tablespoons** and substitute **1 tablespoon ancho chile powder, 2 teaspoons ground cumin, ¼ teaspoon ground cinnamon, ½ teaspoon Mexican oregano,** and **2 tablespoons apple-cider vinegar** for the fennel seeds. Shape into 4 burgers. If you have time, let the mixture sit overnight. Toppings: **chopped onions, fresh cilantro,** and **lime juice.**

Cumin-Chile

Substitute **1 tablespoon toasted cumin seeds, 1 tablespoon toasted sesame seeds,** and **1 teaspoon chili powder** for the garlic and herbs. Omit the cheese. Shape into 4 burgers and grill. Topping: **cilantro leaves.**

Shrimp, Scallop, Corn, and Bacon

Substitute **1 pound shrimp** and **½ pound scallops** for the tuna (no need to chop them), and **½ cup corn kernels** for the mustard, mayo, and capers. After the shrimp and scallops are chopped, stir another **½ cup corn kernels** into the mixture. Grill 4 to 8 minutes total. Toppings: **bacon, lettuce, tomato,** and **mayo.**

Dumpling Style

Substitute **½ cup thinly sliced scallions** for the fennel bulb; **minced ginger** for the garlic; and **1 tablespoon soy sauce, 1 tablespoon Chinese rice wine,** and **1 tablespoon sugar** for the fennel seeds. Shape into 4 burgers and grill. Toppings: **Sriracha and cilantro.**

Kofte Style

Substitute **1 egg** for the garlic and mint; up the **parsley to ¼ cup.** Pulse the meat mixture until it is quite smooth, and form the 4 burgers with wet hands. Grill for 10 minutes total, and omit the cheese. Topping: a mixture of **minced shallots, lemon juice,** and more **parsley.**

VEGETABLES

You can probably tell by the length of this chapter that I'm a little obsessed with vegetables. Not only are they what we should be eating more of than anything else, but there are nearly countless varieties that can be prepared (cooked or not) in an endless number of ways. The wondrous versatility of vegetables is evident in the fact that most of those included here come with at least eight different recipes (celery and bell peppers each have a whopping sixteen).

This chapter is ordered largely by season, which is meant to facilitate the kind of ingredient-driven cooking that I highly recommend when it comes to produce. Rather than finding a recipe that looks good and then shopping for the ingredients, you find ingredients that look good and then shop for a recipe. While the list of produce included here is by no means exhaustive, it does cover a lot. So, whether you come home from the market with beets or cabbage, artichokes or asparagus, tomatoes or corn (just to name a few), you'll find no shortage of options for what to do with them, using ingredients that are likely already in your pantry and fridge.

Of course, if you prefer to map out your recipes ahead of time, by all means do so; there are even some recipes that can benefit from a little advanced planning, like any of the Vegetable Showstoppers (page 112) that substitute for meaty main courses. In the end, it doesn't much matter which veggies you buy and how you cook them; as long as you're putting them at the center of your plate, you can't really go wrong.

SALAD GREENS
+12 WAYS

From late spring until at least Thanksgiving, myriad fresh greens flood our markets, each worthy of the euphoria we tend to reserve for other seasonal produce like spring's first radishes.

Romaine is fine. But dandelion, tender lettuces, chard, and arugula (real arugula, not the "baby" kind they sell in most supermarkets) can be as flavorful as the juiciest tomato. You can make a different salad with these greens every day for weeks without repeating yourself.

The chart that follows highlights twelve of the most available (and wonderful) greens, divided into four categories—tender, crunchy, sturdy, and bold—though the distinctions are often blurred. (Watercress is arguably bold, crunchy, and sturdy.) In any case, don't be constrained by my recommendations. And remember that this is not an exhaustive list; endive, radicchio, chicory, mizuna, mâche, and others are also fresh and flavorful in early summer and will fill in here just fine.

You can turn any salad into a chopped salad by adding chopped things, but all you really need beside greens is vinaigrette—that basic French sauce of oil and acid (usually vinegar or citrus juice). The standard ratio is three parts oil to one part acid, but there's wiggle room; four to one can be too mild, and two to one downright assaultive, so this is an apt occasion for the phrase "to taste."

To make any of the vinaigrettes described here, process all the ingredients, along with salt and pepper, in a blender or food processor until the mixture becomes thick and creamy. Or, you can finely chop everything and whisk them together in a bowl. Hand-mixed vinaigrette isn't as creamy as machine-blended, but it tastes just as good.

Green Salad with Mustard-Shallot Vinaigrette

Toss 6 cups torn Boston or loose-leaf lettuce with MUSTARD-SHALLOT VINAIGRETTE: ⅓ cup olive oil, 2 tablespoons sherry vinegar, 1 teaspoon Dijon mustard, and 1 minced small shallot.

Romaine Salad with Croutons and Anchovy Vinaigrette

Cut 4 thick slices good bread into cubes and cook in 2 tablespoons olive oil over medium heat, tossing occasionally, until browned. Toss with 6 cups torn romaine lettuce, 1 cup grated Parmesan, and ANCHOVY VINAIGRETTE: ⅓ cup olive oil, 2 tablespoons sherry vinegar, and 3 minced anchovy fillets.

Spinach Salad with Bacon and Eggs

Use spinach instead of lettuce. Cook ¼ pound chopped bacon in 2 tablespoons olive oil until crisp. Put 4 large eggs in a saucepan, add water to cover, and bring to a boil; turn off the heat and let sit, covered, for 9 minutes. Rinse the eggs, peel, and chop. Toss with the spinach, bacon, and the Mustard-Shallot Vinaigrette (above).

Mesclun and Herb Salad

Use 5 cups mesclun and 1 cup tender fresh herbs (like dill, parsley, chervil, basil, or a combination) instead of lettuce. Toss with LEMON-SHALLOT VINAIGRETTE: ⅓ cup olive oil, 2 tablespoons lemon juice, and 1 minced small shallot.

Iceberg Salad with Thai Flavors

Use shredded iceberg lettuce instead of romaine; skip the croutons, Parmesan, and anchovy vinaigrette. Toss the lettuce with 2 sliced Thai chiles, ½ cup torn fresh mint leaves, ½ cup torn fresh basil leaves, 1 cup sliced radishes, and THAI VINAIGRETTE: ⅓ cup peanut oil, 2 tablespoons lime juice, and 2 teaspoons fish sauce.

Escarole Salad with Hazelnuts and Grapes

Use escarole instead of romaine and skip the croutons and Parmesan. Toss with 2 cups halved grapes, ¾ cup toasted and crushed hazelnuts, and HAZELNUT VINAIGRETTE: ⅓ cup hazelnut oil and 2 tablespoons sherry vinegar.

STURDY	BOLD

Cooked Chard Salad with Lemon-Caper Vinaigrette

Cook **1 to 1½ pounds trimmed chard** in boiling salted water until tender, 2 to 3 minutes, then drain, rinse, squeeze dry, and chop. Drizzle with **LEMON-CAPER VINAIGRETTE**: **⅓ cup olive oil, 2 tablespoons lemon juice, 1 teaspoon capers with a drop of their brine, and 1 tablespoon chopped fresh parsley.**

Dandelion Salad with Feta

Toss **6 cups torn dandelion greens** with **⅓ cup olive oil, 2 tablespoons lemon juice, and ¾ cup crumbled feta** (or ricotta salata).

Kale Salad with Raisins and Blue Cheese

Use kale, not chard; instead of cooking, chop and drizzle the kale with **1 teaspoon each olive oil and sherry vinegar;** massage and squeeze until tender. Toss with **2 grated carrots, ½ cup raisins, ½ cup crumbled blue cheese,** and **HONEY-GARLIC VINAIGRETTE**: **⅓ cup olive oil, 2 tablespoons sherry vinegar, 1 chopped garlic clove, and 2 teaspoons honey.**

Cooked Collard Salad with Peanut Vinaigrette

Use **collards** instead of chard (collards take longer to cook). Drizzle with **PEANUT VINAIGRETTE**: **⅓ cup peanut oil, 2 tablespoons lime juice, 3 tablespoons dry-roasted peanuts, and 1 chopped garlic clove.** Garnish with **¼ cup chopped scallions.**

All-Green Watercress Salad

Use **watercress,** not dandelions; skip the olive oil, lemon juice, and feta. Cook **1 cup snow peas** in boiling salted water until bright green; rinse and dry. Toss with the watercress, **1 cup sliced cucumber, 1 tablespoon toasted sesame seeds,** and **SOY-SESAME VINAIGRETTE**: **⅓ cup neutral oil, 1 teaspoon sesame oil, 2 tablespoons rice vinegar, and 2 teaspoons soy sauce.**

Southwestern Arugula Salad

Use **arugula,** not dandelions; skip the lemon juice and feta. Cook **1 cup corn kernels in 1 tablespoon olive oil** over medium-high heat until brown, about 5 minutes; cool slightly. Toss with the arugula, **½ cup cooked black beans,** and **CHIPOTLE VINAIGRETTE**: **⅓ cup olive oil, 2 tablespoons lime juice, and 1 canned chipotle chile with a drop of its adobo.**

ASPARAGUS
+12 WAYS

It takes effort to maintain a sense of seasonality with asparagus, given that it has become a year-round product. But in springtime even the stuff in supermarkets may come from a local source—so that the stalks snap rather than bend when you apply pressure and the aroma and flavor are fresh rather than simply strong.

Still, even the best asparagus needs something, if only a little olive oil and lemon. Hence the following, with the best cooking methods—steaming (or poaching; in the case of asparagus, they're roughly equivalent), roasting, grilling (or broiling, which is always an alternative because the broiler is nothing but an upside-down grill), and stir-frying—and flavors well suited to each method.

Asparagus comes in many colors, including white, which is, in my experience, overrated. The most relevant difference for most of us is thick versus thin, and you can use either in any recipe here. In the 1990s, I considered skinny asparagus far superior to fat because it requires no peeling and cooks in a flash. A few years ago, I began to better appreciate the delicious snap of thick spears, as well as their relative sturdiness. Certainly if you're steaming or grilling, thick is the preferable size. They really should be peeled—they will look, taste, and bite more nicely if you take the time. With either thick or thin, you can snap the bottoms off or go the easier route and just chop off the last inch or two with a knife.

You might prefer asparagus crisp-tender rather than softer, but either way, it's done when you can pierce the thickest part of a spear with a sharp knife without much resistance. This might take less than 5 minutes for very slender asparagus, twice that for thicker. (Roasting is the slowest of the cooking methods here.) For all of these recipes, use 1½ to 2 pounds of asparagus to serve four people.

STEAMED	ROASTED

With Brown Butter

Put **asparagus** in a covered pot with 1 inch of water (they may stand, lean, or lie flat) and turn heat to high. Put **2 to 4 tablespoons butter** in a small saucepan over medium heat; stir occasionally until the foam subsides and the butter turns nut brown. When asparagus is done, drain, drizzle with butter, and serve.

With or Without Bacon

Heat the oven to 450°F. Toss **the asparagus** with **2 tablespoons olive oil** (more if you don't use bacon) and **4 ounces bacon, chopped** (optional) in a roasting pan. Roast, turning the asparagus once or twice, until done. Garnish: **grated Parmesan.**

With Aïoli

Skip the brown butter. Put a **large egg yolk** in a food processor with **2 teaspoons Dijon mustard, 1 to 4 garlic cloves, 1 tablespoon fresh lemon juice,** and **1 teaspoon grated lemon zest.** Turn it on and drizzle in **1 cup olive oil**; an emulsion will form. Serve asparagus dipped in aïoli.

With Fried Eggs and Ham

Skip the brown butter. Melt **2 tablespoons butter** in a large skillet over medium heat. Add **4 slices good ham** and warm gently on both sides; remove. Add **2 more tablespoons butter** to the skillet and fry **4 large eggs** until whites are firm. Serve the asparagus topped with ham, eggs, and any pan juices.

With Carrots, Sesame, and Soy

Skip the bacon. Substitute **sesame oil** for the olive oil, and add **2 thinly sliced carrots** to the roasting pan. After 5 minutes of roasting, sprinkle with **1 tablespoon sesame seeds.** When asparagus is done, drizzle with **soy sauce** and toss. Garnish: **crumbled toasted nori.**

With Blue Cheese and Bread Crumbs

After 5 minutes of roasting, turn **the asparagus** and top with **½ cup fresh bread crumbs** and **¼ cup crumbled blue cheese.** Continue to roast without turning until the asparagus is done. Turn on the broiler and broil until the tops brown, about 1 minute.

STIR-FRIED	GRILLED

With Shallots and Fish Sauce

Cut **the asparagus** into 2-inch pieces. Put a large skillet over high heat for 3 minutes. Add **2 tablespoons peanut oil,** then the asparagus and **10 halved shallots.** Cook, stirring, until the asparagus and shallots are dry and beginning to brown. Add 2 tablespoons water and **1 tablespoon fish sauce;** continue to cook until done, 2 or 3 minutes more. Garnish: **chopped peanuts.**

With Lemon Marinade

Heat a grill; position the rack 4 to 6 inches from the flame. Combine **2 tablespoons olive oil** and **the zest and juice of 1 lemon;** brush onto the **asparagus.** Grill the asparagus, turning once or twice and brushing with sauce until done, 8 to 10 minutes. Garnish: **lemon wedges.**

With Scallops and Black Beans

Soak **1 tablespoon fermented black beans in sake or white wine** to cover while the skillet heats. Substitute **1 tablespoon minced garlic** for the shallots and **soy sauce** for the fish sauce. Add the **black beans** and ½ **pound sliced or cubed scallops** to the pan along with **soy sauce** and water and cook just until the scallops are cooked through, 2 to 3 minutes. Garnish: **chopped chives.**

With Chicken and Shiitakes

Skip the shallots. When the skillet is hot, add **the oil,** then ½ **pound cubed chicken thighs.** Cook, stirring occasionally, until browned; remove. Add **the asparagus** and ½ **pound trimmed and sliced fresh shiitake mushrooms;** sauté, substituting **oyster sauce** for the fish sauce, then add the chicken along with the oyster sauce and water, and cook until the chicken is cooked all the way through, 3 or 4 minutes. Garnish: **more oyster sauce.**

With Grape Tomatoes and Pesto

Skip the lemon; **skewer 1 pint of grape tomatoes** and grill with **the asparagus,** brushing all with **olive oil.** Purée **1 cup fresh basil leaves, 1 small garlic clove, 1 tablespoon pine nuts, ¼ cup (or more) olive oil,** and ¼ **cup grated Parmesan** in a mini food processor. Serve the vegetables with the pesto.

With Red Pepper Glaze

Substitute **lime zest and juice** for the lemon; add **1 tablespoon honey** and ½ **teaspoon (or more) hot red chile flakes.** Grill **1 yellow bell pepper**—cut into thick strips—and **4 trimmed whole scallions** along with the **asparagus,** brushing all with the glaze. Garnish: **lime wedges.**

CELERY
+16 WAYS

I used to hate celery. Even as an adult, even recently. I hated the strings, the smell, and the taste. No longer. Part of my coming around to celery was developing a taste for celery's cousin, celeriac, which is harder to clean but easier to enjoy. But I now also find the green stringy stuff to be such a marvelous taste that I'm never without a bunch in the fridge.

Americans don't use celery much, or at least we don't feature it often. Yes, we eat it in cold salads, though it's rarely a dominant feature. You see celery braised with about the same frequency as you see braised leeks, which is to say now and then at a French restaurant that's striving to be traditional.

Well, that can change. I've put together 16 ideas for using celery as a main ingredient (or close to it). I like all of them, but my favorites are celery salt, braised, salsa, marinated, grilled, and soup.

You'll want to use a paring knife or a peeler to remove the toughest outer strings from the ribs. And do not forget the leaves; their flavor is ultra-strong, but used in moderation, they make a fine garnish. Use Chinese celery, if you like; the flavor is excellent, but be aware that it's generally more fibrous, so you might want to blanch it first. Celery hearts—paler, more tender, milder, less stringy—are the best for using raw.

Finally, celery's cheap, so you can use lots.

Celery Salt

Heat the oven to 275°F. Arrange the **celery leaves** on a parchment-lined baking sheet and bake just long enough to dehydrate, about 20 minutes. Crumble the leaves and mix with an equal amount of **coarse salt**.

Mussels

Sauté **chopped celery and leaves** with **onions** (and fennel, if you like) in **butter**; add a **drop of white wine** and some **mussels**, then steam until the mussels open, 5 to 10 minutes; discard any unopened mussels. Serve with **toasted baguette**.

Pasta

Render some **bacon** in **olive oil**; remove the bacon and cook the **chopped celery** until tender. Toss with cooked **orecchiette**, **chopped celery leaves**, and a little **olive oil** if you like; top with **grated Parmesan**.

Braised

Braise **sliced celery**, slowly, in a covered pan with **sesame oil**, **soy sauce**, **minced fresh ginger**, and **garlic** for 30 minutes or until very tender. This is excellent with pork.

Slaw

Grate equal parts **celery**, **apple**, and **fennel** or jícama (grating is easiest with a food processor). Toss with **top-quality olive oil**, **lemon juice**, and perhaps a pinch of **sugar**.

Salsa

Finely chop lots of **celery**, **fresh cilantro**, a grated red **onion**, chopped ripe **tomato**, and **a few fresh green chiles**. Toss with **lime juice** and **olive oil**. Serve with **toasted pita**. Garnish: **minced celery leaves**.

Marinated

Marinate **1 pound chopped celery** in **2 tablespoons each sesame oil and soy sauce**, **2 teaspoons apple-cider vinegar**, and some **minced garlic** and **cayenne**. Serve at room temperature.

Sichuan Tofu and Celery

Heat **peanut oil** with some **ground cinnamon, cloves, coriander, cumin, star anise, peppercorns**, and **hot red chile flakes**, then strain. Blanch the **Chinese celery**, then chill and dry. Toss with **smoked tofu** and drizzle with the **oil**.

Grilled or Broiled

Brush **celery ribs** with **olive oil** and grill or broil until slightly browned. Garnish: **chopped black olives.**

Celery and Shrimp Salad

Chop a handful of **peeled and cooked shrimp.** Combine with some **mayo,** lots of **chopped celery** (leaves, too), **mustard,** and **red onion.** Serve with **pita.**

Soup

Sauté **chopped celery** and **potato in butter;** cover with **vegetable stock** and let simmer 15 minutes. Add some **cream** and purée. Top with **blue cheese, toasted croutons,** and **celery leaves.**

Stir-Fried

Stir-fry some **rice, celery** (leaves, too), **chopped onion,** and **ground lamb** with some **ground cumin, peanut oil,** and **fresh hot chiles.**

Orange and Celery Salad

Peel and thinly slice **a couple of oranges;** drizzle with **olive oil** and **red-wine vinegar,** and refrigerate for 2 hours. Toss the mixture with **finely chopped celery** and a few **chopped, pitted black olives.**

Celery Raita

Whisk some **Greek yogurt** with a bit of **sugar, ground cumin, dry mustard,** and **salt.** Stir in some **chopped celery** and a handful of **chopped fresh mint** leaves. Serve with **pita.**

Asparagus and Celery

Grate **lots of celery** and **asparagus;** toss with **lemon juice** and **olive oil.** Garnish: **crumbled blue cheese.**

Celery Noodles

Use a vegetable peeler to shave the **celery** into thin strips; put them in a covered skillet with a splash of water over medium heat and cook until soft, 3 to 5 minutes; toss with **fresh tomato sauce** and **grated Parmesan.**

SPINACH
+12 WAYS

Spinach has many charms—truly singular flavor, the ability to be transformed by cooking in myriad ways, its famous health benefits—but salad is probably the least convincing.

Here, spinach undergoes four completely distinct treatments (none of which involve leaving it raw). A few pointers: fresh spinach is a given, but *really* fresh spinach—dirty leaves, in bundles rather than bags—is preferable. Make sure to wash it thoroughly in several changes of water. Two pounds is not too much for four people; less than a pound is not enough. For these recipes we started with 1½ pounds.

In these groups of recipes, the wilted and the braised are more likely to make satisfying main dishes; the other two, steamed and super-slow, produce dishes that feel like sides, although they're hardy enough for a main course, especially those in the last group.

WILTED

With Skirt Steak

Sear an 8-ounce skirt steak in a large skillet. Remove, let the pan cool a bit, then add 2 tablespoons butter and the chopped spinach; stir until it wilts. Add 3 tablespoons olive oil, 1 tablespoon balsamic, 2 chopped tomatoes, and ½ chopped red onion; cook for 1 minute. Toss and top with the steak (sliced). Garnish: crumbled blue cheese.

With Bacon

Render 4 thick bacon slices in olive oil until nearly crisp, then remove. Toss the spinach with a sprig of tarragon in the rendered fat to wilt; add ½ pound chopped fresh mushrooms instead of the tomatoes and onion. Garnish: crumbled bacon.

With Chicken

Substitute chicken breast for the steak; cook in the olive oil, browning well. Wipe the pan clean. Melt 3 tablespoons butter and add the spinach to wilt. Add the tomatoes and a handful of chopped scallions; skip the rest. Top with sliced chicken and lemon juice.

STEAMED

With Parmesan

Put washed-and-still-wet spinach in a covered pot over medium-high heat. Put 2 to 4 tablespoons butter in a small saucepan over medium heat; stir occasionally until the butter turns nut brown. When the spinach is tender, 3 to 5 minutes, drain, drizzle with the butter, and add ½ cup each toasted bread crumbs and shaved Parmesan; toss.

With or Without Anchovies

Toast 2 garlic cloves in the butter, then add ½ cup raisins and 2 tablespoons pine nuts. (Anchovy lovers, now's your chance.) Toss the spinach with this mixture instead of the bread crumbs and cheese.

With Cashews

Use 2 tablespoons sesame oil instead of the butter, and stir in 1 chopped green chile. Add ¾ cup cashews; cook until the cashews brown lightly. Toss with the spinach, then add ¼ cup chopped scallions and 2 tablespoons lime juice. Garnish: lime wedges.

BRAISED

With Eggs

Melt 4 tablespoons butter in a large saucepan over medium heat. Add the spinach, one handful at a time, stirring, and sauté until it wilts, about 5 minutes. Form 4 nests in the spinach and crack an egg into each. Cover and cook until egg whites are set, about 4 minutes. Garnish: shaved Parmesan.

With Mussels

Chop 1 white onion and sauté it in the melted butter; add 3 tablespoons white wine. Cook the spinach in this as above, and substitute 1 pound mussels for the eggs; cook until they open; discard any unopened mussels. Garnish: chopped fresh parsley.

With Soy and Ginger

Skip the butter. Put 2 tablespoons sesame oil in a large saucepan along with 2 minced garlic cloves, 1 tablespoon grated fresh ginger, and 1 tablespoon soy sauce. Add the spinach and braise until completely wilted and soft, about 10 minutes.

SUPER-SLOW

With Cream

Melt 2 tablespoons butter in a deep skillet over medium-low heat; add one-fourth of the spinach and cook, stirring occasionally, until the spinach has absorbed the butter; then add another tablespoon butter and more spinach, and stir; repeat until all the spinach is cooked. Add 1 cup heavy cream and cook until the cream is thickened, at least 15 minutes.

With Indian Spices

Use neutral oil. Sauté 2 onions, 1 minced garlic clove, and 1 teaspoon each ground cumin, coriander, and cardamom. Add the spinach and 1 cup coconut milk. Cook, stirring occasionally, until the mixture thickens, 1 hour. Add ½ cup cooked chickpeas and heat through.

With Rice and Carrots

Bring ½ pound carrots and 6 cups water to a boil, then add ½ cup rice. When it returns to a boil, add the spinach. Simmer, stirring, until carrots are tender, 30 minutes. Stir in 3 minced garlic cloves and 2 tablespoons butter.

ARTICHOKES
+9 WAYS

True story, from the wedding of two friends, circa 1977: The bride's father, a louche sophisticate and, perhaps needless to say, an alcoholic, asked of the groom's grandmother, a Russian immigrant of peasant stock: "Isn't eating an artichoke just like sex?" There was, as you can imagine, no reply.

The artichoke has always inspired such lyrical flights. Is it not the most versatile of vegetables as well as the most miraculous? Is it not incredible that this thistle keeps its treasure so well hidden and protected that people can spend their lives blissfully eating only the outer leaves, never getting past the choke to the heart?

Rhetorical questions, I recognize.

It's almost all in the trimming, because cooking artichokes (or eating them raw) is the simple part. Getting them ready for cooking may require several different processes. To prepare artichokes for the raw recipes here, chop off the prickly top parts (more than you would for the other preparations), and peel away or cut the outer leaves until you get all the way to the choke. Cut or scrape it out; thinly slice the heart with a knife or a mandoline. For the stuffed preparations, snap off the harder outside leaves and chop off the prickly top parts. Use a spoon to dig out the choke, rotating it and pulling out the hairy, spiny stuff until it looks clean inside. Finally, to quarter artichokes for sautéing, snap off the harder outside leaves and chop off the prickly top parts. Quarter vertically, then scrape the choke out from each quarter with a spoon or paring knife.

If you're not trying to set a speed record, these preparations are all easy enough. After that, there's only the cooking and the eating—whether it's sexy or not is for you to determine.

General Tips

To keep artichokes from browning (which they'll start to do as soon as you cut into them), prepare a bowl of ice water with a little lemon juice or vinegar (about 10 percent), and put the artichokes in the water as you trim them. Always start by chopping off the dried-out bottom of the stem and trimming the tough outer skin of the rest of the stem, starting at the bottom and peeling upward.

RAW	STUFFED	SAUTÉED

Fennel and Parmesan

In a large bowl, combine the **sliced artichoke hearts (from at least 2 artichokes)** with **thinly sliced fennel, shaved Parmesan cheese, lemon zest, lemon juice,** and **olive oil.** Gently toss to combine. Season to taste with **salt** and **pepper.** Garnish: **chopped fresh parsley.**

With Crab

Heat the oven to 400°F, and put **4 hollowed-out artichokes** upright in a roasting pan. Combine **2¼ cups bread crumbs, 1½ cups lump crabmeat, 1 tablespoon chopped garlic, ¼ cup chopped parsley,** and **4 tablespoons melted butter.** Mix, then stuff artichokes (in center and between leaves) with the mixture. Add 1 inch of water to the pan. Cover the artichokes with foil (poke a few holes in the top), and bake until tender, about 1½ hours (you should be able to pierce them easily with a paring knife).

Anchovies and Garlic

Boil the **artichoke quarters from 4 large artichokes** in salted water until tender, 5 to 15 minutes; drain and pat dry. Heat **3 tablespoons olive oil** in a large skillet over medium-high heat. Add **a few anchovy fillets, lots of chopped garlic,** and **some hot red chile flakes;** cook for 30 seconds. Add the artichokes, sprinkle with **salt** and **pepper,** and cook, turning until lightly browned all over, about 10 minutes (If the garlic starts to get too dark, add **a splash of white wine.**) Garnish: **chopped fresh parsley** and **grated lemon zest.**

Scallions and Soy Sauce

Substitute **chopped scallions** for the fennel, a **splash of soy sauce** for the Parmesan, **lime zest and juice** (or rice vinegar) for the lemon juice, and **sesame oil** for the olive oil. Garnish: **chopped fresh cilantro.**

Pine Nuts and Ricotta

Substitute a mixture of **¾ cup ricotta cheese** and **¼ cup toasted pine nuts** for the crab, **fresh mint** for the parsley if you like, and **olive oil** for the butter.

Shrimp and Garlic

Skip the anchovies and substitute **pimentón** (smoked paprika) for the red chile flakes. When the artichokes start to brown, add **4 ounces of shrimp** and cook until they are pink, about 3 minutes. Add **a splash of white wine** and cook until it reduces a bit. Garnish: **chopped fresh parsley.**

Fresh Peas and Mint

Substitute **fresh peas** for the fennel; use the peas raw if you like, or boil them for a minute or two, then shock in ice water. Add a **generous handful of chopped fresh mint,** and keep the lemon and olive oil (and even the cheese, if you like).

With Sausage

Substitute **ground pork or Italian sausage** for the crab, and **olive oil** for the butter. Add a generous amount of **grated Parmesan.**

Provençal

Add **1 cup chopped tomatoes, ⅓ cup pitted olives,** and **2 tablespoons capers** to the anchovies and garlic. Go easy on the salt. Add **the artichokes** and cook, tossing gently, until the tomatoes break down a bit and release their juice (the artichokes don't need to brown). Garnish: **fresh parsley or basil.**

ZUCCHINI
+12 WAYS

Nobody complains about having too many cucumbers, tomatoes, or eggplants. But zucchini, summer's most under-loved vegetable (yes, technically it's a fruit), gets a lot of grief. It's so prolific! It's so cheap! What are we going to do with all of it?

I suppose it's not just zucchini's omnipresence but also its mild flavor—and indeed, the difficulty of bringing out some of its character—that makes us feel challenged. But zucchini is the workhorse of late summer, firm enough to stand up to all cooking methods, tender enough to eat raw, and quick-cooking and amenable to all kinds of flavors. And there's something else in zucchini's favor: it maintains firmness and freshness longer than any of the more beloved summer vegetables.

When buying, look for the smallest zucchini and yellow squash; they don't have to be designated "baby," but something under 6 inches long and 1 inch or so in diameter will have better flavor and smaller, less cottony seeds. If a zucchini is tender enough, you can even eat the stem. You may also come across pattypan squash; their flying-saucer shape make them a bit trickier to cut up, but they can be used in any of the recipes here, as can yellow summer squash.

No doubt you have grilled and sautéed zucchini, and have probably also eaten it raw (even if it's just a bite taken while chopping it to be sautéed), but it's possible you've yet explored the wonders of zucchini in the microwave. Microwaving makes zucchini silky and tender with the push of a button. If you're without a microwave, you can move those recipes to a saucepan over medium heat.

Appreciate the zucchini. In the scope of summer's bounty, it may not steal the show, but you'll miss it when it's gone.

RAW

Carpaccio

Peel **1 pound zucchini** into ribbons with a vegetable peeler, then spread out on a platter. Whisk together **¼ cup olive oil** and **the juice of 1 lemon**. Drizzle over the zucchini ribbons and scatter **shaved Parmesan** over the top.

Crostini with Ricotta and Mint

Shred **the zucchini**. Toss together the zucchini, **1 cup ricotta, 2 tablespoons olive oil,** and **the lemon juice**. Skip the Parmesan and serve on **toasted crusty bread**. Garnish: **chopped fresh mint**.

Tahini Salad

Slice **the zucchini** into thin rounds with a knife or mandoline. Whisk **2 tablespoons tahini** into **the olive-oil-and-lemon mixture**, adding water as needed to thin to a pourable consistency. Toss the zucchini slices with the dressing. Garnish: **chopped fresh parsley**.

GRILLED

Za'atar Spiced

Make a medium-low fire in a grill with the rack 4 inches from heat. Cut **1½ pounds zucchini** into ½-inch slices. Combine **¼ cup za'atar** and **2 tablespoons olive oil**. Rub the zucchini with the za'atar, and grill, turning once, until browned and tender, 6 to 8 minutes. Garnish: **parsley**.

Barbecue

Skip za'atar and olive oil. Combine **½ cup ketchup, 2 tablespoons each red wine and brown sugar, 1 tablespoon rice vinegar,** and **1 teaspoon each Worcestershire, dry mustard,** and **chili powder**. Quarter the zucchini lengthwise, then cut crosswise into 3-inch wedges. Baste with sauce as it grills.

Fresh Tomatoes and Mozzarella

Skip the za'atar; grill using **¼ cup olive oil**. Slice **1½ pounds ripe tomatoes** and **1 pound mozzarella** into ¼-inch-thick rounds. Toss (or layer) with **the grilled zucchini,** and drizzle with **balsamic vinegar** and **olive oil**. Garnish: **chopped fresh basil**.

SAUTÉED

Pasta with Sausage

Cook **2 minced garlic cloves** and **8 ounces chunked Italian sausage** in **3 tablespoons olive oil** in a skillet over medium heat; remove. Cook **1½ pounds cubed zucchini** until lightly browned, 10 minutes. Toss with the sausage and **1 pound cooked pasta**. Garnish: **parsley** and **olive oil**.

Panzanella

Omit the garlic, sausage, and pasta. Sauté **3 slices cubed stale bread** until crisp; remove. Add **2 tablespoons olive oil** before cooking the zucchini. Toss the bread and zucchini with **1 pint halved cherry tomatoes, shaved Parmesan, basil leaves, 1 tablespoon red-wine vinegar,** and **¼ cup olive oil**.

Dip

Omit the garlic, sausage, and pasta. Cook the zucchini until nicely browned; cool. Purée in a food processor with **½ cup toasted pine nuts, ¼ cup lemon juice, ½ teaspoon minced garlic, pepper,** and **2 tablespoons tahini** until smooth. Add a few teaspoons **water** or **olive oil** to thin, if necessary.

MICROWAVED

Vegetable Soup

Put **1 pound chopped zucchini, 1 cup corn kernels, 2 sliced garlic cloves, 2 chopped tomatoes,** and **a splash of stock** in a microwave-safe bowl. Season, cover, and microwave on high until vegetables are tender, 8 to 10 minutes, stirring after 4 minutes. Garnish: **basil and olive oil**.

Curried

Substitute **5 ounces baby spinach** for corn, **minced ginger** for garlic, and **¾ cup coconut milk** plus **¼ cup stock or water** for tomatoes. Mix in **1 tablespoon curry paste**. Cover and microwave until zucchini is tender, 8 to 10 minutes, stirring after 4 minutes. Serve with **rice**. Garnish: **cilantro**.

Zucchini Confit

Cut **1½ pounds zucchini** into ½-inch pieces, put in a bowl with **¼ cup (½ stick) butter or olive oil** (or a little of both), cover, and microwave until tender, 4 to 6 minutes, stirring halfway. Garnish: **chopped fresh parsley**.

TOMATOES
+12 WAYS

For those of us who grew up eating mealy, pink winter tomatoes harvested hundreds or thousands of miles away, a perfectly ripe, local summer tomato eaten with a drizzle of olive oil, a sprinkle of salt, or nothing at all is a revelation. And if that's still your preferred way to handle summer tomatoes, you might as well stop reading right now. However, once you've eaten them plain for the umpteenth time and tomato season isn't even halfway over, you might be ready to explore some other ways to make

tomatoes even more interesting. While the ideas on the following pages are not all strictly authentic, they are all authentically inspired. There is a mix of cooked recipes and raw ones—not only for salads but also for the classic Sicilian raw-tomato pasta sauce that's one of the first things I make when the season's tomatoes start coming in. Some of these dishes work best as appetizers, some are intended to be condiments, and some are hearty enough for main courses.

Ricotta and Mint

Cut **1½ pounds ripe tomatoes** into ¼-inch slices and arrange on a serving dish. Top with **4 ounces fresh ricotta** and **½ cup torn fresh mint**. Garnish: **drizzle of olive oil**.

Cold Cream of Tomato and Peach

Cook **1 chopped onion** in **2 tablespoons butter** for 5 minutes. Add **2 pounds chopped ripe tomatoes** and **½ pound chopped peeled peaches**. Simmer until the tomatoes break up. Add **½ cup heavy cream** (optional but good), purée the mixture, and chill. Garnish: **chopped fresh tarragon**.

Soy Sauce, Scallions, and Edamame

Boil **1 cup shelled edamame** in salted water for 3 minutes; drain and rinse with cold water. Toss with **1½ pounds chopped ripe tomatoes**, **2 tablespoons soy sauce**, **1 tablespoon sesame oil**, and **½ cup sliced scallions**. Garnish: **more sliced scallions**.

B.L.T. Style

Cook **½ pound chopped bacon** in **1 tablespoon olive oil** until crisp; drain on paper towels and reserve some for the garnish. Toss with **4 cups torn romaine lettuce, 1 pound chopped ripe tomatoes**, and **⅓ cup mayonnaise** whisked with **2 tablespoons sherry vinegar**. Garnish: **crumbled bacon**.

Garlicky Pappa al Pomodoro

Cook **1 chopped onion** and **3 or more tablespoons minced garlic** in **¼ cup olive oil** for 5 minutes. Add **2 pounds chopped ripe tomatoes** and **2 cups vegetable or chicken stock**. Simmer until the tomatoes break up, 15 to 20 minutes. Stir in **2 cups torn day-old bread**, cover, and let sit off the heat for 10 minutes. Garnish: **torn fresh basil**.

Moroccan Style with Chickpeas

Cook **1 chopped onion** and **1 tablespoon each garlic and fresh ginger** in **2 tablespoons olive oil** for 5 minutes. Add **2 teaspoons each ground cumin, coriander, and cinnamon**; cook for 1 minute. Add **2 pounds chopped ripe tomatoes, 2 cups stock**, and **1½ cups cooked chickpeas**. Simmer until saucy, 15 to 20 minutes. Garnish: **chopped fresh parsley or cilantro**.

With Mozzarella

Heat the oven to 450°F. Cut a ¼-inch slice from the stem end of **4 large tomatoes** and scoop out the insides. Chop the pulp and mix it with **8 ounces chopped mozzarella, 1 cup fresh bread crumbs, ¼ cup chopped fresh basil,** and **2 tablespoons olive oil.** Stuff the tomatoes, reposition the top slices, drizzle with **olive oil,** and roast in a greased baking pan until the tomatoes are shriveled and the filling is bubbly and browned, about 30 minutes. Garnish: **more chopped basil.**

Salsa Cruda for Pasta (or Anything Else)

Mash together **1½ pounds chopped ripe tomatoes, 3 tablespoons olive oil, 3 lightly crushed garlic cloves,** and **½ cup chopped fresh basil.** Let sit while you cook **½ pound pasta.** Discard the garlic, then toss the pasta with the sauce (add some pasta-cooking water, if necessary). Garnish: **more chopped basil.**

With (Sort of) Salad Niçoise

Boil **1 medium potato** in salted water until tender, 15 to 30 minutes; drain, peel, and chop. Cut a ¼-inch slice from the stem end of **4 large tomatoes** and scoop out the insides. Chop the pulp and top slices, and mix them with the potato, **7 ounces good canned tuna, ¼ cup chopped black olives, ⅓ cup olive oil,** and **2 tablespoons red-wine vinegar.** Stuff the tomatoes and serve raw. Garnish: **chopped chives.**

With Tofu and Spinach

Heat the oven to 450°F. Cut a ¼-inch slice from the stem end of **4 large tomatoes** and scoop out the insides. Chop the pulp and mix it with **8 ounces crumbled tofu, 2 cups chopped spinach leaves, 2 tablespoons melted butter,** and **1 tablespoon curry powder.** Stuff the tomatoes, replace the sliced ends, drizzle with **2 tablespoons melted butter,** and roast. Garnish: **chopped fresh cilantro.**

Salsa Borracha

Cook **2 chopped medium onions, 2 tablespoons minced garlic,** and **1 to 2 minced fresh jalapeños** in **¼ cup neutral oil** for 5 minutes. Add **2 pounds chopped ripe tomatoes,** a **12-ounce bottle of beer,** and **1 packed tablespoon brown sugar.** Simmer until the mixture is thick, 20 to 30 minutes. Purée with **¼ cup each lime juice and chopped fresh cilantro,** and stir in **2 tablespoons tequila.** Serve with **tortilla chips.**

With Eggplant, Caponata Style

Cook **1 cubed medium eggplant** in **2 tablespoons olive oil** until browned and tender, about 15 minutes. Add **1½ pounds chopped ripe tomatoes** and **1 tablespoon each minced garlic, drained capers,** and **sugar;** simmer until the tomatoes break up, 15 to 20 minutes. Serve spread on **toasted bread.**

CORN
+12 WAYS

I don't need to tell you that there are alternatives to eating corn straight on the cob; you've probably adored creamed corn for most of your life. (Possibly you've never made it from scratch, and if that's the case, throw some kernels in a pan with some butter, and after a little while, add some cream along with seasoning. Heat. Eat.) But it's equally probable that you haven't done much else with corn kernels off the cob. This isn't a revolutionary process (it's as old as corn), nor is it difficult: Stand shucked corn upright in a bowl and use a paring knife to cut down along the kernels, as close to the cob as you can. Really dig that knife in—you want everything you can get from the cob.

These 12 dishes are ideas—starting points. As for most of the recipes in this book, you should feel free to use what you have and what you like. When making corn and seafood salad, for example, remember that scallops, shrimp, or crab is just as good as lobster; so is a white fish, for that matter. (And you can bear all of that in mind when producing Corn Crab Cakes, too.) For corncob stock (an appropriate, easy, and delicious base for any dish that contains both corn and liquid), longer cooking time won't hurt, nor will adding an onion (don't bother to peel it) or a sprig of rosemary, tarragon, or oregano.

For most of these recipes, use 4 to 6 ears of corn, which should work out to between 3 and 4 cups of kernels, depending on the size of the ears, enough to serve four amply.

COLD SALADS

Tomatoes and Basil

Combine the **raw corn kernels** with **sliced cherry tomatoes or chopped plum tomatoes** and **lots of chopped fresh basil** in a large bowl. Add **olive oil** and **lemon juice** or any good vinegar; toss. Garnish: **more basil.**

Avocado and Herbs

Substitute a **chopped avocado** for the tomatoes. Use **basil, cilantro, or mint.** Use **lime juice** for acidity and top with **crumbled feta or cotija cheese.**

Seafood and Tarragon

Include tomatoes or not; add **bits of cooked, cooled shrimp, lobster, or scallops.** Use (a little) **fresh tarragon** instead of basil, along with **lemon zest** and **minced shallot.** Garnish: **lemon wedges.**

WARM SALADS

With Saffron

Melt **butter** in a skillet over medium-high heat. Add **corn kernels** with **1 chopped onion** and **a pinch of saffron.** Sauté until each kernel is deeply browned on at least one surface. Garnish: **Parmesan.**

With Bacon

Render **1 cup chopped slab bacon** in **olive oil** until nearly crisp; remove with a slotted spoon and pour off excess fat. (You define "excess.") Add **the corn** and brown the kernels, skipping the saffron and onion. Return the bacon to the pan along with some **chopped tomatoes** if you like, **chopped scallions,** and **parsley.**

Mexican Style

No butter, no saffron. Sauté **1 chopped onion** in neutral oil until soft; add **1½ cups cooked or canned black beans** with their liquid; cook for at least 5 minutes, then add the corn to heat through. Fry **4 large eggs**; divide the salad in bowls and top each with an egg and some **chopped fresh cilantro.** Garnish: **lime wedges.**

SOUPS

  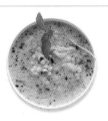

Corn and Green Chile

Simmer **4 stripped corncobs** in 6 cups water, 15 minutes; remove. Sauté **1 cup scallions** and **1 chopped green chile;** add to broth with **¼ cup cornmeal,** corn kernels, and **2 chopped potatoes.** Cook until soft, 20 minutes.

Corn and Tomato

Use just **5 cups water or stock.** Substitute **1 chopped sweet onion** for the scallions, and **1 chopped garlic clove** for the chile. After stirring in the cornmeal, add **2 chopped ripe tomatoes** along with the potatoes. (Skip the cream.) Garnish: **chopped fresh parsley.**

Corn and Coconut Milk

Use **2 cups coconut milk** and 4 cups water for the stock. Substitute **neutral oil** for the olive oil, and **chopped Thai basil** for the scallions; add **2 tablespoons chopped lemongrass.** Skip the cornmeal and cream; add **lime juice** instead. Garnish: **more chopped Thai basil.**

FRIED CAKES

Corn Cakes

Combine ¾ cup cornmeal, ½ cup flour, 2 teaspoons baking powder, 1 beaten egg, ¾ cup milk, and 2 cups corn kernels. Cook batter like pancakes in a skillet with neutral oil until brown on both sides.

Arepas

Substitute **butter** for oil. Use **1 cup cornmeal;** skip the flour and baking powder. Beat the egg with **1 cup milk** and add **1 cup grated Cheddar;** use just **½ cup corn kernels.** (Batter will be thinner.) Cook over medium heat like pancakes, until golden and fluffy, 5 or 6 minutes per side. Garnish: **Cheddar** and **avocado.**

Corn Crab Cakes

Use **olive oil;** skip the cornmeal and baking powder. Beat **1 egg;** add **2 cups corn, ½ pound lump crabmeat, ¼ cup mayonnaise,** and **1 tablespoon Dijon mustard;** skip the milk. Stir in **½ cup bread crumbs** to bind. Shape into patties, dredge in flour, then brown on both sides, 8 minutes total. Garnish: **lemon wedges.**

GRILLED EGGPLANT
+12 WAYS

If you don't love eggplant, it may be because you've never tried grilling it. The very best way to heighten its silky texture and smoky flavor is to cook it with fire, and you can do so in almost any form, over almost any level of heat, with spectacular results.

Real charcoal (preferably not briquettes) is best, but all these recipes can be cooked over gas or wood. Build a hot fire with the grate about 4 inches from the heat source, and place the whole eggplant directly above the coals. The skin will blister, blacken, and burst, and the interior will become dreamy and creamy. If you practice, you can hold it by its stem and peel the charred skin right off; otherwise, use a spoon to scoop out the flesh.

Or, stem the eggplant and cut it into long planks, halves, or rounds. (I never peel eggplant; the skin, on some varieties, is the best part.) Then salt it to remove some bitterness (though with firm, seedless, young, beautiful eggplant, that's not necessary). You can cook these recipes any way you like, but I find thick planks take well to direct heat—that is, an uncovered grill, though not a blazing hot fire. Halves and rounds take well to indirect heat (where the food is not directly above the coals) on a covered grill.

Similarly, most of these recipes will work nicely no matter how you cut the eggplant, but I do love rounds layered with other things, like grilled tomatoes, mozzarella, cooked ground meat, and onions. Halves are sturdy enough to "stuff" (you just shove flavorings into the scored flesh) with strongly flavored combinations. And planks just need to be brushed with the delicious mixture of your choice. For all of these recipes, use two medium or one large eggplant (1½ to 2 pounds) to serve four.

Italian Style

Cut **the eggplant** into 1-inch-thick rounds; make shallow cuts on both faces and rub with a mixture of **⅓ cup olive oil** and **1 tablespoon minced garlic.** Grill, covered, until tender and lightly browned, turning and brushing with more oil as needed, about 20 minutes. Layer with **grilled tomato** and **mozzarella slices.** Garnish: **chopped fresh basil.**

With Herbs

Slice the eggplant in half lengthwise; make shallow cuts on the flesh side. Combine **⅓ cup olive oil** and **¼ cup each minced onion** and **fresh parsley;** brush all over eggplant, pushing into slits. Grill, covered and turning as needed, until the flesh is soft and the skin is crisp, 20 to 30 minutes. Garnish: **more chopped parsley.**

North African Style

Reduce the **oil** to 3 tablespoons; add **2 tablespoons honey** and **1 tablespoon ground cumin.** Forget the mozzarella; layer with **onion and/or tomato slices** and if you like, **cooked ground beef, or lamb.** Garnish: **chopped fresh parsley.**

Parmesan and Bread Crumbs

Add **hot red chile flakes** to the **olive oil** and **garlic.** At the end of the grilling, top with **bread crumbs** and **shaved Parmesan** to melt. **Tomatoes** are nice, though optional. (Mozzarella is overkill.)

Greek Style

Substitute **minced or puréed olives** (or tapenade) for the parsley. Garnish: **crumbled feta** and **more olives.**

Japanese Style

Brush with **neutral oil.** In a saucepan, heat **¼ cup miso** and **2 tablespoons each sugar, mirin,** and **sake** until the sugar dissolves; add **1 tablespoon grated fresh ginger.** Brush the mixture over the eggplant after it's half cooked. Garnish: **chopped scallions.**

Simple

Cut the **eggplant** into planks ½ to ¾ inch thick. Combine **⅓ cup olive oil** and **1 teaspoon minced garlic**; brush all over the planks and place directly on the grill. Cook until the eggplant is dark brown on both sides, about 10 minutes total, turning as needed.

Baba Ghanouj

Grill the **whole eggplant,** turning occasionally, until blackened and collapsed, 20 to 30 minutes. Cool, peel (or scoop), and mash the flesh; combine the flesh with **½ cup toasted pine nuts; ⅓ cup tahini or yogurt, ⅓ cup olive oil, 2 tablespoons lemon juice;** and **1 minced garlic clove.** Serve with **pita.**

Lebanese Style

Prepare as above, but in the last few minutes of grilling, brush **the eggplant** with a mixture of **thick yogurt and lemon juice.** Garnish: **chopped fresh mint.**

Chinese Style

Instead of olive oil, use **1 tablespoon sesame oil, 4 tablespoons hoisin sauce,** and **1 teaspoon each rice vinegar and soy sauce;** add a **dash of chili powder** and **minced fresh ginger.** Garnish: **chopped fresh cilantro.**

With Ground Meat

Instead of pine nuts, add **sautéed ground lamb, beef, or chicken.** Omit the tahini and lemon juice; add **chopped fresh parsley** and **chili powder.**

Bruschetta

Instead of pine nuts, add **roasted whole garlic cloves** to taste and mash them with the eggplant. Omit the tahini and add **1 diced ripe tomato.** Spread onto **slices of baguette.**

BELL PEPPERS
+16 WAYS

Salsa Sofrito

Sauté **chopped roasted peppers, 1 onion,** and minced garlic until soft. Add **1½ cups chopped tomatoes.** Simmer to thicken, 15 minutes; stir in **2 teaspoons chopped oregano** and **1 tablespoon red-wine vinegar.**

Rouille

Put **1 egg yolk, 1 tablespoon lemon juice, 2 teaspoons Dijon,** and **2 teaspoons garlic** in a food processor. Add **1 cup olive oil** in a steady stream to form an emulsion. Add **cayenne** and **1 roasted pepper;** blend.

With Sausage and Rice

Render **12 ounces Italian sausage** in oil. Remove; stir-fry **4 cups cooked rice.** Toss the sausage and rice with **chopped roasted peppers** and more oil, if necessary. Top with **shaved Parmesan** and **fresh oregano.**

Bisque

Boil **4 cups of stock;** add **5 chopped roasted peppers,** a pinch of paprika, and **1 minced garlic clove;** simmer until the peppers are very tender, about 5 minutes. Purée, then whisk in **heavy cream** to taste.

The sweetness of bell peppers is especially pronounced in summer, which is also when you're most likely to wind up with one that was grown locally.

Unless noted, each recipe calls for 1 pound of peppers (use any color you like) to serve four. That's roughly equivalent to two large whole bell peppers, or 3 cups sliced or 2½ cups chopped. Core and seed the peppers first. My favorite method is to stand the pepper up and slice down around the core from the outside.

One of the most basic and wonderful preparations for bell peppers is roasting. Put whole peppers on a baking sheet lined with foil and roast in a 450°F oven, or broil, turning the peppers as each side browns, until they have darkened, even blackened, and collapsed. (A charcoal grill is even better.) Gather the corners of the foil and wrap the peppers; let them cool until you can handle them, about 15 minutes, then remove the blackened skin and seeds. (Do this under running water to make it easier; you probably won't get all the skin off, and that's okay.)

Warm Pickled Peppers

Bring 2 cups water, ½ cup red-wine vinegar, ¼ cup olive oil, a few bay leaves, a pinch of dried oregano and salt to a boil. Add sliced fresh peppers and cook for 1 minute; turn off heat, cover for 10 minutes. Drain.

Muhammara

Pulse roasted peppers, ½ cup walnuts, 2 tablespoons olive oil, 1 tablespoon chopped garlic, the zest of a lemon, and a pinch of ground cumin in a food processor. Add a dash of hot red chile flakes and lemon juice.

Paste

Boil 3 whole fresh peppers to soften, 10 minutes. Drain, cool, core, and purée. Put a few tablespoons olive oil in a skillet over medium heat; cook the paste, stirring until deeply colored, about 2 minutes. Use as a condiment.

Roasted Dip

In a bowl, smash together equal parts chopped roasted peppers and peeled roasted eggplant, and as much roasted garlic as you like. Add olive oil and lemon juice to moisten, and stir to combine. Garnish with parsley.

Frittata

Sauté 2 sliced fresh peppers, a sliced onion, and a pinch of paprika until the peppers are tender. Beat 6 to 8 large eggs and add to the skillet; cook until the frittata will slide from the pan. Flip over and cook until set.

With Anchovies

Sauté thickly sliced fresh peppers over medium heat, turning so the peppers brown without burning, about 10 minutes. Drizzle with red-wine vinegar, and add a few whole anchovies or capers.

Stuffed

Hollow out the peppers; stuff with 1 pound browned ground beef, 2 cups rice, and chopped parsley; replace the pepper caps. Coat with olive oil, stand in a pan, and add ¼ inch stock. Roast at 450°F, 30 to 40 minutes.

With Lamb

Brown 1 pound boneless lamb in oil; remove. Sauté sliced fresh peppers until soft. Return the lamb and add 1 tablespoon each minced garlic, ginger, and soy sauce. Cook for 2 minutes. Toss with scallions; serve over rice.

With Killed Onions

Put 1 large sliced red onion in a bowl, sprinkle with salt, and add red-wine vinegar to cover. Let sit for at least 15 minutes, stirring occasionally. Drain and toss with sliced roasted peppers and toasted bread crumbs.

In Foil with Fish

Oil a large piece of foil; make a bed of sliced fresh peppers and onions. Top with 1½ pounds thick white fish fillet. Fold over and seal the edges of the foil. Grill over medium heat until fish is opaque, 10 to 15 minutes.

Peperonata

Sauté sliced onions until soft. Add sliced fresh peppers, and cook until wilted; add 1 cup chopped fresh tomatoes (with juices) and fresh basil leaves. Bring to a boil, then simmer until thick, 15 minutes.

Vietnamese Style

Heat neutral oil in a skillet over medium heat, and add 4 chopped fresh peppers. Sauté until soft, then add lime juice, fish sauce, and fresh chiles; cook until fragrant. Toss with Thai basil or mint, and serve with rice.

SLAW
+8 WAYS

"Slaw" has come to mean any shredded vegetable with dressing. Maybe you salt the vegetable and maybe you don't. Maybe you chill it a while after dressing it, which softens the vegetable and helps the flavors meld. Maybe you even let it sit in the fridge for a day or two, which doesn't hurt it a bit.

You can shred any vegetable by hand, but the shredding blade of a food processor is faster, easier, more precise, and less dangerous than a box grater.

Some of the recipes call for salting, which draws out water (and bitterness) from the veggies and makes them sweeter (in theory), crunchier (for sure), and more tender (not a contradiction). You can skip the salting if you're short on time, and you can add salt to recipes if your vegetables aren't perfect specimens. In general, most vegetables benefit from salting, but that's a refinement. The flavors of these recipes range from Asian to Mediterranean, to New-Age, to "American." They're all, however, considerably more interesting than standard coleslaw, no matter what definition you use.

All of these will serve six to eight.

Kohlrabi-Sesame Slaw

Peel and shred **2 pounds kohlrabi**. Toss with **1 tablespoon salt** and let sit in a colander for 15 minutes or longer; rinse, drain, and pat dry. Whisk together **2 tablespoons tahini, 2 tablespoons neutral oil, 1 tablespoon sesame oil, 2 tablespoons lime juice, 1 minced fresh hot chile,** and **2 tablespoons minced fresh garlic.** Toss with the kohlrabi, **½ cup chopped scallions,** and **¼ cup chopped cilantro.** Garnish: **sesame seeds.**

Brussels Sprouts Slaw with Peanuts

Shred **1½ pounds Brussels sprouts.** Whisk together **½ cup mayonnaise, ¼ cup lime juice, 2 tablespoons fish sauce,** and **2 teaspoons sugar.** Toss with the sprouts, **½ cup chopped scallions, ½ cup chopped roasted peanuts,** and **¼ cup chopped fresh cilantro.** Garnish: **more scallions.**

Banh Mi Slaw

Shred **1 pound daikon radish** and **½ pound carrots.** Toss with **1 tablespoon salt** and let sit in a colander in the sink for 15 minutes or longer; rinse, drain, and pat dry. Whisk together **¼ cup mayonnaise, 1 tablespoon rice vinegar, 1 teaspoon sesame oil, 1 teaspoon sugar,** and **½ teaspoon or more Sriracha sauce.** Toss with the daikon and carrots, **½ cup fresh cilantro,** and **¼ cup chopped scallions.** Garnish: **more cilantro.**

Broccoli and Seaweed Slaw

Peel the stem of **1 large head broccoli;** chop the florets fine and shred the stem. Toss with **1 tablespoon salt** and let sit in a colander for 15 minutes; rinse, drain, and pat dry. Combine **¼ cup mayonnaise, 2 tablespoons lemon juice, 1 tablespoon soy sauce,** and **1 teaspoon honey.** Toss with the broccoli, **½ chopped red onion, ¼ cup snipped dried wakame** or **hijiki,** and **¼ cup chopped cilantro.** Garnish: **cilantro.**

Fennel and Celery Slaw with Grapefruit

Shred **2 medium fennel bulbs** and **2 celery ribs.** Toss with segments of **1 grapefruit, ¼ cup olive oil, 3 tablespoons lemon juice,** and **2 teaspoons minced fresh tarragon.** Garnish: **chopped fennel fronds.**

Carrot and Raisin Slaw with Cumin-Yogurt Dressing

Shred **1½ pounds carrots.** Whisk together **⅓ cup yogurt, 1 tablespoon olive oil, 1 tablespoon lemon juice, 1 teaspoon minced garlic, ½ teaspoon ground cumin,** and **½ teaspoon ground coriander.** Toss with the carrots, **½ cup raisins,** and **¼ cup chopped fresh mint.** Garnish: **more mint.**

BBQ Slaw

Shred **1½ pounds cabbage.** Whisk together **6 tablespoons mayonnaise, 3 tablespoons barbecue sauce,** and **1½ teaspoons Dijon-style mustard.** Toss with the cabbage, **½ chopped red onion, ½ cup chopped dill pickle,** and **¼ cup chopped fresh parsley.** Garnish: **more parsley** and **barbecue sauce,** if you like.

Beet Slaw with Saffron Aïoli

Shred **1½ pounds beets.** Whisk together **⅓ cup mayonnaise, 2 tablespoons lemon juice, 2 teaspoons minced garlic,** and **a crumbled pinch of saffron.** Toss with the beets, **1 chopped shallot,** and **¼ cup chopped fresh parsley.** Garnish: **more chopped parsley.**

CABBAGE
+12 WAYS

Cabbage
Caesar

Here's one foolproof way to guarantee that you don't overcook cabbage: don't cook it at all. While raw cabbage most often suffers the fate of being drowned in mayonnaise (and sugar), there are tastier and less heavy-handed ways to go than a lump of traditional coleslaw. (For some truly delicious—and dare I say more refined—versions of slaw, see page 90.)

The other three methods here do apply heat, ranging from the hot blast of the wok, to the gentleness of a braise, to a quick bath in a bubbling broth. Taste often for doneness; the key is to let the cabbage soften and lose its raw edge while still retaining some of its crunch.

I've made suggestions for which type of cabbage to use in which recipes, but you should feel free to substitute. No matter what kind of cabbage you buy, look for tightly packed heads; they should feel heavy for their size and not have any loose or yellowing leaves.

To shred cabbage, cut the head into quarters, slice out the hard white core, and cut crosswise into thin strips (to shred napa cabbage, just cut the whole thing crosswise). Whatever method you use to shred cabbage for coleslaw (maybe you have one of those old-fashioned wooden graters) will work here.

These recipes should serve four generously.

BRAISED

Unstuffed Cabbage

Sauté **1 pound ground beef, 1 chopped onion,** and **1 chopped carrot** in **2 tablespoons olive oil** until browned. Add chopped leaves of **1 small savoy cabbage** (about 6 cups), **¼ cup raisins,** and **a pinch of cinnamon.** Cover and cook until the cabbage wilts, then add a **28-ounce can of whole tomatoes** (with juice) and **½ cup stock.** Simmer, partly covered, until the cabbage is tender and the sauce thickens. Garnish: **parsley.**

Curry

Use **green cabbage.** Substitute **chicken thigh chunks** for beef; **1 tablespoon each minced garlic, ginger,** and **fresh chile** for carrot; **1 tablespoon curry powder** for cinnamon; and **15 ounces coconut milk** for tomatoes. Garnish: **cilantro and lime.**

Sausage and Beer

Substitute chunks **of kielbasa** for ground beef, **butter** for olive oil (skip the carrot). Use **red cabbage.** Skip the raisins, cinnamon, and tomatoes, and substitute **1 to 2 cups of beer,** plus **¼ to ½ cup cider, red-wine,** or **sherry vinegar** for the stock.

RAW

Thai Style

Put about **12 cups shredded napa cabbage** in a large bowl with **½ cup chopped peanuts** and **1 cup chopped mint.** Combine **3 tablespoons fish sauce, 1 to 2 tablespoons rice vinegar, 1 tablespoon neutral oil, 1 tablespoon brown sugar,** the **juice of 1 lime,** and some **minced fresh hot chile** to taste; whisk to dissolve the sugar. Add the dressing to the cabbage and toss.

Apples and Bacon

Substitute **red cabbage** for napa, **walnuts** for peanuts, and **a sliced green apple** for mint. Skip the Thai flavors. Crisp **4 ounces chopped bacon** in olive oil. Stir in **1 tablespoon Dijon,** chopped **shallot,** and lots of **pepper;** toss with cabbage.

Cabbage Caesar

Forget everything but the cabbage. Rub the bowl with **a garlic clove;** add **1 egg yolk, a few chopped anchovies, ½ cup grated Parmesan,** the **juice of 1 lemon, 6 tablespoons olive oil,** and **salt** and **pepper.** Whisk; add the **cabbage** and toss.

SOUP

Hot and Sour

Bring **8 cups chicken stock** to a boil with **2 tablespoons each minced garlic and fresh ginger.** Add **8 ounces sliced fresh shiitakes** and **5 cups shredded napa cabbage;** cook until softened, 5 minutes. Add **3 tablespoons soy sauce, ¼ cup rice vinegar, 1 cup tofu cubes,** and **black pepper.** Cook 3 to 4 minutes. Garnish: **chopped fresh cilantro, scallions.**

Pho

Use **napa cabbage.** Add **1 cinnamon stick, 4 cloves,** and **4 pieces star anise.** Substitute **8 ounces thinly sliced beef** for shiitakes, **fish sauce** for soy, **lime juice** for vinegar, and **4 ounces soaked rice noodles** for tofu. Garnish: **cilantro, mint, sliced chiles.**

Beans and Ham

Keep the stock, skip the rest. Brown **8 ounces chopped ham** and **1 chopped onion** in **olive oil.** Add the stock and **3 cups cooked white beans;** bring to a boil. Add **green cabbage** and some **thyme;** simmer until tender. Garnish: **Parmesan.**

STIR-FRIED

  *(plus two additional plate images)*

Shrimp and Mushrooms

Put **3 tablespoons neutral oil** in a large skillet over high heat. When hot, add **1 tablespoon each minced garlic and fresh ginger,** and cook for 15 seconds; add **1 small shredded napa cabbage** and **8 ounces sliced mushrooms;** cook, stirring, until soft and slightly brown, 5 minutes. Add **8 ounces shrimp** and cook until pink, 3 to 5 minutes. Turn off the heat and stir **soy sauce** to taste. Garnish: **scallions.**

Pork and Peanuts

Use **napa cabbage.** Brown **8 ounces ground pork** in the oil before adding the **garlic** and **fresh ginger.** Skip the mushrooms and shrimp (add **a handful of peanuts** when you'd add the shrimp, and cook until lightly toasted). Garnish: **scallions.**

Egg and Tomato

Use **napa cabbage;** skip the mushrooms and shrimp. Once the cabbage is soft, push it to one side of the pan, add more oil, and scramble **2 or 3 eggs** in the empty spot until firm. Stir in **1 cup chopped tomatoes.** Garnish: **scallions and soy.**

ROOT
VEGETABLES
+6 WAYS

There was a time when the only root vegetables anyone paid attention to were carrots and potatoes. (I know potatoes are tubers. Whatever.) Turnips were déclassé, celeriac unheard of, beets a pain to clean. The unpopularity has disappeared—in part because it was all wrong; in part because if you're going to eat seasonal and local, you are going to eat roots in winter, even if you live in California; and in part because roasted root vegetables, which most of us have discovered only recently, are the greatest thing ever.

Here's one more reason: they're interchangeable. Color aside, many of the root vegetables actually look the same. (Even colorwise, it's confusing because there are white carrots, yellow beets, and purple potatoes.) Their density is quite similar, so they cook at about the same rate. Most contain starchy sugars, so they brown beautifully and become sweet after cooking. (Only carrots and beets are sweet raw.) All of this can be disclosed simply by substituting just about any root vegetable you like in your favorite potato recipe. The treatment won't be identical (the more sugar, the quicker the browning), but it will be similar and the results will almost always be startling and good.

Each of the six recipes here, to serve four, is based on a given root vegetable, but the point is this: mess around. Bake beets instead of celeriac; make creamy potato soup, braise carrots, grate parsnips, and so on. And don't stop there: please consider turnips, rutabaga, and yams, as well as taro, yucca, boniato, and cassava.

If you have more root vegetables than you know what to do with, make pickles, a purée (also good for baby food), or a simple chutney. By the time you've worked your way through all that, it'll be spring.

Baked Whole Celeriac

Heat the oven to 350°F. Thoroughly wash a **celeriac** and pat dry; brush the outside with **olive oil**, sprinkle liberally with **coarse salt**, and bake for 1 to 2 hours (for celeriac, longer is better; other vegetables will be done sooner), until the outside is roasted and evenly crisp and the inside is tender. Remove it from the oven and cut it up if you like (you can also sprinkle with more oil and salt). (Yes, you can eat the skin.)

Creamy Carrot Soup

Sauté **1 chopped small onion** and **1 smashed garlic clove** in **2 to 3 tablespoons butter** in a large pot over medium heat until the onion is soft, about 3 minutes. Add **1½ to 2 cups chopped carrots** and **a pinch of salt**, and continue cooking for another 5 minutes. Add **6 cups hot chicken or vegetable stock**, **¼ cup heavy cream**, **1 bay leaf**, and **1 teaspoon chopped tarragon**, and bring to a boil. Simmer and cook until the vegetables are tender, about 5 minutes. Cool, remove the bay leaf, and then purée the mixture. Reheat, adding **a cup of minced raw carrot** (or greens); cook until barely tender, about 5 minutes. Garnish: **chopped fresh parsley**.

Mixed Root-Vegetable Sauté

Cook **a thinly sliced medium onion in olive oil** over medium-high heat until tender, about 5 minutes. Meanwhile, **peel and grate a few carrots, sweet potatoes, and radishes or turnips;** add them, along with some **minced garlic,** to the pan and continue to cook, stirring occasionally, for another 5 minutes. Add the **juice of ½ lime** (this will loosen the mixture a bit), and add **a sprinkle of chili powder, a handful of chopped scallions,** and **fish sauce** to taste. Garnish: **lime wedges.**

Potato Nik

Peel and grate **2 pounds all-purpose potatoes** and **1 medium onion;** drain in a colander. Mix with **2 large eggs, 2 tablespoons bread crumbs, salt,** and **pepper.** Put **neutral oil** in a large, deep skillet (nonstick or cast-iron is best) on medium-high heat and, when hot, add the batter. Cook, shaking the pan occasionally; adjust the heat so the mixture sizzles but does not burn. Continue cooking until the bottom is nicely browned, at least 15 minutes, then turn. Slide the nik onto a plate, cover with a second plate, and invert. Return to the pan. Add a bit more oil, and cook until nicely browned, about 15 minutes. Garnish: **Parmesan.**

Braised Beets

Peel about **1 pound of beets** and chop into 1-inch cubes. In a large saucepan, combine **2 to 3 tablespoons butter** with the beets and enough **chicken or vegetable stock to cover** (½ cup or more). Add a **splash of white wine** and some **chopped fresh tarragon;** bring to a boil. Cover and adjust the heat so the mixture simmers, cooking until the vegetables are tender, 15 to 20 minutes. Add **salt and pepper to taste.**

Parsnip Gratin

Heat the oven to 375°F. Put **2 or 3 cups heavy cream** in a pot and heat until hot. Peel and separately slice **1 pound each parsnips and potatoes.** Grate enough **Gruyère** to have 1 to 1½ cups. Layer the parsnips, potatoes, and cheese in an ovenproof dish, sprinkling every other layer with **salt, pepper,** and **chopped fresh thyme.** Pour in enough hot cream to come about three-fourths of the way up the vegetable layers. Bake until the vegetables are tender and easily pierced with a fork, 45 to 50 minutes; the top should be nicely browned. Let stand for a few minutes.

BEETS +12 WAYS

Give a cook a beet, and he or she will probably do one of two things with it: reject it for fear of turning the kitchen into a juicy red crime scene, or roast it and serve it with goat cheese. Ever since its ascendance, the beet-and-goat-cheese salad has been as ubiquitous a combination as tomato and mozzarella. I can take this marriage or leave it, but even if you love it, you must admit that it only scratches the surface of what beets have to offer.

There are some roasted-beet recipes here—*sans* goat cheese—but the rest treat the root in less familiar ways. More than half the time that I prepare beets, I shred them in a food processor and serve them raw with a simple dressing or stir-fry them to brown slightly, which brings out their sweetness like nothing else.

Size doesn't matter much with beets: the big ones taste just as good as the little ones, and they're easier to handle and peel. A better indication of quality is when beets are attached to their greens, which ensures that they're reasonably fresh. Only the braised recipes here call for the greens, but there's plenty more you can do with the greens. You'll never go wrong sautéing them with garlic and olive oil, or cooking them any way you'd cook Swiss chard.

The beet's notoriety for staining your hands and kitchen is well deserved (unless you use golden beets; feel free), but there are easy ways to mitigate the mess. You can wear disposable gloves to stop the beets from tinting your hands, though that's overkill—the redness does wash off with soap and water. More lasting is a beet stain on a wooden cutting board. Lay wax paper over the board while cutting, or opt for plastic boards that won't absorb the juice. Work over or in the sink when possible, and wear an apron.

Or don't worry too much. A red stain is a cook's badge of honor.

These recipes each serve four.

RAW

With Sherry Vinaigrette

Peel and grate **1 pound beets**. Make a vinaigrette with **1 minced shallot**, **2 teaspoons Dijon mustard, 2 tablespoons olive oil, 1 tablespoon sherry vinegar**, and some **chopped fresh parsley or tarragon** (really nice). Toss with the beets, taste, and adjust the seasoning. Garnish: **more parsley.**

With Creamy Dill Dressing

Substitute **¼ cup sour cream** for the oil and vinegar, and **chopped fresh dill** for the herbs. Add **lemon juice to taste**. (You can skip the mustard if you like, but I prefer to keep it). Toss with the beets. Garnish: **more dill.**

Borscht Salad

Peel and grate **½ pound beets**. Substitute **¼ cup sour cream** for the oil and vinegar and **dill** for the herbs. Add about **2 cups shredded cabbage** and a **chopped hard-boiled egg**. Toss with the beet. (Or, use 1 pound beets and make a bigger salad; this keeps well.) Garnish: **chopped fresh parsley.**

ROASTED

Pine Nuts and Parmesan

Wash **2 pounds beets**; wrap each in foil. Roast at 400°F on a baking sheet until a knife pierces with little resistance, 45 to 90 minutes. When cool enough to handle, peel and cut into chunks; toss with **¼ cup pine nuts, shaved Parmesan, lemon juice,** and **olive oil.** Garnish: **parsley.**

Moroccan Carrots

Replace half the beets with **carrot chunks** (wrap the beets only). Toss carrots with **olive oil** and roast with the beets until tender, 30 to 45 minutes for carrots, longer for beets. Substitute **chopped almonds** for pine nuts, and **½ teaspoon each ground cumin and coriander** and **a pinch of allspice** for the Parmesan. Garnish: **mint.**

Pears and Pistachios

Replace half the beets with **pears cut into quarters** (wrap the beets only). Toss the pears with **olive oil** and roast with the beets until tender, 25 to 35 minutes for pears, longer for beets. Skip the Parmesan. Substitute **pistachios** for the pine nuts and **red or white wine vinegar** for the lemon juice. Garnish: **chopped mint.**

BRAISED

Butter and Dill

Peel **2 pounds beets**; chop into 1-inch chunks. Chop the beet greens. Put both in a saucepan with **3 tablespoons butter** and **½ cup stock**. Bring to a boil, reduce heat, cover, and simmer until beets are tender, 20 to 25 minutes. Boil off excess liquid; toss with **chopped dill.**

Sour Cream and Chives

Reduce the **butter** to 1 tablespoon. When the beets are tender, stir in **¼ cup sour cream**; substitute **chopped fresh chives** for the dill. (This is fantastic served over egg noodles.)

Ham and Beer

Add **½ cup chopped smoked ham hock or ham steak** to the saucepan, and reduce the **butter** to 1 tablespoon. Substitute **beer** for the stock. Omit the dill. Garnish: **caraway seeds.**

SAUTÉED

Buttered

Peel and grate **1½ pounds beets**. Put **3 tablespoons butter** in a large skillet over medium-high heat. When hot, add **1 chopped medium onion** and cook until tender, 5 minutes. Add the beets and stir occasionally until tender and lightly browned, about 10 minutes. Garnish: **parsley.**

With Pasta and Brown Butter

Increase the **butter** to 4 tablespoons and skip the onion. Heat the butter until it turns nutty brown, then add **20 fresh sage leaves** along with the beets. When the beets are done, add some **cooked pasta** and toss. Garnish: **grated Parmesan.**

Red-Eye Hash

Replace half the beets with **grated potatoes**; add **½ cup chopped ham** with the **onion**. Cook until the beets and potatoes are tender, 15 minutes; remove from the skillet. Deglaze the skillet with **⅓ cup coffee** and **2 tablespoons heavy cream**. Spoon over the vegetables. Garnish: **chopped scallions.**

POTATOES
+12 WAYS

Latkes

There are the up-and-coming root vegetables with near-celebrity status—celeriac, parsnips, beets—and then there is the potato.

A good potato can be incredibly delicious sautéed in a little garlicky olive oil, simmered in stock, boiled and drizzled with the tiniest amount of butter and a sprinkle of mint, or mashed with greens. And those are just the start. In the something like 10,000 years since the potato was first cultivated (it has been in the hands of Europeans and their descendants for only 500 years), there have been something like 10,000 different ways of cooking it. Here are a mere twelve, but at least a few of them are bound to be new to you. All these recipes are based on using about 2 pounds of potatoes, or roughly four medium to large spuds.

There was a time when the term "all-purpose,"

Mashed
with
greens

Braised
with wine

applied to potatoes, was really wishful thinking: no potato combined waxy and mealy properties in a pleasing balance, at least not one grown in North America. The Yukon Gold changed all that. Developed in Ontario in the 1960s (but only on the market since the 1980s), it is similar to potatoes grown in northern Europe—starchy enough to bake and firm enough to boil—making it as close to the "everything potato" as exists.

That said, mashed dishes are best made with russet varieties, and new potatoes are better for cooking in fat. (Use the latter type of potato for the labor-intensive Tater Tots, which are little short of a revelation.)

You can peel the potatoes in these recipes or not; thin-skinned potatoes, especially, are just fine with a good scrubbing (use a brush).

All of the recipes serve four.

BAKED	BRAISED

Pommes Anna

Heat the oven to 400°F. Peel and thinly slice **2 pounds all-purpose potatoes** (consider using a food processor). Toss with **3 tablespoons melted butter or oil** and neatly layer in a 10- or 12-inch ovenproof skillet. Bake for 30 minutes; slide the cake out onto a plate, cover with another plate, invert it, and slide it back into the skillet, with a little more butter or oil if necessary. Continue cooking until potatoes are done and top is browned, 20 to 25 minutes; cut into wedges.

Simple

Cut **2 pounds potatoes** into chunks. Heat **3 tablespoons butter** in a deep skillet over medium-high heat; add the potatoes, **1 chopped onion, 1 teaspoon chopped garlic,** and **a sprig of thyme or rosemary;** cook, stirring, until the potatoes begin to turn golden, 10 minutes. Add enough **chicken or vegetable stock** to barely cover the potatoes. Bring to a boil, then simmer until the potatoes are tender and the liquid mostly evaporates, 30 minutes. Garnish: **chopped fresh thyme or rosemary.**

Anchovy and Pesto

Heat the oven to 375°F. Slice **the potatoes** up to ¼ inch thick. Skip the butter. In a food processor, combine **2 cups fresh basil leaves, 1 garlic clove, 2 tablespoons pine nuts, 4 anchovy fillets, ¼ cup olive oil,** and **½ cup grated Parmesan;** pulse until blended, adding another 2 to 4 tablespoons oil until smooth. Toss with the potatoes; layer in an 8 by 10-inch baking dish and bake until the top is browned and the potatoes are done, about 55 minutes.

Gratin

Heat the oven to 400°F. Slice **the potatoes** up to ¼ inch thick; layer in an ovenproof skillet. Dot with **2 tablespoons butter;** add enough **half-and-half** to come three-fourths to the top (2 to 3 cups). Place the skillet on the stove and bring to a boil; simmer for 10 minutes. Put in the oven and bake until the top browns, 10 minutes; reduce the heat to 300°F and cook until tender and browned, 10 minutes. Garnish: **grated cheese** (sprinkled on in the last 2 minutes of cooking) and **nutmeg.**

Curried in Coconut Milk

Substitute **neutral oil** for the butter; omit the thyme. Add **1 tablespoon chopped fresh ginger** and **2 teaspoons curry powder** along with the **onion** to the **potatoes.** Substitute **1½ cups coconut milk thinned with ½ cup water** for the stock. Garnish: **chopped fresh cilantro or Thai chile** or both.

With Wine

Sauté **¼ pound diced pancetta** in **a little olive oil** until crisp; remove with a slotted spoon. Add **1 tablespoon chopped garlic** and **the onion;** cook for a moment, then add **the potatoes.** Use **1 cup dry white wine** and **1 cup stock** for the liquid and cook until done. Garnish: pancetta crisps and **chopped fresh parsley.**

MASHED	FRIED

Blowout

Boil **2 pounds of starchy or all-purpose potatoes** until soft, 15 to 30 minutes, and drain. Wipe the pot and return to very low heat. Mash potatoes with **½ cup (1 stick) butter**; then stir in **½ cup heavy cream**. Garnish: **chopped fresh parsley or chives.**

Rosti

Grate **2 pounds all-purpose potatoes**; squeeze out excess liquid. Melt **2 tablespoons butter** in a skillet (preferably nonstick) over medium heat and add the potatoes; shape into a disk. Cook until golden brown, about 10 minutes, adjusting heat as necessary. Slide the cake onto a plate, cover with another plate, and invert. Add more butter to the pan and slide the cake back in. Cook until browned all over, turning again, if necessary. Garnish: **chopped fresh parsley.**

Lean but Good

While **the potatoes** boil, heat **¼ cup olive oil** in a skillet with **1 tablespoon minced garlic** and **a sprig of rosemary or thyme.** When the garlic is colored (not brown), add the drained potatoes to the olive oil and mash, adding a bit more oil if you like; skip the cream. Garnish: **chopped chives.**

With Greens

Following the recipe for Lean but Good, mash in **1 pound chopped cooked dandelion greens, spinach, or other bitter greens.** Garnish: **buttered bread crumbs.**

Tater Tots

Heat the oven to 400°F. Parboil **the potatoes** until tender before grating. Mix with **1 tablespoon cornstarch** and **1 teaspoon each salt, pepper, and garlic powder.** Add **neutral oil** to a depth of ½ inch in a skillet. Form small cylinders the shape and size of gnocchi and fry until golden, 15 seconds per side. Drain on paper towels, let cool, then bake until crisp, about 30 minutes, turning once. (Makes 40 tots)

Latkes

To the **grated potatoes**, add **1 grated medium onion, 2 lightly beaten eggs,** and **2 tablespoons bread crumbs** (or matzo meal). Substitute **neutral oil** for the butter (be liberal). Spoon the potato mixture into the oil to form small pancakes; fry until brown and crisp on both sides, 6 to 8 minutes per side. Serve with **sour cream** and **apple-sauce.** (Makes about 12 latkes)

PUMPKIN
+3 WAYS

Almost no one in this country cooks with fresh pumpkin.

Yet the pumpkin—or those squashes whose non-English names translate as "pumpkin"—is a staple the world over, turned into substantial dishes celebrated for their sweetness and density. So-called sugar pumpkins, which are smaller and more flavorful than anything you might carve, are the best for cooking and available even in super-markets. But you can tackle the big boys, too.

All three of the recipes are global classics, and all use cubes of pumpkin flesh, though you can use any orange-fleshed winter squash, like butternut or Kabocha, in any pumpkin recipe. But let's assume you're working with a pumpkin. Getting at the good stuff is the tricky part. Start just as if you were carving a jack-o'-lantern: cut a circle around the stem, then pull up on the stem and discard it. Using the cavity as a handle, peel the pumpkin with a sturdy vegetable peeler. Yes, it will take a while.

Then cut the pumpkin in half and scrape out the seeds with an ice cream scoop or heavy spoon. You can discard the seeds or roast them. Cut or scrape off any excess strings and cut the pumpkin into approximately 1-inch cubes. (A 4-pound pumpkin will yield about 8 cups of cubes.)

These recipes are substantial, even if you make them vegetarian. (To make them with-out meat, simply skip the beef in the Afghan recipe, substitute more pumpkin for lamb in the Moroccan dish, and use vegetable stock for all.)

Afghan Style (with Yogurt Sauce)

SERVES: 4 to 6

2	tablespoons neutral oil
1	medium onion, chopped
1	teaspoon ground turmeric
1	tablespoon minced fresh ginger
1	minced fresh hot chile (like jalapeño or Thai), seeds removed
8	cups (1-inch) cubed pumpkin flesh
1½	cups chicken, beef, or vegetable stock, plus more as needed
	Salt and freshly ground black pepper
2	tablespoons olive oil
2	garlic cloves, crushed
1	pound ground beef (optional)
1	14½-ounce can crushed tomatoes (double if omitting the meat)
¼	teaspoon ground coriander
1	cup yogurt, preferably whole milk
¼	cup chopped fresh mint, plus more for garnish
1	teaspoon minced garlic

1. Put the oil in a pot or deep skillet over medium-high heat. When hot, add the onion and cook until browned, about 10 minutes. Add the tur-meric, ginger, and chile, and cook for another 2 minutes, until aromatic.

2. Add the pumpkin and stock; sprinkle with salt and pepper. Bring to a boil, cover, and turn heat to low. Cook, stirring once or twice, until pumpkin is tender, 15 to 30 minutes. Check periodically to make sure there is adequate liquid; if the pumpkin is done and the liquid is thin, remove the lid and turn the heat to medium-high, boiling the mixture until thick; taste and adjust seasoning.

3. Heat the olive oil in a skillet over medium heat. When hot, add the crushed garlic. If using ground beef, add it and sprinkle with salt and pepper. Cook, stirring occasionally, until the meat begins to brown, about 5 minutes. Add the tomatoes and coriander, and reduce the heat to low; simmer until the mixture thickens, 5 to 10 minutes.

4. Combine the yogurt, mint, minced garlic, salt, and pepper in a bowl and stir.

5. Spoon the ground beef and tomato sauce over the pumpkin. Top with yogurt sauce and more fresh mint.

Risotto con la Zucca

SERVES: 4 to 6

5	cups (1-inch) cubed pumpkin flesh
6	tablespoons butter or olive oil
1	large or 2 medium onions, diced
1	tablespoon minced garlic
¼	teaspoon grated nutmeg
1	tablespoon minced fresh sage or rosemary
1½	cups arborio or other short-grain rice

	Salt and freshly ground black pepper
½	cup dry white wine
4	to 6 cups chicken, beef, or vegetable stock
½	cup freshly grated Parmesan, plus more for garnish
¼	cup thinly sliced almonds or chopped pistachios

1. Bring a large pot of water to a boil and add the pumpkin; boil until soft, 15 to 20 minutes. Drain the pumpkin and purée it until smooth in a blender or food processor.

2. Put 2 tablespoons butter in a large, deep skillet over medium heat. When hot, add the onion and cook until softened, about 5 minutes. Add the garlic, nutmeg, and sage, and continue cooking another minute or so; do not brown.

3. Add 2 tablespoons more butter; raise the heat to medium-high and add the rice. Cook, stirring occasionally, until it is glossy and coated, 2 to 3 minutes. Sprinkle with salt and pepper; stir in the wine and let most of it bubble away.

4. Begin adding the pumpkin purée and stock alternately, ½ cup or so at a time, stirring after each addition. When the liquid is just about evaporated, add more; the consistency should not be soupy or dry. Stir frequently.

5. Taste the rice after about 20 minutes. You want it to be tender but still have some bite; this can take up to 30 minutes. When the rice is done, turn off the heat and stir in the remaining 2 tablespoons butter and the Parmesan; taste and adjust the seasoning. Heat a dry skillet and add the nuts; toast until fragrant. Sprinkle the risotto with the toasted nuts and more Parmesan.

Moroccan Style (with Lentils)

SERVES: 4 to 6

2	tablespoons olive oil, plus a little more if necessary
1	pound boneless leg of lamb, cut into 1-inch cubes and trimmed of fat
	Salt and freshly ground black pepper
1	large or 2 medium onions, roughly chopped
6	cups (1-inch) cubed pumpkin flesh
2	teaspoons minced garlic
1	teaspoon ground turmeric

1	teaspoon ground cinnamon
1	teaspoon ground cumin
2	fresh bay leaves
½	cup dry white wine
2	cups chicken, beef, or vegetable stock
1½	cups chopped ripe tomatoes with juices (canned are fine)
1	cup green lentils
	Chopped cilantro, for garnish

1. In a heavy pot with a lid, heat 2 tablespoons olive oil on medium-high heat. When hot, add the lamb; sprinkle with salt and pepper and cook until browned on all sides, 5 to 8 minutes total, stirring as needed. Remove the lamb to a plate and reduce the heat to medium.

2. If the pan is dry, add a little more oil. Add the onion and cook, stirring occasionally, until soft, 5 minutes. Add the pumpkin, garlic, turmeric, cinnamon, and cumin; cook until the pumpkin begins to soften, about 10 minutes.

3. Add the bay leaves, wine, stock, and tomatoes, and return the lamb to the pan. Bring to a boil, then reduce the heat and cook for at least 45 minutes on medium-low, partly covered. Stir occasionally; add more stock if needed to keep mixture moist.

4. Add the lentils and bring the mixture back to a boil. Adjust the heat to a simmer. Continue to cook, uncovered, stirring occasionally, until the lentils are tender and the liquid is thick, about 30 minutes. (If at any point the mixture threatens to become too thick, add a bit of stock or water.) Taste and adjust the seasoning. Remove the bay leaves, and garnish with cilantro before serving.

MUSHROOMS
+3 WAYS

If the word *mushroom* conjures for you those white buttons in supermarket tubs, you're not alone. But there is a big world of mushrooms out there, and you don't have to be a forager to live in it. In recent years, the availability of mushroom varieties, particularly shiitake, has exploded. And the ease with which you can buy dried mushrooms—not just porcini but also morels, lobster mushrooms, and another dozen even more exotic types—is a revelation.

I'm not suggesting you abandon fresh mushrooms. Even though the only fresh mushroom you can buy that remotely rivals dried wild mushrooms in flavor is the shiitake, fresh mushrooms offer a texture and "brownability" that you cannot really duplicate with dried. Hence, the technique of combining fresh and dried mushrooms in the same dish captures the best qualities of both. Especially in the soup that follows and the Pasta with Funghi Trifolati, I like a combination: button or shiitake for the fresh, and porcini, morel, and maybe even lobster for the dried. The resulting assortment of sensations may keep you from ever thinking of mushrooms the same way again.

Mushroom Soup

SERVES: 4

2   to 3 ounces dried mushrooms (cremini, morel, whatever you like)

4   tablespoons (½ stick) butter

1   fresh thyme or rosemary sprig

1   large onion, or 3 or 4 shallots, chopped

1   tablespoon minced garlic

1   pound fresh mushrooms (shiitake or button—a variety is nice), sliced

    Salt and freshly ground black pepper

⅓   cup sherry or Madeira

5   cups chicken stock, mushroom-soaking liquid, or a combination

1   cup heavy cream (optional)

    Chopped fresh parsley leaves, for garnish

1. Soak the dried mushrooms in 5 cups very hot water until soft, anywhere from 5 to 15 minutes. When they are tender, remove the mushrooms from the soaking liquid with a slotted spoon, reserving the liquid; slice or chop if the pieces are large, and discard the stems if you are using shiitakes.

2. Meanwhile, put the butter in a large pot over medium heat. When it melts, add the thyme, onion, and garlic and sauté, stirring occasionally, until soft, about 5 minutes. Turn the heat to medium-high, and add the fresh mushrooms. Stir in the soaked mushrooms, sprinkle with salt and pepper, and cook until the fresh mushrooms have given off their liquid and begun to brown, about 20 minutes, stirring occasionally.

3. Add the sherry to the pot and cook, scraping up any browned bits from the bottom as the liquor starts to bubble. Add the stock and bring to a boil, then lower the heat to a steady simmer and cook, covered, until flavors have melded, about 15 minutes.

4. Discard the thyme sprig. Reduce the heat to low, and use an immersion blender to purée the liquid to desired consistency (I like it half-puréed). Add the cream if you're using it; stir to combine and let simmer for a few minutes. Taste and adjust the seasoning; garnish with chopped parsley.

Mushroom Stir-Fry

SERVES: 4 to 6

2   ounces dried mushrooms, preferably shiitakes

2   cups chopped broccoli florets and stems (in bite-size pieces)

3   tablespoons neutral oil

2   tablespoons minced garlic

2   tablespoons minced fresh ginger

1   large onion, halved and sliced

1   pound fresh mushrooms (button, cremini, shiitake—a variety is nice), sliced

2   carrots, peeled and roughly chopped

2   celery ribs, roughly chopped

1   teaspoon cornstarch (optional)

2   tablespoons soy sauce

    Salt and freshly ground black pepper

¼   teaspoon hot red chile flakes (optional)

½   cup chopped scallions

1. Soak the dried mushrooms in 3 cups very hot water until soft, anywhere from 5 to 15 minutes. When they are tender, remove the mushrooms from the liquid with a slotted spoon, reserving the liquid and discarding the stems; slice or chop if the pieces are large.

2. Meanwhile, set a pot of water to boil for the broccoli. Cook the broccoli for 2 minutes in the boiling water, then drain.

3. Put a large, deep skillet over medium-high heat; add the oil and swirl it around, then add the garlic and ginger. Cook for 15 seconds; add the onion and cook, stirring occasionally, until beginning to soften and brown, 3 to 5 minutes. Add the fresh and soaked dried mushrooms, and allow them to cook down 2 or 3 minutes before adding the carrots and celery. Cook, stirring occasionally, until vegetables are tender but not at all mushy, 10 to 12 minutes. Add the broccoli after about 6 minutes of cooking.

4. If you're using the cornstarch, dissolve it in the soy sauce; stir into the pan and sprinkle with salt and pepper. Add the red chile flakes if you're using them, and pour in ¾ cup of the mushroom-soaking liquid. Stir the mixture, and scrape the bottom of the pan, then turn off the heat; the liquid should be mostly absorbed. Sprinkle with the scallions.

Pasta with Funghi Trifolati

SERVES: 3 to 4

1   ounce dried mushrooms (cremini, porcini, whatever you like)

1   tablespoon olive oil

3   tablespoons butter

2   teaspoons minced garlic

1   medium onion, chopped

1   pound fresh mushrooms (shiitake or button—a variety is nice), sliced

½   cup dry white wine

½   pound dried cut pasta (ziti or penne)

½   cup chopped fresh parsley, plus more for garnish

    Salt and freshly ground black pepper

    Fresh-shaved Parmesan (optional)

1. Soak the dried mushrooms in very hot water until soft, anywhere from 5 to 15 minutes. When they are tender, remove the dried mushrooms from the soaking liquid with a slotted spoon, reserving the liquid; slice or chop if the pieces are large.

2. Set a large pot of salted water to boil for the pasta. Put a large skillet over medium-high heat, and add the olive oil and 2 tablespoons of the butter. When it is hot, add the garlic and onion; cook, stirring occasionally, until the onion begins to soften, 3 to 5 minutes. Add the fresh and the soaked mushrooms, and cook until the fresh give up their liquid and start to brown, at least 15 minutes. Add the white wine or ½ cup of the mushroom-soaking liquid to the pot and cook, scraping up any browned bits from the bottom as the liquid starts to bubble.

3. Meanwhile, cook the pasta in the boiling water until tender.

4. Reduce the skillet heat to low. Add the remaining tablespoon of butter and the ½ cup parsley, and stir to combine; sprinkle with salt and pepper. When the pasta is done, drain it, reserving a bit of the cooking water. Add the pasta to the mushroom mixture, and toss until well combined. If the mixture is dry, add a little pasta water or more mushroom-soaking liquid. If you like, garnish with Parmesan and more parsley.

VEGAN ENTREES
+10 WAYS

Sometime in your life (I'm guessing even within this year) you've probably made the pledge to eat better. With the ascendance of clashing fad diets, defining what's "better" has become increasingly more difficult, but the core of the answer is, or should be, known to everyone: eat more plants. And if the diet that most starkly represents this—veganism—is no longer considered bizarre or unreasonably Spartan, neither is it exactly mainstream. (For the record, vegans don't simply avoid meat; they eschew all animal products in their diet, including dairy, eggs, and even honey.)

Many vegan dishes, however, are already beloved: we eat fruit salad, peanut butter and jelly, beans and rice, eggplant in garlic sauce. The problem faced by many of us—brought up as we were with plates whose center was filled with a piece of meat—is in imagining less traditional vegan dishes that are creative, filling, interesting, and not especially challenging either to put together or to enjoy.

You can make semi-veganism work for you. Once a week, let bean burgers stand in for hamburgers, leave the meat out of your pasta sauce, make a risotto the likes of which you've probably never had—and you may just find yourself eating "better."

This is not a gimmick or even a diet. It's a path, and the smart resolution might be to get on it.

Each of the recipes here will serve four hearty appetites as a main course, more as an appetizer or side dish.

Loaded Miso Soup

Bring 6 cups water to a bare simmer in a large pot and add **1 kombu strip** (dried kelp); let it soak 10 minutes, then remove and chop it; reserve the kombu water. Meanwhile, sauté **a handful of sliced shiitake mushrooms** in **2 tablespoons neutral oil** until crisp, about 10 minutes. Whisk 1 cup of the kombu water with ½ cup miso in a bowl until smooth. Pour the miso mixture into the kombu water and add **½ pound silken tofu**, along with **a few cups shredded carrots, turnip, and ginger,** the chopped kombu, and **a handful of cooked shelled edamame** (frozen are fine). Let stand long enough to heat the tofu through, about 1 minute. Add some **chopped scallions** and the crisp shiitakes.

Fried Rice

Prepare **3 cups cooked and cooled rice.** Heat **3 tablespoons neutral oil** in a sauté pan over medium-high heat. Add **½ pound cubed extra-firm tofu,** then add **a handful each of snow peas, chopped carrot, and peanuts,** stirring more or less constantly until the carrot is just becoming tender, 3 to 5 minutes. Add **a teaspoon each of grated garlic and ginger,** followed by the rice. Cook, stirring, until the rice begins to brown, about 5 minutes. Add enough water to loosen the mixture a bit, then add **soy sauce** to taste.

Bean Burgers

Cut **a medium onion** into chunks and put it in a food processor along with **2 cups drained canned beans** (white are best here, but any will work), **½ cup old-fashioned rolled oats, 1 tablespoon chili powder,** and **salt and pepper.** Pulse on and off, stopping occasionally to scrape the sides as necessary, until the mixture holds together. Taste; if it's too dry, add a little water; if it's too wet, add more oats, 1 tablespoon at a time. Shape the mixture into 4 patties. Heat **2 tablespoons olive oil** in a skillet and cook the burgers until nicely browned each side, about 5 minutes per side. Serve on **toasted buns** with **lettuce** and **tomato** and **onion slices.**

Spinach and Chickpeas

Heat **2 tablespoons olive oil** in a large skillet and cook **2 minced garlic cloves** until fragrant, about a minute. Add **1 cup fresh bread crumbs** (made from 4 or 5 slices of crusty bread, pulsed in a food processor); cook, stirring frequently, until evenly toasted, about 5 minutes, then remove from skillet. Add **a little more oil** and sauté **1 pound spinach leaves,** along with **1 teaspoon each ground cumin** and **pimentón** (smoked paprika). When the spinach begins to wilt, in 2 or 3 minutes, add a **14-ounce drained can of chickpeas** (or 2 cups cooked dried chickpeas), and cook for 5 minutes or so. When you're ready to serve, stir in **1 tablespoon sherry vinegar** and sprinkle with the toasted bread crumbs.

Tomato-Rice Soup

Heat **¼ cup olive oil** in a large pan and add **1 tablespoon chopped garlic, 1 chopped onion, 1 cup each chopped carrot and celery,** and some **chopped parley;** cook until the onion is translucent, about 5 minutes. Add **½ cup white or brown rice** and cook, stirring, until fragrant, then add **2 tablespoons tomato paste** and stir. Add **4 cups vegetable stock** or water and **2 cups chopped ripe or canned tomatoes.** Bring to a boil, reduce the heat, and simmer until the rice is half-tender, about 10 minutes for white rice and 25 minutes for brown. Add **1 cup chopped collard greens** and a few tablespoons **red wine,** and cook until the greens are tender, 2 to 3 minutes more.

Pasta, Beans, and Tomatoes

Heat **3 tablespoons olive oil** in a large, deep skillet over medium heat. Sauté **2 table-spoons chopped garlic** until fragrant, about a minute. Add **2 cups chopped ripe or canned tomatoes** and cook for 5 minutes, or until saucelike. Add **1½ cups canned white beans** or 1 cup cooked dried beans and heat until bubbly. Add **1 pound cooked penne pasta** and stir. Add **a handful of fresh basil** and a bit more olive oil.

Saffron and Mushroom Barley Risotto

Heat **3 tablespoons olive oil** in a large, deep skillet over medium heat. Cook **1 chopped onion** until soft, about 5 minutes. Add **1½ cups pearled barley,** and cook, stirring, until it's glossy, 2 to 3 minutes. Add **a pinch of saffron, a splash of dry white wine,** and **a handful of dried porcini.** Stir well, then let the liquid bubble away over medium heat. Add **4 cups hot vegetable stock,** 1 cup at a time, stirring after each addition and waiting until the mixture is nearly dry before adding the next. Meanwhile, sauté **2 cups sliced shiitake mushrooms in olive oil** until lightly crisped, about 10 minutes; stir into the barley when it's done and garnish with **chopped parsley.**

Brussels Sprouts with Walnuts and Croutons

Heat **2 tablespoons olive oil** in a large skillet over medium heat. Lay **1 pound halved Brussels sprouts** cut side down in the skillet and add a little **water or vegetable stock,** cover, and cook undisturbed until sprouts are browned and tender, 20 to 30 minutes. (Lower the heat or add more water if the sprouts threaten to burn.) Put in a serving bowl and drizzle with **a little balsamic.** Add **½ cup chopped walnuts** and **2 minced garlic cloves;** cook, stirring, for about 5 minutes, then add to the sprouts. Add **a bit more oil** to the skillet and **1 smashed garlic clove,** then **1 cup bread cubes,** and brown lightly, about 5 minutes. Toss with the sprouts.

Sweet Potato Stew

In a large, deep skillet, sauté **1 pound cubed sweet potatoes, 1 peeled and cubed apple, 1 chopped onion, 1 minced dried or fresh chile,** and **1 tablespoon minced fresh ginger,** along with **a sprinkle of curry powder** in a large saucepan until the onion is soft, 5 or 6 minutes. Add enough **coconut milk thinned with vegetable stock or water** to come about halfway up the sides of the mixture in the pan; cook until the potatoes are soft, 20 to 30 minutes. Mash about half of the mixture, and stir back into the remainder. Garnish with **chopped peanuts** and **cilantro.**

Roasted Squash with Kale and Vinaigrette

Heat the oven to 425°F. Halve and seed **2 small to medium winter squash** (acorn, butternut, etc.). Place in a deep baking pan, drizzle with **olive oil,** and bake until just tender, 20 to 30 minutes. Coarsely chop **a bunch of kale** (about 3 or 4 cups); add to the squash and bake an additional 10 to 20 minutes. Meanwhile, make a vinaigrette by combining **6 tablespoons olive oil** and **2 tablespoons wine vinegar** with salt and pepper and **1 chopped shallot** in a blender until a creamy emulsion forms. When the vegetables are tender and easily pierced with a fork, cut into 1-inch pieces, toss with the kale, then dress with vinaigrette.

VEGETABLE SHOWSTOPPERS

Imagine this: Your dinner guests are seated around the table, waiting for you to parade out the main course. You triumphantly carry it in on a platter. Oohs and ahs ensue.

What did you picture on that platter? A bronzed turkey, perhaps? A hulking roast? Lobster à l'Américaine? It probably wasn't vegetables, which have long been relegated to side-dish territory. But the WOW factor isn't restricted to animal flesh. I argue that elevating vegetables to star status is a better display of your culinary chops— and a more unconventional and surprising one— than showcasing a piece of meat.

The recipes here are vegetarian and nearly vegan. (I love carrots with olive oil, but butter makes them otherworldly.) They don't rely on either animal products or heavy carbs as belly-filling crutches, but instead allow the vegetables to become the centerpieces. There's squash stuffed with more squash that has been enriched with dried porcini; a whole head of cauliflower parboiled and then roasted until gloriously browned; and the aforementioned carrots, slow-roasted until soft and deeply caramelized. (These are an adaptation of the "forgotten carrots" served by Neil Borthwick at Merchants Tavern in London; they actually do require a little bit of attention.)

And, yes, they can be main courses. The squash is quite substantial, with plenty of extra stuffing to serve on the side. The cauliflower and carrots could just as easily accompany larger dishes, but their supple textures and rich sauces—Romesco and Brown Butter Vinaigrette, respectively—help them register as meaty and filling. This isn't to say that they don't need side dishes, just that they're beautiful and complex enough to command center stage. If that makes you nervous, you can always serve a little bit of meat on the side.

Slow-Roasted Carrots with Brown Butter Vinaigrette

SERVES: 4

2 pounds large carrots	Salt and freshly ground black pepper
3 tablespoons olive oil	3 tablespoons sherry vinegar
½ cup (1 stick) plus 3 tablespoons unsalted butter	1 teaspoon Dijon mustard
2 cardamom pods	3 tablespoons chopped fresh chervil or parsley
2 star anise	

1. Heat the oven to 325°F. Scrub the carrots and peel them if you like (it really doesn't matter). Set a long roasting pan over two burners on medium heat; put the olive oil in the pan. When the oil is hot, add the carrots and cook, turning as they brown in the oil, until lightly caramelized all over, 10 to 15 minutes.

2. Add 3 tablespoons butter, the cardamom and star anise, salt, and pepper. Transfer the roasting pan to the oven, and cook, shaking the pan once or twice, until the carrots are crinkly on the outside and you can pierce them easily with the tip of a sharp knife, 45 to 60 minutes.

3. Meanwhile, melt the remaining ½ cup butter in a small saucepan over medium heat. Cook, stirring occasionally, until the foam subsides and the butter turns nut brown, about 5 minutes. Turn off the heat.

4. Put the brown butter, the vinegar, mustard, salt, and pepper in a standing blender. Blend until a creamy emulsion forms, about 30 seconds; taste and adjust the seasoning. Put the carrots on a platter, drizzle the vinaigrette over the top, and garnish with the chervil or parsley.

Stuffed Butternut Squash

SERVES: 4

2   medium butternut squash

¼   cup olive oil, plus more for rubbing squash

    Salt and freshly ground black pepper

½   cup dried porcini or other mushrooms

1   medium onion, chopped

½   cup dry red wine

1   cup vegetable stock or water

10 fresh sage leaves, chopped

    Zest of 1 lemon

1. Heat the oven to 400°F. Peel and trim the squash; separate the long necks from the bulbous bases. Scoop out the seeds, and reserve. Roughly dice the necks into pieces no bigger than ½ inch.

2. Rub the hollowed-out bases inside and out with olive oil; sprinkle with salt and pepper. Stand them up on a rimmed baking sheet, and roast, flipping once, until they are browned all over and you can easily pierce the flesh with the tip of a sharp knife, about 1 hour.

3. Meanwhile, soak the porcini in 1 cup hot water until soft; remove and chop, reserving the liquid. Put 3 tablespoons olive oil in a large skillet over medium-high heat. When hot, add the onion and cook, stirring occasionally, until soft, 5 minutes. Add the chopped squash and the porcini, and sprinkle with salt and pepper. Cook, stirring occasionally, until the squash is browned, 8 to 12 minutes.

4. Add the red wine, stirring to scrape up any browned bits from the bottom, and let it bubble away until it almost disappears. Add the mushroom-soaking liquid (leave any sediment behind) and the stock. Bring to a boil, then reduce to a simmer. Cover partly and cook, adding more liquid if the pan gets too dry, until the squash is very tender, 10 to 15 minutes; taste and adjust seasoning.

5. Put 1 tablespoon olive oil in a separate small skillet. When the oil is hot, add the squash seeds and cook, stirring occasionally, until golden brown and crisp, 4 to 6 minutes. Turn off the heat, add the chopped sage, lemon zest, and a sprinkle of salt and pepper. Toss.

6. When the squash bases are done, spoon the chopped squash mixture into the cavities (save the leftover stuffing or serve it on the side). Sprinkle with the squash seeds.

Whole Roasted Cauliflower with Romesco

SERVES: 4

3   red bell peppers

1   medium to large cauliflower

¼   cup olive oil, plus more for drizzling

    Salt and freshly ground black pepper

½   cup Marcona almonds

1   small garlic clove, peeled

1   tablespoon sherry vinegar

1. Fill a large pot two-thirds full with water and set to boil; turn on the broiler, and put the rack about 4 inches from the heat source. Put the peppers on a foil-lined baking sheet and broil, turning as each side browns, until they have darkened and collapsed, 15 to 20 minutes. Wrap the peppers in the same foil that lined the pan; when they are cool enough to handle, remove the skins, seeds, and stems (this is easiest under running water).

2. Heat the oven to 450°F. Remove any leaves from the cauliflower. When the water boils, salt it generously. Submerge the cauliflower in the water, reduce the heat to a simmer, and cook until you can easily insert a knife into the center, 15 minutes or more. Don't overcook.

3. Using two spoons or a shallow strainer, transfer the cauliflower to a rimmed baking sheet and pat dry with paper towels. Drizzle all over with olive oil, sprinkle with salt, and roast until nicely browned all over, 40 to 50 minutes.

4. Meanwhile, combine the roasted red peppers, the almonds, garlic, vinegar, and a sprinkle of salt and pepper in a standing food processor. Turn the machine on and stream in ¼ cup olive oil; purée into a thick paste. Taste and adjust the seasoning.

5. When the cauliflower is browned, transfer it to a serving platter. Cut the cauliflower into slices or wedges, and serve the sauce on the side for dipping.

PASTA, GRAINS, AND BEANS

Any chapter (in this or any book) that combines three categories as gigantic and diverse as pasta, grains, and beans will necessarily be a bit of a catch-all. Taking that as a given, I'll say that among the recipes included here are some of my all-time favorites to cook and eat, period. Take socca, for instance, the giant chickpea-flour pancake from Provence that could very well be part of my last meal on earth (if I had control over such things). Then there are homemade corn tortillas (a revelation if you're used to store-bought), and any of the dal recipes from my Indian cooking guru Julie Sahni.

Don't worry that I've given short shrift to more familiar categories. You'll find plenty of things to do with pasta (including eight versions of primavera and four flavors of gnocchi), rice (twelve recipes using brown), and that twenty-first-century darling, quinoa (which, among other things, can be turned into my new obsession, addictively crunchy crumbs).

For the most useful information in the whole chapter, see the Grain Salad recipe generator (page 122), where my method for cooking just about every grain you will come across is outlined. Learn that, and you're pretty much set for life.

PASTA PRIMAVERA
+8 WAYS

Pasta primavera, which means "springtime pasta," is an American invention—at least as American as, say, fettuccine Alfredo. It first appeared on the menu at Le Cirque in the 1970s, and Sirio Maccioni, that restaurant's owner, was quoted in 1991 in the *New York Times* saying, "It seemed like a good idea and people still like it."

But with all due respect to Mr. Maccioni, is pasta primavera still a good idea? I'm all in favor of pasta with vegetables, but I want to be able to taste them, not toss together every vegetable under the sun and smother them under heavy cream. I want them to be prepared thoughtfully.

So I created these vegetable pasta dishes that are made in a more traditional Italian way—simply, and in a skillet—with just enough additional ingredients to heighten the flavors of the dish.

The basic pasta-cooking technique is simple and consistent from dish to dish. As for the vegetables, sauté them in a large skillet until they're just barely tender. When the pasta's tender but not mushy, drain it, reserving about 1 cup of cooking water, then add the pasta to the skillet and toss, pouring in enough of the reserved water to cook through both the pasta and the vegetables.

I have not recommended specific pasta shapes for these sauces, because the shape doesn't matter. Use what you like and don't worry about it.

Pasta Primavera Universal Instructions

Bring a large pot of water to a boil, salt it, then add ½ to 1 pound of pasta. (Vary the amount depending on your preferred pasta-to-sauce ratio; the quantity of sauce in the recipes that follow will sauce up to 1 pound of pasta, or enough to serve four at minimum.) When the pasta is tender but not mushy, drain it, reserving 1 cup of cooking water.

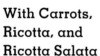

With Peas, Pecorino, Chile, and Mint

Before cooking the pasta, add **2 cups shelled peas** to the pot of boiling water and cook until tender, 3 to 5 minutes; remove, Then cook **the pasta.** While it cooks, sauté **1 tablespoon minced fresh hot chile** (like Thai) and the peas in **2 tablespoons olive oil** over medium heat, stirring occasionally, for a minute or two. Toss with the pasta, **½ cup chopped fresh mint,** and **½ cup grated pecorino romano cheese.** Garnish: **chopped fresh mint** and **grated pecorino.**

With Carrots, Ricotta, and Ricotta Salata

Cook **4 thinly sliced carrots** in **2 tablespoons olive oil** and 2 tablespoons water over medium-high heat, stirring as necessary, until the carrots are tender and lightly browned, 8 to 10 minutes. Toss with cooked **pasta** and **1 cup ricotta.** Garnish: **crumbled ricotta salata** and **chopped fresh parsley,** if you like.

With Creamed Spinach

Before cooking the pasta, add **2 pounds spinach** to the pot of salted boiling water; cook for 1 minute, then remove, cool, and chop. While **the pasta** cooks, boil **1 cup heavy cream, 3 tablespoons butter,** and **the chopped spinach** over medium heat and cook until thick, 5 minutes or more. Toss with the cooked pasta. Garnish: **grated nutmeg.**

With Dandelions and Smoked Sausage

Cook **1 tablespoon minced garlic** and **8 ounces chopped smoked sausage** (like chorizo or kielbasa) in **2 tablespoons olive oil** over medium heat until the sausage browns, 8 to 10 minutes; remove. While **the pasta** cooks, add **1 pound chopped dandelion greens,** cover, and cook until wilted but still somewhat firm, about 5 minutes. Uncover, add a little pasta-cooking water, and continue to cook, stirring, until the greens are tender, about 5 more minutes. Toss with the cooked pasta and the sausage, adding more olive oil if needed. Garnish: **ground black pepper.**

With Favas, Watercress, and Brown Butter

Shell **3 pounds fresh fava beans,** then rinse (or use 3 cups shelled favas). Simmer in water to cover until tender, 12 to 15 minutes. Drain, cool slightly, and peel each bean. Melt **4 tablespoons butter** over medium heat and stir until the foam subsides, then add the favas and cook for 2 minutes. Toss with the cooked **pasta** and **1 bunch chopped watercress** (reserve a handful for garnish). Garnish: **chopped watercress.**

With Butter-Braised Turnips and Sage

Cook **1 pound peeled and diced turnips** in **2 tablespoons butter** over medium heat, stirring, until they begin to brown, about 10 minutes. While **the pasta** cooks, add **1 tablespoon chopped sage** and **⅔ cup vegetable or chicken stock, white wine, or water;** boil until the turnips are tender and the liquid is almost entirely evaporated, 10 to 20 minutes. Toss with the cooked pasta. Garnish: **chopped fresh sage.**

Carbonara with Leeks

Cook **4 ounces chopped pancetta or good bacon** in **2 tablespoons olive oil** over medium heat, stirring occasionally, until browned, 8 to 10 minutes; remove with a slotted spoon. While **the pasta** cooks, add **chopped white and tender green parts of 3 cleaned leeks** (about 1 pound) to the pan and cook until softened and beginning to brown, about 15 minutes. Make 4 wells in the cooked leeks, add a little olive oil to each, and crack **4 large eggs** into the wells. Fry until the whites are barely set. Toss with cooked pasta, the pancetta, and **½ cup grated Parmesan.** Garnish: **chopped fresh parsley.**

With Chard and Roasted New Potatoes

Heat the oven to 425°F; toss **1 pound diced new potatoes** with **2 tablespoons olive oil** in a roasting pan. Roast, stirring occasionally, until browned and very tender, about 30 minutes. Meanwhile, cook **the pasta.** Chop **1 pound chard,** keeping the stems and leaves separate. Cook **1 chopped onion** in **2 tablespoons olive oil** over medium heat, stirring, for 5 minutes. Add the chard stems and cook until they soften, a minute or two, then add the leaves, cover, and cook until tender, about 5 minutes. Toss with the cooked pasta and the potatoes. Garnish: **grated Parmesan.**

GNOCCHI
+4 WAYS

Carrot gnocchi with brown butter, sage, and parmesan

A phrase often used (overused, really) to describe well-made gnocchi is "light as a cloud." It's not an especially instructive description for a piece of real food, and for cooks hoping to try their hands at gnocchi for the first time, it can be daunting.

It's all in the dough. There are just a few key things to remember:

1. Use starchy potatoes, like regular old russets. It's the starch from the potatoes—along with the gluten from the flour—that holds the dough together.

2. You don't want overcooked, waterlogged potatoes; the wetter they are, the more flour you'll need.

I bake them whole, which is effortless, but you could also boil them whole and unpeeled. If time allows, you might dry them in a low oven for a little while, once they're fully tender.

3. Use as little flour as you can get away with to make the dough hold its shape. Add the flour a little at a time, and test-boil a piece of dough—even if you think it's not ready yet—to see if it holds together.

4. Be gentle when mixing and kneading; the idea is to avoid overdeveloping the gluten, the offense most likely to make your gnocchi decidedly un-cloudlike.

Gnocchi Universal Instructions

SERVES: 4

1½ pounds starchy potatoes
Salt and pepper

½ to ¾ cup all-purpose flour, plus more as needed

1. Heat the oven to 400°F. Bake the potatoes until tender, about 1 hour. Immediately split them open to let the steam escape. When you can handle the potatoes, scoop out their flesh.

2. Bring a large pot of water to a boil and salt it. Pass the potato flesh through a ricer or food mill, and season to taste. Sprinkle ¼ cup of the flour on a clean counter or cutting board, and knead the potatoes with it, sprinkling in an additional ¼ cup flour, until the dough just comes together. Pinch off a piece of the dough, and boil it to make sure it will hold its shape. If it does not, knead in a bit more flour (no more than necessary), and try again; the gnocchi will float to the top and look a little ragged when ready.

3. Roll a piece of the dough into a rope about ½ inch thick, then cut the rope into ½-inch lengths. Score each piece by rolling it along the tines of a fork; as each piece is ready, put it on a baking sheet lined with parchment or wax paper; do not allow the gnocchi to touch one another.

4. Add the gnocchi to the boiling water a few at a time, and stir gently; adjust the heat so the mixture doesn't boil too vigorously. A few seconds after they rise to the surface, the gnocchi are done; remove them with a slotted spoon or mesh strainer, and finish with any of the sauces.

Beet Gnocchi

Peel and grate **½ pound beets.** Cook in **2 tablespoons olive oil** over medium-low heat, **seasoning** to taste, until very soft, 25 to 30 minutes. Transfer to a food processor, and purée until smooth. Stir into the mashed potatoes in step 2 of the master recipe (you'll most likely need an extra **¼ cup flour**).

Carrot Gnocchi

Peel and grate **½ pound carrots.** Cook in **2 tablespoons olive oil** over medium-low heat, **seasoning** to taste, until very soft, 20 to 30 minutes. Transfer to a food processor and purée until smooth. Stir into **the mashed potatoes** in step 2 of the master recipe (you'll most likely need an extra **¼ cup flour**).

Spinach Gnocchi

Roughly chop **8 ounces spinach leaves.** Cook in **2 tablespoons olive oil** over medium-low heat, **seasoning** to taste and stirring, until soft and wilted, about 5 minutes. Rinse under cold water and squeeze dry. Transfer to a food processor and purée until smooth. Stir into **the mashed potatoes** in step 2 of the master recipe (you'll most likely need an extra **¼ cup flour**).

SAUCES

Olive Oil and Garlic

Cook at least **1 tablespoon minced garlic** in **⅓ cup olive oil,** along with (optional) **hot red chile flakes and/or chopped anchovies** just until the garlic turns golden (but no more than that). Toss with **the gnocchi,** some of their cooking water, and plenty of **chopped fresh parsley.**

Bacon and Cream

Crisp **8 ounces chopped bacon, prosciutto, or pancetta** in **2 tablespoons olive oil.** Stir in **½ cup heavy cream** and **pepper.** Simmer until the cream thickens slightly, 2 to 3 minutes, then add **the gnocchi.**

Tomato Sauce

Cook a **chopped small onion** in **2 tablespoons olive oil** until soft. Add **1 tablespoon minced garlic, 3 to 4 cups chopped canned or ripe tomatoes,** and **salt** and **pepper.** Cook at a steady bubble until sauce-like, 15 to 20 minutes. If the sauce becomes too thick, add a splash of the gnocchi cooking water. Serve with **the gnocchi.** Garnish: **torn fresh basil** and/or **grated Parmesan.**

Brown Butter, Sage, and Parmesan

Put **4 tablespoons butter** and **a handful of fresh sage leaves** (40 wouldn't be too many) in a skillet over medium heat. Cook until the butter is light brown and the sage is sizzling, about 3 minutes. Toss with **the gnocchi,** some of their cooking water, and loads of **grated Parmesan.**

GRAIN SALADS
+RECIPE GENERATOR

A grain salad is more of a concept than a recipe—there are virtually infinite variations. They are the perfect canvas for showcasing pretty much any vegetables that require only chopping, slicing, or grating. All that you'll need to cook are the grains, which don't demand very much of your attention.

I typically opt for heartier grains that retain a chewy texture when cooked, like farro, brown rice or wild rice, pearled barley, wheat berries, bulgur, or steel-cut oats. For grains with a bit more tenderness, quinoa, couscous, and white rice are all excellent options.

The method I use to cook almost every grain—bulgur, couscous, and wild rice are exceptions—is simple: put 2 cups of the grain in a small to medium saucepan with a large pinch of salt and water to cover by about 1 inch. Bring to a boil,

then adjust the heat so that the mixture bubbles gently. Cook, stirring occasionally and adding boiling water if necessary to keep the grains covered; when they're tender, they're done, anywhere from 15 minutes (pearled barley) to an hour (wheat berries). If there is water remaining in the pot when you're done, strain it. Remember that even after you toss the salad, the warm grains will continue to cook, so err slightly on the side of undercooking.

While the grains are cooking, whisk together any vinaigrette you like in the bottom of a large bowl, then prepare whatever veggies and flavorings you're using, and toss them all together. Leftover grains work fine here, though warm grains soak in the vinaigrette and intensify the flavor of the other ingredients.

Grapes

Feta

Citrus zest

Asparagus

Quinoa

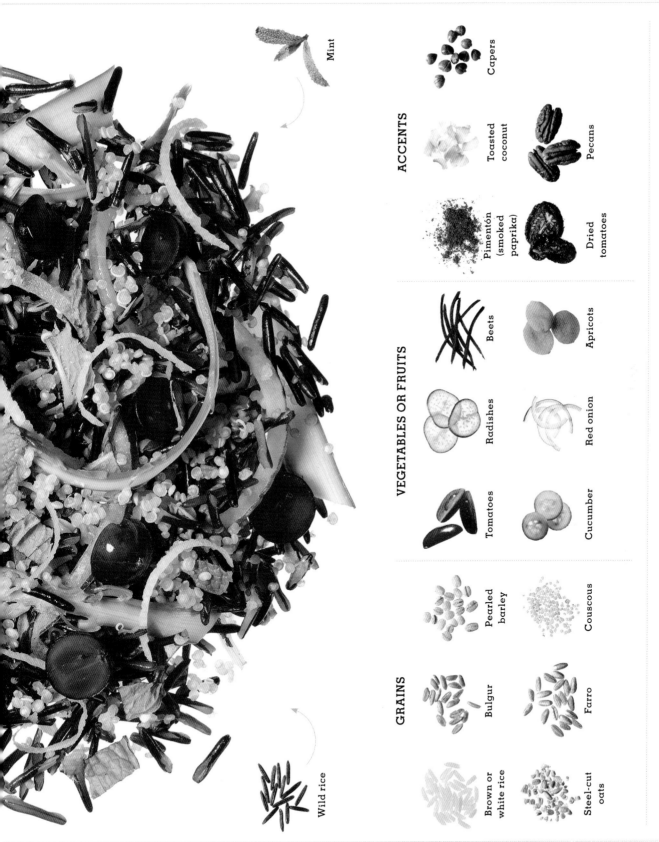

Mint

Wild rice

ACCENTS

Capers

Toasted coconut

Pimentón (smoked paprika)

Pecans

Dried tomatoes

VEGETABLES OR FRUITS

Beets

Apricots

Radishes

Red onion

Tomatoes

Cucumber

GRAINS

Pearled barley

Couscous

Bulgur

Farro

Brown or white rice

Steel-cut oats

Grain Salads Universal Instructions

THE ASSEMBLY: To serve four, combine about 2 cups cooked grains with 1 cup raw vegetables, fruit, or both and flavorful accents. Toss with a vinaigrette, and serve warm or at room temperature. THE DRESSING: basic vinaigrette of 3 parts olive oil, 1 part lemon juice, plus salt and pepper (see page 238).

QUINOA
+10 WAYS

Crisp Quinoa Cakes
with Almonds,
Rosemary and Dijon

Not so long ago, quinoa was as mysterious as dark matter. Few could even pronounce the name of this ancient, disk-shaped "super grain" from the Andes, mistakenly calling it kwih-NO-ah (it's KEEN-wah). It tasted a little strange; home cooks didn't know what to do with it, and only vegan restaurants put it on menus.

Now quinoa is everywhere, and seemingly everyone knows everything about it. You probably recognize its grassy flavor and faintly crunchy texture. If I told you that it's not a grain at all but, rather, a chenopod related to spinach and beets, you probably wouldn't be surprised.

Yet we still don't explore quinoa's full potential, probably because when it's simmered until fluffy and just tender, quinoa is an admirable base for a salad or a pilaf. But real rewards await those who venture a bit outside the box. For example, quinoa makes a delicious risotto. Cook it long enough, and its starches begin to release; cook it even further, and you can form the quinoa into cakes for pan-frying, without adding bread crumbs or eggs (though you should still handle them gently).

My favorite application is transforming quinoa into crunchy crumbs. You boil it, spread the tender grains on a rimmed baking sheet, toss them with seasonings, and roast until crackling and crisp. Sprinkle them on salads, stir-fry dishes, pastas, or anything else you might be inclined to finish with toasted bread crumbs or chopped nuts.

Crisp Quinoa Cakes with Almonds, Rosemary, and Dijon

MAKES: 8 to 10 cakes

1 cup quinoa	1 tablespoon minced fresh rosemary
Salt and freshly ground black pepper	1 tablespoon Dijon mustard
¼ cup chopped almonds	2 tablespoons olive oil
2 tablespoons minced shallots	Lemon wedges, for serving

1. Put the quinoa, a large pinch of salt, and 2¼ cups water in a medium saucepan. Bring to a boil, and then adjust the heat so that the mixture bubbles gently. Cover, and cook, stirring once, until the grains are very tender and begin to burst, 25 to 30 minutes. When the grains are starchy and thick (a few minutes longer), transfer them to a large bowl to cool for a few minutes.

2. Heat the oven to 200°F. Fold the almonds, shallots, rosemary, and mustard into the quinoa, and add a generous sprinkle of salt and pepper. With your hands, form the mixture into 8 patties.

3. Put 1 tablespoon olive oil in a large skillet over medium heat. When the oil is warm, cook 4 cakes at a time until the bottoms are nicely browned and crisp, about 4 minutes. Flip, and brown on the other side, another 4 minutes. Transfer the cakes to the oven to keep warm while you cook the second batch with the remaining tablespoon of oil. Serve with lemon wedges.

Quinoa Cakes with Pine Nuts and Raisins

Omit the almonds, shallots, rosemary, and mustard; instead, use ¼ cup pine nuts, ¼ cup raisins, ¼ cup chopped fresh parsley, and ½ cup freshly grated Parmesan.

Quinoa Cakes with Cilantro, Scallions, and Sriracha

Omit the almonds, shallots, rosemary, and mustard; instead, use ½ cup chopped fresh cilantro, ¼ cup chopped scallions, and 1 tablespoon Sriracha.

Three-Cheese and Mushroom Quinoa Risotto

SERVES: 4 to 6

¾ cup dried porcini mushrooms	½ cup dry white wine or water
3 tablespoons butter or olive oil, plus more to taste	2 to 3 cups chicken or vegetable stock
2 shallots, chopped	¼ cup each freshly grated Parmesan, chopped fontina, and crumbled Gorgonzola
1 cup chopped fresh shiitake caps	
1½ cups quinoa	
Salt and freshly ground black pepper	

1. Cover the dried mushrooms with 1 cup hot water, and set aside until softened, 5 to 10 minutes; drain and chop, reserving the soaking liquid. Put the butter in a large, deep skillet or saucepan over medium heat. When it is hot, add the shallots and dried and fresh mushrooms, and cook, stirring occasionally, until the shiitakes begin to brown, about 5 minutes.

2. Add the quinoa, and cook, stirring occasionally, until it's glossy and coated with butter. Sprinkle with salt and pepper, and then add the wine. Stir, letting the liquid bubble away. Add the porcini-soaking liquid, being careful not to pour in any sediment.

3. Start adding the stock about ½ cup at a time, stirring after each addition and adjusting the heat to maintain a gentle bubble. When the stock is nearly evaporated, add more. Continue to cook, stirring frequently and adding stock as necessary; the mixture should be neither soupy nor dry.

4. Begin tasting the quinoa after about 20 minutes; you want it to be tender but not mushy and to have released some of its starch. Once it reaches that stage, after about 25 minutes, stir in the cheeses, along with a little more butter or oil, if you like. Stir until the cheeses melt; taste and adjust the seasoning, and serve.

Smoky Quinoa Crumbs

MAKES: 2¼ cups

1 cup quinoa	1 tablespoon pimentón (smoked paprika)
Salt	

1. Heat the oven to 375°F. Put the quinoa and a large pinch of salt in a medium saucepan. Add water to cover the quinoa by about 1 inch. Bring to a boil, and then adjust the heat so that the mixture bubbles gently. Cover, and cook, stirring occasionally, until the quinoa is tender and the water is absorbed, 15 to 20 minutes. If any water remains in the pot, strain it off.

2. Spread the quinoa on a large rimmed baking sheet, breaking up any clumps with your fingers. Sprinkle with salt and the pimentón. Toss to combine, and spread the quinoa in as even a layer as possible.

3. Bake, tossing once or twice with a spatula, until the grains dry out and become crisp, 15 to 25 minutes, depending on how crunchy you want them. Use immediately, or cool completely and store in an airtight container in the fridge for up to a week.

Sesame Nori

Instead of the pimentón, use **3 tablespoons sesame seeds, 3 tablespoons finely snipped nori**, and **½ teaspoon Chinese five-spice.**

Garlic

Instead of the pimentón, use **1 tablespoon finely minced garlic.**

Lemon and Herb

Instead of the pimentón, use **the zest of 1 lemon** and **1 tablespoon finely minced fresh rosemary, thyme, sage, or oregano.**

Pumpkin Seed Spice

Instead of the pimentón, use **3 tablespoons chopped pepitas** and **½ teaspoon each ground cinnamon, nutmeg, and allspice.**

Smoky and Spicy

Instead of the pimentón, use **1 teaspoon ground cumin, 1 teaspoon chili powder**, and a **pinch of cayenne.**

MASA
+3 WAYS

Corn
Tortillas

If you're interested in a serious project, you can make the best tortillas you've ever had by soaking and washing dried hominy, then grinding it to produce masa, or "dough." Then you press out small disks and griddle them. Do that, and you'll have my admiration.

Or, you can do what so many people do: start with masa harina, or "masa flour," which you mix with water and a little fat to make masa. The tortillas produced with masa harina are not quite as fabulous as those that begin with dried hominy, but they're very good, especially compared with the chalky disks that pass for tortillas in most places. You'll find masa harina in any supermarket that has even a small Latino clientele, or online. Don't use cornmeal or corn flour to make tortillas; it won't cook properly, and the tortillas won't taste right.

These will taste deeply corny, lightly puffy, and fresh. And they'll open the door to more involved masa projects like pupusas and tamales. Pupusas—a traditional Salvadoran treat—are essentially fat tortillas stuffed with beans, cheese, or meat, and griddled until crisp. Tamales—cornmeal dough wrapped in corn husks and steamed—are more a test of patience than of technique.

Tortillas, which of course can be used in a variety of ways, are also potential tacos. So I've included a recipe for the kind of shredded chile-sauced meat—beef, pork, chicken, or lamb—that you can use as a filling for any of the three.

Corn Tortillas

MAKES: 12 to 16 tortillas

1½ cups masa harina

¼ teaspoon salt

2 tablespoons vegetable oil, lard, or butter

About 1 cup hot water, or more as needed

All-purpose flour, for kneading

1. Combine the masa and salt in a bowl; stir in the oil. Slowly stream in the water while mixing with your hand or a wooden spoon until the dough comes together into a ball.

2. Turn the dough out onto a lightly floured surface and knead until it is smooth and elastic—just a minute or two. Wrap in plastic, and let rest at room temperature for at least 30 minutes or up to a few hours.

3. Break off pieces of the dough (you're shooting for 12 to 16 tortillas total), and lightly flour them. Put them between 2 sheets of plastic wrap, and press them in a tortilla press, or roll them out or press them with your hands to a diameter of 4 to 6 inches. Begin to cook the tortillas as you finish pressing or rolling them.

4. Put a large skillet, preferably cast iron, over medium-high heat for 4 to 5 minutes. Cook the tortillas, 1 or 2 at a time, until brown spots appear on the bottom, about a minute. Flip, and do the same on the other side. Wrap the cooked tortillas in a towel to keep them warm; serve immediately, or cool and store tightly wrapped in the fridge for a few days.

Pupusas

MAKES: 6 pupusas

Masa dough from Corn Tortilla recipe (steps 1 and 2)

Vegetable oil

¾ cup Shredded Red Chile Meat (see recipe, right), or a combination of cooked beans and shredded cheese

1. Divide the dough into 6 balls. With lightly oiled hands, hold a ball in one hand, and use your other thumb to make an indentation. Flatten the edges to create a bowl. Put about 2 tablespoons of the filling into each. Wrap the dough around the filling, and pinch to seal the edge. Pat it back and forth between your hands to flatten into a ¼-inch-thick disk.

2. Cook in an oiled skillet over medium-high heat until browned and slightly puffy, 3 to 4 minutes per side. Serve immediately.

Tamales

MAKES: 24 tamales

24 dried corn husks

3½ cups masa harina

2¼ cups chicken stock, approximately

1 cup lard, cut into cubes

1 teaspoon salt

1 teaspoon baking powder

1½ cups Shredded Red Chile Meat (see recipe below)

1. Soak the husks in warm water for at least 3 hours or overnight. Drain, separate the husks, then continue soaking.

2. Put the masa harina in a bowl and add stock a little at a time until the mixture is crumbly.

3. With a mixer, beat the lard, salt, and baking powder until light. Add the masa mixture, and continue to beat until the dough is fluffy, adding more stock if needed. The mixture is ready when a small ball of it floats in water.

4. Drain a husk, and pat dry. Spread 2 tablespoons of the masa dough in the center of the husk, smooth side up, then wet your fingers and pat into a 4 by 3-inch rectangle along the center of the husk, leaving at least 2 inches on each side. Put 1 tablespoon of the shredded meat lengthwise down the center of the dough rectangle. Wrap by folding the rectangle in half and bringing the right side of the dough over the filling. Continue rolling tightly to the end of the husk, then secure one open end with string or strips of corn husk. Repeat with the remaining ingredients.

5. Prepare a large steamer by setting a steamer rack about 2 inches above gently boiling water. Stack the tamales, seam down, on the rack. Cover and steam until the filling is firm and comes away easily from the husk, about 45 minutes. Serve warm or at room temperature.

SHREDDED RED CHILE MEAT
MAKES: About 3 cups

2 pounds boneless beef chuck, pork shoulder, lamb shoulder, or chicken thigh meat, cut into 1-inch cubes

5 garlic cloves, lightly crushed

1 large onion, quartered

2 dried guajillo chiles, seeds and stems removed

2 dried ancho chiles, seeds and stems removed

2 bay leaves

1 tablespoon ground cumin

Salt and freshly ground black pepper

Cayenne (optional)

1. In a large pot or Dutch oven, combine all the ingredients except the cayenne. Add water to cover and bring to a boil, skimming off any foam that comes to the surface. Partly cover, and adjust the heat so that the mixture bubbles steadily; cook until the meat is very tender, 1 to 2 hours.

2. Transfer the meat to a bowl, reserving the cooking liquid. When the meat is cool, shred it with your fingers. Transfer the garlic, onion, and chiles (discard the bay leaf) to a blender along with a splash of the cooking liquid. Blend until smooth. Add the sauce to the meat and toss. Taste, adding a little cayenne if you want it spicier; you may want to over-season the meat slightly if you're using it as a filling. Use, or store in the fridge for up to 1 week, or in the freezer for up to a few months.

BROWN RICE
+12 WAYS

Once relegated to hippie status, brown rice has become sort of de rigueur (though it's mostly served as a side dish next to something more interesting, a worthy if obligatory "healthful" substitute for white rice). It need not be this way. There are dozens of brown-rice varieties because "brown" simply means "hulled but not stripped of bran layers."

Brown basmati has the same nutty aroma as white basmati, with more chew; most brown long-grains cook just like "regular" long-grain rice; and black, mahogany, purple, and red—all those novelty rices—are "brown" as well and can be treated in pretty much the same ways, and those ways are myriad.

PILAFS

Garlic and Parsley

Cook **1 tablespoon minced garlic** in **2 tablespoons butter** for 2 minutes. Add **1½ cups brown basmati (or other) rice** and cook, stirring, about 3 minutes. Add **3 cups stock**, bring to a boil, lower the heat, and cover. Cook until the liquid is absorbed and the rice is tender, 40 to 50 minutes. Stir in **½ cup chopped fresh parsley**, cover, and let rest for 10 minutes. Garnish: **more chopped parsley.**

Sausage, Red Peppers, and Onions

Use **olive oil** instead of butter. Cook **1 sliced medium onion**, **1 sliced red bell pepper**, and **8 ounces sliced or chunked Italian sausage** in the oil before adding **the garlic**. Substitute **fresh basil** for the parsley.

Shrimp, Scallions, and Snow Peas

Use **neutral oil.** Cook **½ cup chopped scallions** before adding **the garlic.** Add **8 ounces peeled shrimp** (chopped, if large), **1 cup snow peas**, **1 tablespoon soy sauce**, and **1 teaspoon sesame oil** for the last 5 minutes of cooking. Garnish: **cilantro.**

STEWS

Fried Egg and Chives

Combine **1½ cups brown rice** with 3 cups water over high heat. Bring to a boil, lower the heat, and partly cover. Cook, stirring occasionally and adding more water if necessary, until the rice is tender and thick, 45 to 60 minutes. Stir in **½ cup chopped chives.** Meanwhile, fry **4 large eggs** in **1 tablespoon light sesame oil.** Serve the eggs over the rice. Garnish: **more chopped chives.**

Jerk Chicken

Skip the chives and eggs. First, sear **4 bone-in chicken thighs** in olive oil. Add **1 chopped onion**; cook for 5 minutes. Add **1 tablespoon minced ginger**, **1 teaspoon fresh thyme**, **½ teaspoon minced habanero**, **1 teaspoon allspice**, **½ teaspoon cinnamon**, **the rice,** and the water.

Coconut and Molasses

Skip the chives and eggs. Substitute **1 can coconut milk** for 1½ cups of the water and add **½ cup shredded unsweetened coconut** to the rice. Serve drizzled with **molasses.**

SALADS

White Bean, Lemon, and Tomato

Combine **1½ cups brown rice** with 2½ cups water over high heat. Bring to a boil, lower the heat, and cook until the liquid is absorbed and the rice is tender, 40 to 45 minutes. Chill if time allows. Toss with **1 cup cooked white beans**, **1 cup halved cherry tomatoes**, **¼ cup chopped fresh dill**, **¼ cup olive oil**, **2 tablespoons lemon juice**, and **1 tablespoon minced garlic.** Garnish: **more chopped dill.**

Grape and Ricotta

Substitute **ricotta** for the white beans, **grapes** for the cherry tomatoes, **basil** for the dill, and **1 chopped small shallot** for the garlic.

Broccoli–Pine Nut

Steam **2 cups broccoli florets** until just tender, about 5 minutes; shock in ice water, then drain and chop. Substitute **½ cup toasted pine nuts** for the white beans, **the broccoli** for the cherry tomatoes, and **1 tablespoon chopped sage** for the dill.

RICE CAKES

Parmesan and Scallion

Combine **1½ cups brown rice** with 3 cups water. Bring to a boil, then lower heat. Cook, stirring occasionally and adding more water if needed, until the rice is starchy and soft, about 1 hour. Chill for at least 1 hour. Stir in **1 cup grated Parmesan**, **½ cup chopped scallions**, and **¼ cup chopped parsley.** Form patties and cook in **olive oil** over medium-high heat until browned on both sides, about 4 minutes per side. Garnish: **Parmesan.**

Carrot and Parsnip

Skip the cheese, scallions, and parsley. Instead, stir **1 cup shredded carrot**, **1 shredded small onion**, **½ cup shredded parsnip**, and **1 tablespoon minced fresh sage** into the rice; proceed as above. Garnish: **chopped fresh parsley.**

Leek and Spinach

Skip the cheese, scallions, and parsley. Cook the white and tender green parts of **2 chopped leeks** in **2 tablespoons olive oil** until very soft and brown, 15 to 20 minutes. Add **3 cups chopped spinach** and cook just until wilted. Stir the leeks and spinach into **the rice.** Garnish: **lemon wedges.**

SPRING ROLLS+RECIPE GENERATOR

Fresh spring rolls, sometimes called summer rolls, are a staple in Vietnam. They're typically made of rice paper (although nori seaweed and lettuce leaves work well, too) filled with rice vermicelli, cooked meat or shrimp, raw vegetables, basil, cilantro, and mint. I've taken that concept as a jumping-off point and included a wide range of fillings to accompany the noodles and herbs.

Some logistics: Rice paper needs to be soaked for about 10 seconds in a dish or skillet of hot water to become pliable. If you're using nori, spritz each sheet all over with water.

Soaking rice vermicelli—you can use glass (mung bean) noodles if you prefer—in boiled water takes only 5 to 10 minutes. Boiling it on the stove for a minute or two also works. Rinse the cooked noodles in cold water, and drain well.

Rice paper rolls are rolled up like burritos, and nori rolls like sushi (you could even use cooked short-grain rice if you like). Spread the noodles all over the nori, except for the far edge. Pile the fillings closest to you and roll, wetting the far edge of the seaweed with a little more water to seal the roll. I like long rolls, but cut them into small pieces if you prefer.

Sprouts

Asparagus

Arugula

Tuna

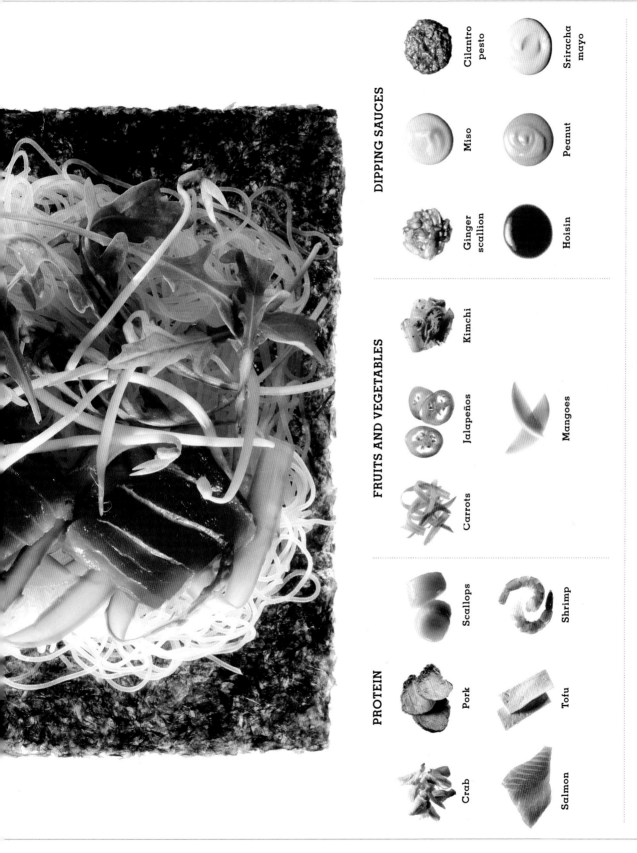

PROTEIN

Crab

Pork

Salmon

Tofu

Scallops

Shrimp

FRUITS AND VEGETABLES

Carrots

Jalapeños

Kimchi

Mangoes

DIPPING SAUCES

Ginger scallion

Miso

Cilantro pesto

Hoisin

Peanut

Sriracha mayo

Spring Rolls Universal Instructions

Select a protein (like seared tofu, grilled skirt steak, or cooked or raw salmon); add some accompaniment (mango, cucumber); put it in a wrapper of nori or rice paper, or in a lettuce leaf, along with vermicelli, basil—Thai basil, if you can find it—and cilantro and mint. For dipping sauces, simple is best: minced ginger and scallions mixed with soy sauce and sesame oil, miso thinned with water, pesto made with cilantro (no Parmesan), straight hoisin sauce, peanut butter and minced ginger thinned with soy sauce and water, or mayo spiked with Sriracha. In many cases, a drizzle of soy sauce will also do the trick nicely. Each serves one as an appetizer.

DAL
+4 WAYS

Khatti
Dal

I'd made and enjoyed dal for many years before I first visited northern India, where I realized dal could be infinitely tastier than my own. As legumes became a more important part of my cooking, however, I decided that my dal problem needed to be remedied. I turned to Julie Sahni, whose first two books, *Classic Indian Cooking* and *Classic Indian Vegetarian and Grain Cooking*, were instrumental in helping me gain a foothold in that cuisine.

From Julie I learned that there are three or four things to know in cooking dal. One is that although you can cook any beans using these techniques and spices, you're not likely to get the ideal consistency unless you shop for Indian legumes.

That texture is enhanced by a *mathani,* a kind of wooden beater or churner. A mathani is fun to use—you rub the dowel end between your palms to twirl the action end in the dal, semi-puréeing it—but a whisk works pretty well, too.

The finishing touch, brilliant in its simplicity, is called a *tadka*—oil heated with seeds, spices, and, usually, some kind of onion, often to a degree that other cuisines might consider "overcooked." The tadka is poured into the dal just before serving, and the whole thing explodes with fragrance and flavor.

Chana Dal (Split Chickpeas), New Delhi Style

SERVES: About 4

1	cup split chickpeas (chana dal)	6	whole cloves
1½	teaspoons turmeric	4	large garlic cloves, thinly sliced
½	teaspoon ground cardamom	1	teaspoon hot red chile flakes (optional)
1	bay leaf, preferably Indian	3	tablespoons chopped fresh cilantro
1	teaspoon salt		
2	tablespoons neutral oil		

1. Combine the chana dal, turmeric, cardamom, bay leaf, salt, and 4 cups water in a large saucepan and bring to a boil. Adjust the heat so the mixture bubbles gently, cover partly, and cook for 40 minutes. The mixture should still be quite moist; if not, add 1 cup water and continue cooking, covered, until the dal is tender, about 20 minutes; turn off heat. Remove the bay leaf. Use an Indian mathani or whisk to purée the dal for 1 minute; the dal should be saucy but not soupy.

2. To make the tadka, put the oil in a small saucepan over medium-high heat. When hot, add the cloves; sizzle for about 30 seconds, until fragrant. Add the garlic and cook, stirring, until medium brown. Stir in the red chile flakes if you're using them, and turn off the heat.

3. Pour the tadka into the dal; stir gently to combine. Garnish with the cilantro and serve.

Khatti Dal (Sour Lentils), Hyderabad Style

SERVES: About 4

1	cup yellow lentils (toor dal)	2	tablespoons neutral oil
1½	teaspoons turmeric	1	teaspoon mustard seeds
1	teaspoon fresh jalapeño, seeded and minced	1	teaspoon minced garlic
1½	teaspoons salt	12	curry leaves (optional)
¼	cup tamarind concentrate, or 1½ tablespoons lime juice	3	tablespoons chopped fresh cilantro

1. Combine the dal, turmeric, chile, salt, and 4 cups water in a large saucepan and bring to a boil. Adjust the heat so the mixture bubbles aggressively and steadily and cook, uncovered, for 25 minutes.

2. Add the tamarind concentrate and ½ cup additional water, and let bubble for another minute. Turn off heat. Use an Indian mathani or whisk to purée the dal for about 1 minute; it should be saucy but not soupy.

3. To make the tadka, heat the oil in a small saucepan over high heat. When the oil is hot, add the mustard seeds and cover the pan; let the seeds pop and sizzle. When the popping begins to subside, add the garlic and cook until lightly browned, about 15 seconds. Add the curry leaves, if you're using them. Cover the pan (to prevent spattering) and cook for about 10 seconds, allowing flavors to meld. Pour the tadka into the dal; stir gently to combine. Garnish with the cilantro and serve.

Chilkewali Mung Dal (Split Green Mung Beans), Mumbai Style

SERVES: About 4

1	cup split green mung beans (chilkewali mung dal)	1½	teaspoons salt
1	teaspoon turmeric	2	tablespoons neutral oil
1	teaspoon minced garlic	1	teaspoon brown mustard seeds
½	teaspoon minced fresh hot green chile	2	tablespoons julienned fresh ginger
¾	cup chopped onion	1	teaspoon ground cumin
1	cup chopped tomato	3	tablespoons chopped fresh cilantro
1½	teaspoons brown sugar		

1. Combine the dal, turmeric, garlic, chile, onion, tomato, brown sugar, salt, and 4 cups water in a large saucepan and bring to a boil. Adjust the heat so the mixture bubbles gently, and cook, covered, for 25 minutes, stirring occasionally. Partly uncover and cook for 15 minutes, until tender; turn off heat. Use an Indian mathani or whisk to beat and purée the dal for 1 minute; the dal should be saucy but not soupy.

2. To make the tadka, heat the oil in a small saucepan over high heat. When the oil is hot, add the mustard seeds and cover the pan; let the seeds pop and sizzle. When the popping begins to subside, add the ginger and cook until lightly browned, about 15 seconds. Turn off the heat and stir in the cumin. Pour the tadka into the dal; stir gently. Garnish with the cilantro and serve.

Makhani Dal (Butter Dal), Mogul Style

SERVES: About 6

¾	cup whole black gram beans (sabat urad)	1	teaspoon cardamom
2	tablespoons adzuki beans	1	teaspoon paprika
2	tablespoons split chickpeas	½	teaspoon chili powder
1	cup plain whole-milk yogurt	2	teaspoons salt
2	cups finely chopped onions	3	tablespoons neutral oil
1½	cups chopped tomatoes	1½	teaspoons minced garlic
2	tablespoons minced ginger	1½	teaspoons ground cumin
1	teaspoon turmeric	¾	teaspoon garam masala
		½	cup plain low-fat yogurt

1. Combine the legumes with 4 cups water in a large saucepan and bring to a boil; cook, uncovered, for 2 minutes. Turn off the heat and cover for 2 hours.

2. Add the yogurt, 1 cup of the onions, the tomatoes, ginger, turmeric, cardamom, paprika, chili powder, and salt to the pot and bring to a boil. Cook, partly covered, over low heat for 90 minutes, or until very soft. Turn off heat; purée with a mathani or whisk as in the other recipes.

3. To make the tadka, heat the oil in a small saucepan over high heat, add the remaining onions, and cook until they begin to soften. Add the garlic and cook, stirring, until medium brown. Turn off the heat; stir in the cumin and garam masala. Transfer the dal to a large bowl, cover with the low-fat yogurt, top with tadka, and stir gently.

CHICKPEAS
+4 WAYS

Panelle

When I was young, my mother would open a can of chickpeas and put them out at parties, with salt and pepper—hardly an inspired hors d'oeuvre. Because of that early exposure—or despite it—I'm partial to chickpeas. They have what to me is an irresistibly robust and nutty flavor, and a texture that can be either crunchy or tender.

Canned chickpeas bear a closer resemblance to cooked-from-dried than any other canned bean: they're sturdy enough to withstand additional cooking without falling apart. If you make the Crisp Spiced Chickpeas here with canned, you'll see what I mean. Even after a 20-minute sizzle in a skillet with olive oil, they stay intact, their exteriors turning crunchy while their insides become creamy.

You'll get a similar result if you start cooking with chickpea flour. Made from nothing more than ground dried chickpeas, it has that same distinct nuttiness as the whole bean; use it to make socca or panelle once, and you'll keep it in your kitchen forever.

Panelle

MAKES: 4 to 6 appetizer servings

Vegetable or olive oil, for greasing and frying

1 cup chickpea flour

Salt and freshly ground black pepper

2 tablespoons olive oil

1 lemon, cut into wedges

1. Grease an 8-inch square baking dish or quarter sheet pan with some oil. Bring 2 cups water to a boil in a small saucepan. Put the chickpea flour in a large bowl. When the water is boiling, gradually add it to the bowl with the chickpea flour, whisking constantly to prevent lumps. Scrape the mixture into the saucepan you used to boil the water, then sprinkle with salt and pepper and bring to a boil. Reduce the heat to a gentle simmer, stir in the olive oil, and cook for just 1 minute.

2. Scoop the chickpea mixture onto the sheet pan and spread it in an even layer. Let it cool, and cover loosely with parchment or plastic. Refrigerate for at least 30 minutes or up to 24 hours.

3. Put at least ¼ inch of oil in a large skillet over medium heat; heat the oil to 250°F. Cut the chickpea mixture into french fries about 3 inches long; blot any excess moisture with a paper towel. Working in batches, gently drop them into the hot oil. Cook, rotating them occasionally, until they're golden all over, 3 to 4 minutes. Drain on paper towels and immediately sprinkle with salt and lots of pepper. Serve hot, with lemon.

Crisp Spiced Chickpeas

MAKES: 2 cups

3 tablespoons olive oil

2 cups cooked or canned chickpeas, well drained and blotted dry on paper towels

1 teaspoon pimentón (smoked paprika), or ground cumin, or curry powder

Salt and freshly ground black pepper

1. Put the oil in a large skillet over medium heat. When the oil is hot, add the chickpeas and cook, shaking the skillet occasionally, until the chickpeas are brown and very crisp, 10 to 20 minutes.

2. Sprinkle with the spices, salt, and pepper, and continue to cook, shaking the pan a bit more frequently, until the spices are toasted and fragrant, 2 to 3 minutes. Drain on paper towels if necessary.

Cold Chickpea-Tahini Soup

SERVES: 4 to 6

1 cup chopped ripe tomato

1 cup chopped peeled cucumber

¼ cup chopped red onion

¼ cup chopped pitted black olives

¼ cup chopped fresh parsley

Salt and freshly ground black pepper

3 cups cooked or canned chickpeas

3 tablespoons lemon juice

1 tablespoon olive oil, plus more for drizzling

¼ teaspoon ground cumin, plus more for garnish

1 small garlic clove

2 to 3 tablespoons tahini

½ cup crumbled feta

1. Combine the tomatoes, cucumber, red onion, olives, parsley, and a sprinkle of salt and pepper in a small bowl; set aside.

2. In a blender, combine the chickpeas, lemon juice, 1 tablespoon olive oil, the cumin, garlic, tahini, and a sprinkle of salt and pepper. Gradually add water (start with 1 cup) and blend until smooth and thin enough to pour. Taste and adjust seasoning. Pour into bowls, and top with the chopped vegetable mixture, sprinkle with some feta, a bit more cumin (if you like), and a generous drizzle of olive oil.

Socca (Farinata)

MAKES: 4 to 6 appetizer servings

1 cup chickpea flour

1 teaspoon salt

1 teaspoon freshly ground black pepper

4 tablespoons olive oil, or more as needed

½ large onion, thinly sliced

2 teaspoons chopped fresh rosemary

1. Heat the oven to 450°F. Put a well-seasoned or nonstick 12-inch pizza pan or cast-iron skillet in the oven.

2. Put the chickpea flour in a bowl; add the salt and pepper. Slowly add 1 cup lukewarm water, whisking to eliminate lumps. (An immersion blender is ideal for this.) Stir in 2 tablespoons of the olive oil. Cover and let sit while the oven heats, or for as long as 12 hours. The batter should be about the consistency of heavy cream.

3. Remove the pan, pour the remaining 2 tablespoons oil into it and swirl. Add the onion, return the pan to the oven, and cook, stirring once or twice, until onion is well browned, 6 to 8 minutes. Add the rosemary. Stir the onion and rosemary into the batter, then immediately pour the batter into the pan. Bake for 10 to 15 minutes, or until the pancake is firm and the edges are set.

4. Heat the broiler and brush the top of the pancake with 1 or 2 table-spoons of oil if it looks dry. Set the pancake a few inches from the broiler, and cook just long enough to brown it in spots. Cut it into wedges, and serve hot or warm.

SLOW COOKER BEANS
+RECIPE GENERATOR

I don't use a slow cooker often, but when it comes to beans, it deserves a second look. In addition to being nearly foolproof, slow cookers don't heat up your kitchen, a boon in the warmer months, and they don't even require you to be in your kitchen—or your house, for that matter.

While slow cookers are best known for their meat-braising prowess, they also work wonders on dried beans, rendering them almost impossibly creamy inside while leaving them completely intact. Throw some liquid, seasonings, and meat in the bottom, place vegetables on top, and you'll wind up with slow-cooked stews that make the most of seasonal produce. That's the "recipe," such as it is.

If you don't have a slow cooker, you can bake the mixture in a covered pot or Dutch oven at 250°F. To brighten up the finished dish, garnish with some chopped fresh herbs like parsley, cilantro, basil, or chives. These recipes serve 6 to 8.

Summer squash

Corn

Onions

Ham hock

Chickpeas

LEGUMES

Black beans

White beans

Lentils

Split peas

VEGETABLES

Chopped greens

Potatoes

MEAT

Chicken

Beef chuck

Sausage

Bacon

SEASONINGS

Parmesan rind

Chiles

Coriander seeds

Garlic

Cumin seeds

Curry

Rosemary sprigs

Peppercorns

Slow Cooker Beans Universal Instructions

In an empty slow cooker, combine 1 pound of any variety of dried, unsoaked beans, ¾ pound meat (or more, or less, or none), and seasonings—including salt and pepper—to taste. Add about 4 cups stock or water—enough to cover the beans by ¼ to ½ inch. (Use closer to 3½ cups liquid if you want the mixture a little less saucy, and feel free to play around with stock combinations that include wine, beer, soy sauce, or other flavorful liquids.) On top of this, add 2 pounds of vegetables (chopped or sliced into bite-size pieces), cover the cooker, and set the temperature to high. Cook for 6 to 8 hours, or until the beans are creamy inside but still intact.

FISH AND SEAFOOD

The hardest part of cooking seafood is buying it. The dizzying variety of species that crop up in most supermarkets these days is enough to overwhelm a fisherman, let alone a regular cook just trying to make some dinner. Add to that the ever-shifting rubric of wild, farmed, fresh, frozen, line-caught, net-caught, local, imported, sustainable, and endangered, and it's not hard to see how making it home with a nice-tasting, morally defensible piece of fish is a challenge all its own.

But your rewards for doing so are the endless (and, for the most part, fast and easy) ways to prepare all types of seafood, from ubiquitous varieties like white fish fillets and shrimp, to short-season delicacies like wild salmon and soft-shell crab. You'll notice that the techniques covered in this chapter often overlap from fish to fish; broiling, roasting, sautéing, frying, poaching, stir-frying, and steaming are methods that work across a huge range of seafood. If you can fry shrimp, you can fry squid; if you can make tartare out of salmon, you can sure as hell make it out of scallops. Here, you'll find all of that and more, including inventive ways to pair fish with meat, and blow-by-blow directions for a clambake on the beach. (Okay, this may not fall into the fast-and-easy category, but it's so worth it.)

SALMON
+12 WAYS

Whether it's farmed (from the Atlantic, available all the time) or wild (from the Pacific, in season from mid- to late summer), salmon is an absolute treat. Farmed salmon comes with two distinct advantages: it's not expensive, and its high fat content makes for not only good eating but also for extremely forgiving cooking. Wild salmon (like King, Sockeye, and Coho) is leaner, much more flavorful, and generally better; but unless you live in Alaska or the Northwest, where it's practically flung onto your doorstep along with the morning paper, fresh wild salmon remains a rare treat. If you can find it, cook it.

As with any seafood, mislabeling is something to look out for. It's not unheard of for purveyors to label any kind of wild salmon—or even farmed salmon—as King. Buy from people you trust.

A good piece of salmon really only needs a hot skillet and a sprinkle of salt, but to make it even more enticing, I've included recipes spanning a wide range of flavors and cooking methods, all of which will work for whatever kind of salmon you can get your hands on. You can also find inspiration for making salmon tartare and kebabs in the recipe generators on pages 16 and 220 respectively.

RAW	POACHED

Cucumbers, Soy, and Ginger

Chop **1½ pounds of skinless salmon fillet** into ½-inch cubes; put in a bowl with **1 cup chopped cucumber, ⅓ cup chopped scallions, 1 tablespoon minced fresh ginger,** and **2 tablespoons sesame seeds.** Drizzle with enough **soy sauce** and **sesame oil** to just moisten everything, and gently toss to coat. Serve on its own or over rice.

Soy Sauce and Scallions

Put a **1½-pound piece of skin-on salmon fillet** in a pan just large enough to hold it. Barely cover with water. Add **1 cup soy sauce, a few slices of ginger,** and some **scallion greens.** Cover and bring to a boil. Reduce to a simmer and cook for 1 minute; turn off the heat and let the salmon sit until tender, about 10 minutes. Carefully remove the salmon, drain, and chill in the fridge (up to a day). Garnish: **scallions** and **sesame oil.**

Chipotle and Avocado

Substitute **chopped avocado** for the cucumber, **fresh corn kernels** for the scallions, and **1 or 2 minced chipotles in adobo** for the sesame seeds. Skip the ginger. Substitute **lime juice** for the soy sauce and **neutral oil** for the sesame oil. Serve with **tortilla chips.**

Crème Fraîche and Caviar

Place **2 tablespoons brown mustard seeds** in a bowl and cover with water, then add a **squeeze of lemon juice.** Let soak until softened, between 3 hours and overnight. Toss the salmon with enough **crème fraîche** to moisten, as well as plenty of **chopped chives.** Serve on blinis or crackers, with a dollop of drained mustard seeds.

Coconut, Curry, and Lemongrass

Substitute **one 14-ounce can coconut milk** for the soy sauce and **several 3-inch pieces of lemongrass** for the scallions; add **1 tablespoon curry powder** and **2 heaping tablespoons salt** to the poaching liquid. Garnish: **chopped fresh cilantro.**

With Tarragon Mayonnaise

Substitute **1 cup dry white wine** for the soy sauce and **lemon slices** for the ginger. Skip the scallions, and add **2 heaping tablespoons salt** to the poaching liquid. Combine **1 cup mayonnaise, 1 tablespoon chopped fresh tarragon,** and **1 tablespoon lemon juice** to spoon over the salmon once it's chilled.

Lemon and Herb

Heat a grill until moderately hot. Stir together the **juice of 1 lemon; 2 tablespoons chopped fresh parsley, basil, or dill;** and **1 tablespoon olive oil.** Rub a **1½-pound skin-on salmon fillet** with **olive oil, salt,** and **pepper.** Grill skin side down until the skin is crisp, 4 or 5 minutes. Turn and cook until the fish is firm but still medium rare, another minute or two. Drizzle with the lemon and herb mixture.

Mustard and Shallots

Cut a **1½-pound skinless salmon fillet** into large chunks. Put one-fourth of it in a food processor with **2 teaspoons Dijon.** Process into a paste. Add the remaining salmon and **1 chopped shallot;** pulse to roughly chop the salmon. Stir in **½ cup bread crumbs.** Shape into 4 burgers; refrigerate for up to a few hours. Grill until firm, 4 minutes on one side, a minute or two on the other side. Serve on **greens** or **buns.**

Harissa

Substitute **1 tablespoon harissa** for the lemon juice and **½ teaspoon ground cumin** for the herbs. Use **2 tablespoons olive oil** (no need to rub extra on the fish) and brush on **the salmon** before grilling. If the glaze gets too dark before the fish is done, move it to a cooler part of the grill. Combine **½ cup yogurt, the juice of 1 lemon,** and **2 tablespoons chopped mint.** Serve the salmon with **yogurt sauce.**

Apricot, Mustard, and Soy

Substitute **¼ cup apricot jam** for the lemon juice, and **1 tablespoon Dijon mustard** for the herbs; add **1 tablespoon soy sauce** and **1 teaspoon minced garlic.** Brush on both sides of **the salmon** before grilling (no need to rub the fish with oil). If the glaze gets too dark before the fish is done, move it to a cooler part of the grill to finish cooking. Garnish: **scallions.**

Curried with Yogurt Sauce

Substitute **1 tablespoon curry powder** for the mustard and **1 tablespoon chopped fresh ginger** for the shallot. Combine **½ cup plain yogurt, the juice of 1 lime, ¼ cup chopped cilantro, salt,** and **pepper** in a bowl. Serve the burgers with yogurt sauce.

With Salsa

Substitute **2 teaspoons chili powder** and **1 teaspoon ground cumin** for the mustard, and **¼ cup chopped scallions** for the shallot. Serve the burgers with any of **the salsas** on pages 240–241 and with **a dollop of sour cream,** if you like.

OIL-POACHED FISH

I used to say that I never invented a dish in my life, but now that would be disingenuous. I know I'm not creative in the same sense that a talented chef is, but I also know that my experience has taken me from slavishly following recipes to rarely looking at them. Now almost every meal begins with a fantasy. I then buy what looks as if it has the potential to fulfill that fantasy—or I simply open the refrigerator and see what's already there. At that point I improvise on an established theme from I guess what you'd call my repertoire. In this regard, cooking is like music, but easier: the basic skills are not difficult to attain, but the creativity comes not in reinventing them but in imagining new ways in which to combine them.

In my experience, the results are sometimes mundane, sometimes bordering on greatness. Sometimes the fantasy is realized, and sometimes reality intervenes—yet the results are still happy. This is one such dish.

It began with a reverie of mixed grilled oysters, squid, scallops, and fish, a dream that was promptly dashed once the downpour started. This gave rise to plan B (which turned out way better than plan A was ever going to be). I poached the oysters just until they popped open, then simmered the squid in the oyster liquid and chopped them both. The fish and scallops I poached in copious olive oil flavored with garlic and thyme, then (not wanting to waste that oil or the oyster poaching liquid), cooked a sauce with those, cherry tomatoes, and the chopped oysters and squid. I tossed the sauce with hot pasta, dressed the fish and scallops with oil and lemon, and that was it. Unexpected, but extraordinary.

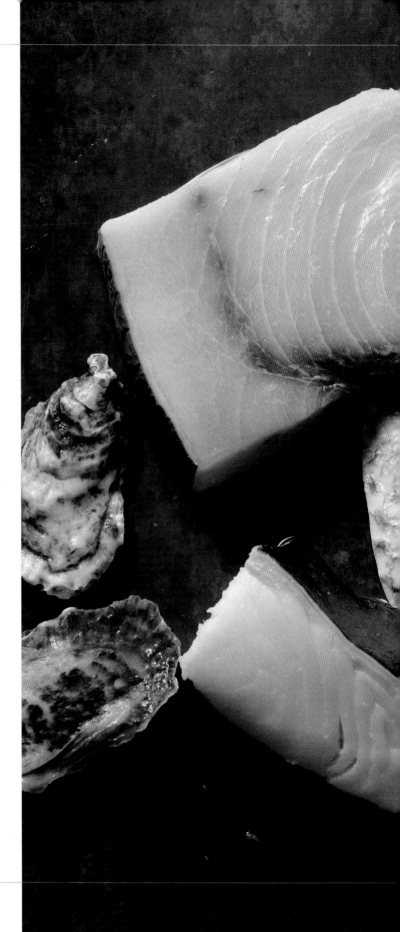

Olive Oil–Poached Fish with Pasta

SERVES: 4 to 6

6	oysters
2	large or 4 medium squid, cleaned and cut up
½	cup good olive oil, plus some for garnish
4	to 8 garlic cloves, peeled and left whole
	Several sprigs of fresh thyme
¼	to ½ pound striped bass, preferably a strip of belly
¼	to ½ pound halibut fillet

¼	to ½ pound swordfish fillet
2	to 4 sea scallops
	Salt and pepper
	Lemon wedges
	Chopped fresh parsley, for garnish
20	cherry tomatoes, cut in half
	Pinch of cayenne (optional)
1	pound cut pasta, like rigatoni
¾	cup shredded fresh basil, or more

1. Steam the oysters in a little water, ¼ inch or less, just until they're easy to open. When they're cool enough to handle, open them, separate from the shells, and cut the meat in half. Meanwhile, cook the squid in the same liquid just until opaque, less than 2 minutes. Take them out with a slotted spoon and reserve the liquid. Turn off the heat.

2. Set a big pot of water to boil for the pasta and salt it. In a broad skillet, add the olive oil, garlic, and thyme and turn the heat to medium-low. Gently cook the fish and scallops in the oil, in batches if necessary, flipping and turning as needed. Don't rush and don't worry about browning anything; just cook until each piece is tender, which will be different for each fish, but not more than 10 minutes for any. Do not overcook. Remove with a slotted spoon, leaving the garlic behind. (Discard the thyme.) Season with salt and pepper and put on a platter with the lemon wedges and parsley. Drizzle with olive oil.

3. Add the tomatoes and cayenne to the oil in the pan and cook at a lively pace, stirring occasionally, until saucy, 10 to 12 minutes. Start the pasta in the meantime. Add the reserved cooking liquid, oysters, and squid to the tomato sauce and cook a bit longer, another 3 or 4 minutes. Taste and season as needed.

4. When the pasta is almost tender, drain it and toss it with the sauce and the basil; cook another minute or so, until the pasta is tender. Serve the pasta in bowls, and pass plates on the side with the fish.

WHITE FISH FILLETS
+12 WAYS

Cooking fish is rife with problems, though maybe not the ones that first come to mind. Sustainability is a big concern for many cooks. After nearly exhausting our cod stocks twenty years ago, we now have fished a dozen or more alternatives practically out of existence. It can be hard to know which fish are managed well enough to eat without guilt. But if you buy from a reliable store, like Target, Wegmans, or Whole Foods, which have adopted seafood-sustainability practices more effectively than many other retailers, or you consult online sources like the Monterey Bay Aquarium, you can eat white-fleshed fish without guilt.

The next problem is that the best-looking (or best-priced) fish may be one with which you're unfamiliar, be it cod, catfish, sea bass, halibut, grouper, tilefish, haddock, or some form of snapper. The good news is that it barely makes any difference which fish you buy. You can cook one white fish fillet the same way you would any other: broiled, sautéed, roasted, or poached. And you can team it up with just about any seasoning you can think of, from the obvious, like tomatoes and capers, to the semi-exotic, like sugar and fish sauce. And this isn't just my offering a barely acceptable compromise. It works.

The chart that follows provides ideas for cooking 1½ pounds of white fillet, whether whole or cut into four individual portions. None of these recipes take more than 30 minutes from start to finish; thicker pieces of fish will cook in 15 minutes or less, thinner pieces in under 10 minutes. You can tell that any fillet is done when it's opaque and a thin-bladed knife meets little resistance when you use it to poke the thickest part.

With Tomatoes and Capers

Heat the broiler. Set an oven rack 4 inches from the heat source. Place the **fish fillet** on an oiled, broiler-safe pan. Toss **1 pound sliced ripe tomatoes** with olive oil to coat and **2 tablespoons each drained capers** and **chopped red onion**. Spread on and around the fish. Broil the fish fillet until opaque and tender, 10 to 15 minutes. Garnish: **chopped fresh parsley** and **lemon wedges.**

Cornmeal-Crisped

Cut **the fish fillet** into 4 pieces and soak in **1½ cups buttermilk.** Combine **1 cup cornmeal** with **1 tablespoon chili powder.** Put a large skillet over medium heat; add **1 tablespoon each olive oil and butter.** Pull half the fish from the buttermilk; drain, then dredge in **cornmeal.** Sauté until golden, turning once, 3 or 4 minutes per side. Wipe the skillet clean, then repeat for the remaining fish pieces. Garnish: **squeeze of lemon juice** and **chopped fresh parsley or cilantro.**

Fish Tacos

Skip the tomatoes and capers. Rub **the fish fillet** with **vegetable oil** and **a mild chili powder.** While the fish is broiling, combine **2 chopped cucumbers,** **½ cup chopped fresh cilantro,** **1 minced hot chile,** and **2 tablespoons lime juice.** Flake the fish and serve in **warm corn tortillas** with cucumber salsa.

Caramelized Fish

Skip the tomatoes and capers. Heat a little **vegetable oil** in a skillet. Dredge **the fish fillet** in a mixture of **brown sugar and (lots of) coarse black pepper.** Broil carefully; the fillet will brown quickly. Drizzle with **fish sauce.** Garnish: **chopped fresh mint** (lots) and **minced hot fresh chile** (optional).

Classic Sautéed

Skip the buttermilk, cornmeal, and chili powder. Beat **2 large eggs** with **¼ cup chopped fresh parsley.** Dredge **the 4 fish pieces** lightly in **all-purpose flour,** then in **the egg mixture.** Sauté in **the butter and oil** in 2 batches. Garnish: **chopped fresh parsley, lemon wedges.**

Prosciutto-Wrapped

Skip the buttermilk, cornmeal, and chili powder. Lay **2 prosciutto slices,** slightly overlapping, on a work surface and top with **basil leaves.** Wrap a piece of **fish** in the prosciutto and basil, then repeat with more prosciutto and the remaining 3 fish pieces. Cook the bundles in **2 tablespoons olive oil** in 2 batches. Garnish: **more basil.**

ROASTED	POACHED

With Herbs

Heat the oven to 475°F. Put **4 tablespoons butter** in an ovenproof pan and place in the oven to melt. Add **4 tablespoons chopped fresh herbs** (a combo is best: parsley, dill, basil, tarragon, thyme, etc.), then add the **fish fillet**. Roast, turning once, until opaque and tender, 10 to 20 minutes. Serve with the pan juices.

With Ginger and Soy

Put a large, deep skillet over medium heat; add **2 tablespoons vegetable oil** and **1 tablespoon minced fresh ginger,** and cook until sizzling. Add the **fish fillet, ½ cup soy sauce,** 1½ cups water, **½ cup chopped scallions, ½ cup chopped fresh cilantro,** and **1 teaspoon rice vinegar.** Bring to a boil, then cover, remove from the heat, and let stand for 10 minutes. Garnish: **chopped scallions.**

With Potatoes

Heat the oven to 425°F. Skip the butter and herbs. Toss **2 pounds sliced new potatoes** with ¼ **cup olive oil.** Roast until brown, about 20 minutes. Add **1 tablespoon chopped sage** and **1 teaspoon minced garlic.** Top with the **fish;** drizzle with **2 tablespoons olive oil.** Roast until fish is done, 10 to 15 minutes. Serve with the pan juices.

Leeks and Bacon

Heat the oven to 425°F. Skip the butter and herbs. Toss the white and tender green parts of **4 sliced leeks** and **2 ounces chopped bacon** with ¼ **cup olive oil.** Roast for 10 minutes. Add **1 tablespoon fresh thyme** and **½ cup white wine;** roast 20 minutes more. Top with the **fish** and **2 tablespoons olive oil.** Roast until fish is done, 10 to 15 minutes.

Curried with Zucchini

Sauté **1 chopped onion** and **2 chunked zucchini** in **the oil** for 5 minutes. Add **the ginger** and **1 tablespoon curry powder** (or to taste), cook for 1 minute, then add **the fish.** Substitute **1 cup coconut milk** for the soy sauce; use only 1 cup water. Skip the scallions and vinegar. Garnish: **chopped cilantro.**

Tomato-Fennel

Skip the ginger; use **olive oil.** When oil is hot, add **1 chopped onion** and **2 chopped fennel bulbs;** cook 5 minutes. Add **the fish, a pinch of saffron,** and **1 tablespoon fennel seeds.** Substitute **1 cup diced tomatoes** for the soy sauce; use only 1 cup water. Skip the scallions, cilantro, and vinegar. Garnish: **chopped fennel fronds.**

FISH STEW WITH MEAT
+3 WAYS

Braised
Fish,
Pot-Roast
Style

I don't subscribe to the belief that everything is better with bacon, but small amounts of meat do often improve many dishes, even those with fish. While there are plenty of classic fish stews that don't use meat for flavoring, there are many that do.

Try, for example, the brilliantly simple dish of rice and aromatics cooked in fish stock, with sausage stirred in to give the lean broth a fatty jolt. If you can't find whiting, use other small whole fish or make a regular fish stock with heads and bones and add chunks of flaky white fish, like cod or halibut, during the last few minutes of cooking.

Then there's the riff on a classic choucroute garni—usually a mess of smoked and fresh meats with sauerkraut—made primarily with fish, but with the addition of ham or bacon.

Interestingly, the meatiest recipe here doesn't include any actual meat. It's fish braised like a pot roast, meaning seared, then simmered with vegetables in red wine and stock. To make this well, you need homemade stock; the canned stuff is overpoweringly bad, so try one of the Quick Stock recipes on pages 36–37. After all, with this dish and the others, the whole point is for the meaty flavors to complement the fish, not drown it.

"Choucroute" of Fish

SERVES: 4

½ cup (1 stick) butter

2 cups rye-bread cubes

1 pound sauerkraut, rinsed and drained

4 ounces chopped smoked ham or slab bacon

1 teaspoon juniper berries, crushed

1 teaspoon caraway seeds

1 teaspoon fresh thyme leaves, or ½ teaspoon dried

3 dried bay leaves

1 cup white wine, not necessarily bone-dry

½ to ¾ pound white fish fillet, like halibut

½ to ¾ pound smoked trout or haddock

½ to ¾ pound salmon without skin

Salt and pepper

1 shallot, minced

½ cup heavy cream

Juice of 1 lemon

Chopped fresh parsley, for garnish

1. Heat the oven to 300°F. Melt 2 tablespoons of the butter. Put the bread cubes on a rimmed baking sheet, and toss with the melted butter. Bake, stirring occasionally, until golden and crisp, 15 to 20 minutes.

2. Meanwhile, put the sauerkraut, ham, juniper, caraway, thyme, bay leaves, and all but 2 tablespoons of the wine in a Dutch oven over medium-high heat. When the mixture bubbles, lower the heat to a simmer and cover. Cook, stirring occasionally, for 40 minutes. Lay the three fish on top, sprinkle with salt and pepper, and cover the pot. The fish will be tender in about 10 minutes.

3. As the fish cooks, put the shallot and the remaining 2 tablespoons wine in a small saucepan over medium-high heat; cook until the liquid has almost evaporated, about 5 minutes. Turn the heat to low, and stir in the cream. Add the remaining 6 tablespoons butter, a little bit at a time, stirring constantly. Once the mixture is creamy, stir in the lemon juice and some salt and pepper; keep the mixture warm over the lowest possible heat.

4. When the fish is tender, spoon it and the sauerkraut onto a platter; pour the sauce over all, scatter the croutons on top and around, garnish with the parsley, and serve.

Fish Stew with Rice

SERVES: 4

1½ pounds small whiting, cleaned

3 large carrots, sliced

1 large onion, chopped

2 fresh mild chiles, preferably Anaheim, chopped

1 dried mild chile

2 inches fresh ginger, peeled and chopped

4 garlic cloves, chopped

½ cup short-grain rice

Salt and pepper

½ pound Italian or other fresh sausage, crumbled

Minced scallions, for garnish

Fresh cilantro or parsley, for garnish

1. In a large saucepan, cover the fish with 5 cups water, and bring to a boil. Turn off the heat, place the lid on, and let sit for 20 minutes. Transfer the fish to a plate; when the fish is cool enough to handle, carefully remove the meat from the bones, and set aside; discard the bones, head, fins, tail, and so on. Strain the broth and return to the pot.

2. Add the remaining ingredients except the sausage and garnishes. Simmer gently, stirring occasionally, until the flavors are blended and the carrots and rice are tender, about 15 minutes.

3. Add the reserved fish, along with the sausage, and cook another couple of minutes, or until the sausage is cooked through. Turn off the heat, taste and adjust seasoning, and let rest for a few minutes, or eat piping hot, with the garnishes.

Braised Fish, Pot-Roast Style

SERVES: 4

3 tablespoons olive oil

1½ to 2 pounds monkfish, halibut, or swordfish, as thick as possible and preferably in 1 piece

Salt and pepper

1 onion, chopped

2 thyme sprigs

Pinch of saffron (optional)

3 medium carrots, cut into 1-inch chunks

1 small fennel bulb, cut into chunks

1 pound potatoes, cut into 1-inch chunks

2 tablespoons tomato paste

1 teaspoon pimentón (smoked paprika)

½ cup red wine

2½ cups Flavorful Fish Stock or other Quick Stock (pages 36–37)

Chopped fresh parsley, for garnish

1. Put the olive oil in a Dutch oven over medium-high heat. When it is hot, sprinkle the fish with salt and pepper, and add it to the pot. Cook, undisturbed, until it is well browned, 5 or 6 minutes. (If you're using halibut fillet, and it has skin, brown the flesh side.) Transfer it to a plate, browned side up.

2. Add the onion, thyme, saffron, carrots, fennel, and potatoes; sprinkle with salt and pepper. Cook, stirring occasionally until the onion begins to soften, about 5 minutes. Add the tomato paste and pimentón, and cook, stirring, until the tomato paste darkens a bit, 2 or 3 minutes. Add the wine, scraping up any browned bits from the bottom of the pot, and let it bubble away until it almost disappears.

3. Add the stock, bring to a boil, and let it bubble vigorously until the liquid reduces by one-third, 10 minutes. Adjust the heat so the mixture simmers; when the vegetables are nearly tender—about 10 minutes later— nestle the fish, browned side up, among the vegetables; keep the browned crust above the liquid. Cook, undisturbed, until the fish and vegetables are tender, 10 to 15 minutes.

4. Transfer the fish to a cutting board, and divide the vegetables among shallow bowls. Slice the fish and put it on top. Taste the cooking liquid, and adjust the seasoning; ladle it over, garnish with parsley, and serve.

SHRIMP
+12 WAYS

Rustic
shrimp
cocktail

Shrimp is now the most popular seafood in America, and there is no wrong way to eat it. Wild shrimp from the Pacific or the Gulf of Mexico is a treat if you can find it. Fresh local shrimp from Maine or the Carolinas is an even rarer gem. (These are all preferable from a sustainability perspective.) A vast majority, of course, is farmed and frozen, but you might as well buy it frozen and thaw it yourself to get the freshest shrimp possible.

If you buy it "individually quick frozen" in resealable bags, you can take out only as many as you want and thaw them by leaving the shrimp in the fridge for 24 hours or running them under a trickle of cool water for an hour or less.

Shrimp is also the most versatile seafood. Peeled shrimp certainly wins the prize for convenience, but the shells give you a shot at one of the choicest by-products in all of cooking: shrimp

Greek-style
shrimp

Fried shrimp
with cornmeal
batter

stock. Cover the shells with water, simmer for
10 minutes, and strain. Refrigerate or freeze, then
use for risotto, seafood stews, or bisques.

Peeling the shells for stock is a much better use
of your time than deveining. (For those who find
this a repulsive statement, make a shallow cut on
the back side of each shrimp with a paring knife,
and pull out the black, threadlike vein.)

The twelve fast recipes on the following pages

serve four and are just a sampling of the possibilities. Incredibly, the cooking time for each of
these is less than 15 minutes. For the most part,
the shrimp will tell you when they're done.
Certainly they're ready once they have turned
pink, though very large shrimp may need an
extra minute to cook through. To check, slice one
in half; if it's opaque, or even nearly so, season to
taste and start eating.

Garlic and Saffron

Put ¼ cup olive oil in a large skillet over medium-low heat. Add **3 sliced garlic cloves** and cook until golden. Stir **1½ pounds peeled shrimp,** **1 teaspoon each pimentón** (smoked paprika) **and ground cumin,** and **a pinch of saffron** (optional). Cook, turning the shrimp once or twice, until they are pink, 5 to 10 minutes. Garnish: **fresh parsley.**

Rosemary and Lemon

Heat the oven to 500°F. Lay a **bunch of fresh rosemary branches** in the bottom of a roasting pan, and put **1½ pounds peeled shrimp** on top. Drizzle with **a few tablespoons olive oil** and **the juice of a lemon.** Roast, turning the shrimp once, until they're pink all over, 10 to 15 minutes. Garnish: **lemon wedges.**

Fermented Black Beans

Substitute **2 tablespoons vegetable oil** for olive oil, and **2 teaspoons minced fresh ginger** and **3 tablespoons fermented black beans** soaked **in 2 tablespoons mirin** for the pimentón, cumin, and saffron. When **the shrimp** are pink, stir in **2 tablespoons soy sauce** and serve. Garnish: **chopped scallions.**

Capers and Olives

Add **2 tablespoons capers** and **½ cup chopped pitted black olives** along with **the garlic;** omit the pimentón, cumin, and saffron. Add **½ cup chopped fresh tomatoes** with **the shrimp.** Garnish: **fresh basil.**

With Bread Crumbs

Omit the rosemary. Put **the shrimp** in the bottom of a roasting pan, and toss with the **olive oil** and **lemon juice.** Scatter **¼ cup bread crumbs** on top, and drizzle with **more oil.** Roast until the shrimp are pink, 10 to 15 minutes. Garnish: **fresh parsley** and **lemon juice.**

Rustic Shrimp Cocktail

Omit the rosemary and lemon. Put **the shrimp** and **1 pint cherry tomatoes** in the pan; toss with **the olive oil.** Roast for 10 to 15 minutes. Mash **the tomatoes** in a bowl. Add **2 tablespoons olive oil,** and **lemon juice, Worcestershire, horseradish,** and **hot sauce** to taste. Dip the shrimp in the warm sauce.

FRIED	BROILED

Tempura

Heat **2 inches peanut or neutral oil** in a deep pan to 350°F. Slice **1 pound peeled shrimp** lengthwise. Combine 1½ cups water with some ice cubes; measure 1½ cups water from that, and put it in a bowl. Beat with **1 cup flour** and **2 large egg yolks**. Dredge the shrimp in the flour, then dip in the egg batter. Fry until crisp, less than 5 minutes. Drain on paper towels. Serve with **soy sauce** for dipping.

Cajun Style

Turn on the broiler, and put the rack close to the heat. Mash **1 garlic clove** with **1 teaspoon salt** until it forms a paste. Add to it **½ teaspoon cayenne, 1 teaspoon paprika, 1 tablespoon lemon juice, 2 tablespoons olive oil,** and **lots of black pepper.** Rub the paste all over **1½ pounds peeled shrimp.** Broil for 2 to 3 minutes per side. Garnish: **lemon wedges.**

Cornmeal Batter

Skip the tempura batter. Combine **1 cup milk** with **1 large egg,** and beat. Dip **the shrimp** in the liquid, then dredge in a mixture of **1 cup cornmeal** and **½ cup flour.** Fry as above. Garnish: **lemon wedges.**

Shrimp Toast

Batter and fry **the shrimp** as for the Tempura recipe. In a small bowl, combine **⅓ cup mayonnaise, 1 teaspoon soy sauce, 2 teaspoons sesame oil,** and **some chopped scallions.** Spread the mixture on **buttered toast** (white bread is classic), and top with the shrimp.

Greek Style

Substitute **1 tablespoon chopped fresh oregano** for the cayenne and paprika. (Everything else stays the same.) Garnish: **chopped ripe tomatoes** and **crumbled feta.**

Thai Style

Mince and mash **a few Thai chiles** along with **the garlic and salt.** Substitute **1 teaspoon sugar** for the cayenne and paprika, **fish sauce** for the lemon juice; skip the olive oil and use **lime juice** instead. Use only a little **black pepper.** Broil as above. Garnish: **fresh cilantro** and **mint.**

SCALLOPS
+12 WAYS

Miso Glaze

Creamy and sweet, briny and meaty all at the same time, scallops are the most user-friendly of mollusks, and the recipes here won't unnecessarily complicate things. Half of them call for grilling, and the remainder leave the scallops raw.

Much more difficult than cooking scallops is buying scallops. As with most seafood these days, unless you're on the boat yourself—or have a trustworthy source—it's hard to know exactly what you're getting. Scallops are often soaked in a phosphate solution that plumps them up with water (thereby adding weight for determining the selling price), so it's important to look for scallops that are labeled "dry" or "dry-packed." A waterlogged scallop doesn't sear well, and a phosphate-marinated scallop may taste like soap, especially when it's raw, so make sure to ask for dry.

In most parts of the country, at most times of year, you want sea scallops—the big ones that are harvested year-round. True bay scallops—possibly the best and certainly the priciest—are mostly caught off Long Island and Cape Cod in the winter. (Other "bay" scallops, like the calicos or other smallish varieties, are not really worth buying. West Coast pink scallops are lovely, if you can find them.) Scallops are also sold individually quick-frozen (IQF), but opt for fresh if you can.

One note on preparation: err on the side of undercooking. Take the scallops off the grill before they're opaque all the way through. If you undercook a scallop, it will still be delicious. If you overcook a scallop, however, it will get rubbery and you probably will get sad.

Buying tasty scallops is more than half the battle. Treating them simply once you get them to the kitchen is the rest.

Grilled Scallops Universal Instructions

Heat a charcoal or gas grill until very hot. Rub the grill grate with a little oil, and set it 3 or 4 inches from the heat. Grill the scallops until they're browned on the bottom and release easily from the grill, 2 to 3 minutes. Turn and brown on the other side; total cooking time should be 3 to 5 minutes. You want to take the scallops off the grill a little before their interior becomes totally opaque. The raw recipes make 4 appetizer portions; the grilled recipes are main courses serving 4. For grilled, use 12 large sea scallops (about 1½ pounds); the raw recipes specify the number of scallops to use. Bay scallops are usually too small for the grill, but they are great raw. Use them for the raw recipes if you like (no need to chop or slice them, except for the tartare).

GRILLED	RAW

GRILLED

Miso Glaze

Whisk together **2 tablespoons miso, 2 tablespoons mirin,** and **some black pepper.** Thread **the scallops** onto skewers. Brush with **vegetable oil,** and grill until almost done. Brush the miso mixture on both sides, and continue to cook, turning once or twice, until the glaze caramelizes a bit and the scallops are done. Garnish: **sesame seeds** and **sliced scallions.**

Kale and Olives

Brush **the scallops** with **olive oil,** sprinkle with **salt** and **pepper,** and grill as directed. Toss with **1 bunch chopped kale, ½ cup pitted olives, ½ cup thinly sliced red onion, olive oil** and **lemon juice** to moisten everything, **salt** (go light because of the olives), and **lots of black pepper.**

Mango Skewers

Thread **the scallops** onto skewers, alternating them with **1-inch chunks of mango, chunks of red bell pepper,** and **wedges of red onion.** Brush with **vegetable oil,** sprinkle with **salt** and **pepper,** and grill as directed. Garnish: **chopped fresh cilantro** and **lime wedges.**

Panzanella

Brush **3 slices crusty bread, 2 large halved tomatoes,** and the **scallops** with **olive oil;** season. Grill until the scallops are done, the bread is browned, and the tomatoes are lightly charred. Chop the bread and tomatoes into large cubes; toss with the scallops, **olive oil, lemon juice.** Garnish: **basil leaves.**

Olive Oil and Lemon

Rub the **scallops** with **olive oil;** thread onto skewers. After a few minutes on the grill, turn them, and squeeze **lemon juice** over them. For a sweeter version, char **lemon halves** cut side down on the grill before squeezing over the scallops. Garnish: **chopped parsley** or **basil.**

Peaches and Corn

Brush **2 shucked ears of corn** and **2 halved peaches** with **olive oil;** grill until browned. Strip the kernels into a bowl; add the chopped peaches. Brush the **scallops** with **olive oil;** season and grill. Toss the halved scallops with the corn and **1 cup chopped tomatoes, chopped basil,** and **olive oil.**

RAW

With Bacon

Cook **4 slices bacon** until fully cooked but not completely crisp; drain on paper towels and cut each slice into 4 pieces. Quarter **4 big scallops,** and toss them with **½ teaspoon lemon juice, salt,** and **pepper** (a pepper mix is nice). Top each piece of bacon with a piece of scallop, and serve with napkins.

Tartare

Chop **8 large scallops** into small bits, and toss with **2 chopped hard-boiled eggs, 2 tablespoons each minced red onion** and drained **capers, ¼ cup minced fresh parsley, 1 teaspoon Dijon mustard,** and **Worcestershire sauce** to taste. Serve with **toast points.**

Salsa Cruda

Quarter **8 large scallops,** and gently toss them with **1½ cups chopped ripe tomatoes, 1 teaspoon minced garlic, ½ cup chopped fresh parsley, 2 tablespoons olive oil,** and **2 tablespoons balsamic vinegar.**

Seaweed Salad

Rinse **1 ounce dried seaweed** and soak it in a large pot of water until tender, 5 minutes. Drain, and gently squeeze dry. Quarter **8 large scallops,** and toss with the seaweed, **½ cup chopped cucumber, 2 tablespoons soy sauce,** and **2 teaspoons sesame oil.** Garnish: **scallions** and **sesame seeds.**

Ceviche

Slice **6 large scallops** into thin rounds, and put them on a plate. Scatter some **thinly sliced red onion** and **rounds of fresh hot chiles** (like serrano or Thai) over the top. Sprinkle with a **generous amount of lime juice.** Serve right away, or wait for up to 30 minutes. Garnish: **chopped fresh cilantro.**

Pesto

Slice **6 large scallops** into thin rounds, and put them on a plate. Put **1 cup fresh basil leaves** in a food processor with **¼ cup olive oil, 1 tablespoon lemon juice, ½ small garlic clove,** and **¼ cup grated Parmesan.** Process until smooth. Spread the pesto over the scallops. Garnish: **toasted pine nuts.**

CLAMS
+12 WAYS

There's no wrong time to eat clams. You can cook them in a pit on a beach in summer (see page 172), in a warming chowder in the dead of winter, and everywhere in between.

These recipes all use hard-shelled clams, which are called by a thousand different names depending on their size, including littlenecks, cherrystones, Manilas, cockles, and quahogs (littlenecks and cherrystones are the best ones to use here). They require almost no work to get ready: rinse or scrub off any sand on the shells, discard any that can be pried open with your fingers (or those with smashed shells), then wash in several changes of cold water—as you would salad greens—until all traces of sand are gone.

To shuck a clam raw takes a bit of practice; I can't really do it, so I can't expect you to. But there are two alternatives: you can steam them (actually, the microwave works like a charm) until they just barely open; or you can have someone else shuck them for you. Either method will work if you need a considerable quantity of raw, shelled clams, as you do for the fried delicacies here. To get 1½ pounds of shucked clams to serve four, you will need about 8 pounds of clams in the shell.

Conventional wisdom states that clams cooked in their shells shouldn't be eaten if they don't open during cooking. That's a waste of money, and of what's likely a perfectly good clam. Pry the shy ones open at the table as if you were shucking them. If they don't look or smell right, chuck 'em; otherwise, enjoy.

STEAMED

White Wine and Garlic

Put **4 pounds of clams** and **½ cup white wine** in a large pot with **4 chopped garlic cloves**; turn the heat to high. (One cup total of chopped **celery** and/or **onion** is also good in here.) Cover, and cook, shaking the pot occasionally, until all (or nearly all) of the clams open, about 10 minutes. Serve with **crusty bread**. Garnish: **chopped fresh parsley**.

Chorizo and Tomatoes

Before starting, sauté **8 ounces chopped Spanish chorizo** in **olive oil** until nicely browned. (You can do this in the big pot.) Add **1 cup chopped ripe tomatoes** along with **the wine**. Garnish: **fresh parsley**.

Thai Curry

Before starting, sauté **2 tablespoons minced fresh ginger**, **1 minced fresh green chile**, and **1 minced lemongrass stalk** (tender parts only), along with **the garlic**. Substitute **beer** for the wine, and add **½ cup coconut milk**. Garnish: **fresh cilantro** and **Thai basil**.

BAKED

Parsley Bread Crumbs

Heat the oven to 450°F. Mix **2 cups bread crumbs** and **½ cup chopped fresh parsley**; moisten with **olive oil**. Steam open **24 clams** and discard the top shells. Cover the clams with bread crumbs, packing tightly, and bake until browned, 10 minutes. Garnish: **lemon wedges**.

Casino

Chop **the clams**, and add them to **the bread-crumb mixture** along with **½ cup crumbled cooked bacon**, **1 tablespoon minced garlic**, and **½ cup grated Parmesan**. Stuff the mixture back into the bottom shells, and bake. Garnish: **lemon wedges**.

Wasabi Bread Crumbs

Use **panko bread crumbs**. Substitute **a teaspoon of wasabi powder** for the parsley, and **soy sauce** for the olive oil; add a **drizzle of dark sesame oil** too. Garnish: **chopped chives**.

PAN-ROASTED

Potatoes, Bacon, and Cream

Heat the oven to 400°F. In a roasting pan, combine **1½ pounds small new potatoes** and **½ pound chopped bacon**; toss with **pepper**. Roast for 20 minutes, stirring occasionally. Add **½ cup heavy cream**, **½ cup seafood or chicken stock**, and **4 pounds clams**; roast 20 minutes, or until the clams open. Garnish: **fresh chives and parsley**.

Potatoes, Corn, and Andouille

Substitute **3 shucked ears of corn**, cut crosswise into 2-inch rounds, for half the potatoes, and **sliced Andouille sausage** for the bacon. Toss everything with **olive oil** and **Old Bay Seasoning** before roasting, and substitute **¾ cup beer** for the liquids.

Kale and Linguica

Substitute **linguiça or chorizo** for the bacon. Substitute **¾ cup white wine** for the liquids, and add **1 pound chopped kale** for the last 20 minutes of roasting. Garnish: **lemon wedges**.

FRIED

Cornmeal-Dredged

Heat **2 inches of neutral oil** in a deep pot over medium-high heat. Soak **1½ pounds shucked clams** in milk; in a separate bowl, combine **1 cup cornmeal**, **1 cup flour**, **salt**, **pepper**, and **a pinch of cayenne**. When the oil is hot, dredge the clams in the cornmeal; fry in batches until golden, 2 minutes. Drain on paper towels. Garnish: **lemon wedges**.

Clam Rolls

Fry **the shucked clams** as above. Combine **1 cup mayonnaise**, **¼ cup combined chopped sweet pickles and capers**, and **1 tablespoons mustard**. Spread the tartar sauce on **toasted and buttered hot-dog buns** (or something better), and stuff with the clams.

Curry-Fried with Cilantro

Soak **shucked clams** in a mixture of half **coconut milk** and half **dairy milk**; add **2 tablespoons curry powder** to the cornmeal. Toss the fried clams with lots of **cilantro leaves**, almost as if it were a salad. Top with **lime juice**; eat with a fork.

SQUID
+12 WAYS

Old-time fish experts always said about squid: "Cook it for two minutes or two hours." It's good advice. For tender squid, cook it lightning-fast or very slowly; anything in between may produce something akin to rubber bands. This is hardly a problem, though, because it means that recipes run only 15 minutes, or allow you time to do something else while the squid simmers.

Truly fresh squid is better than frozen, but frozen squid—available everywhere—is usually pretty good, and cheap. It freezes well—about this the old-timers would say, "Seafood without blood freezes best"—and defrosts quickly in a cold-water soak.

When you're buying it fresh, squid should be purple to white—not brown—with a clean, sweet smell; you'll know if it's gone bad. Cleaning your own is an option, but a time-consuming one, and these days, most are cleaned before sale. If you ask me, the tentacles are the best part, but if they make you squeamish, ask for bodies only.

All the recipes here serve four and should be made with 1½ to 2 pounds of squid (it shrinks a lot during cooking), blotted dry with paper towels in every case except for stewing. Fried, broiled, and stir-fried squid are done as soon as they turn opaque, while slow-stewed squid is done when it's tender.

Here's one nice option: Make a pot of soup or stew, and when it's bubbling hot and ready to go, stir in thinly sliced rings of squid and small pieces of tentacles. By the time you ladle it into bowls and bring it to the table, the squid will be done. Squid may seem like a daunting ingredient, but cooking doesn't get any easier than that.

STIR-FRIED

Garlic, Parsley, and Lemon

Cut the **squid bodies** into rings; halve the tentacles, if large. Add **3 tablespoons olive oil** to a skillet over high heat. Add **2 tablespoons minced garlic**, then the squid. Cook until it turns opaque, 2 minutes. Stir in **¼ cup chopped parsley** and the **zest and juice of a lemon.**

Scallions and Ginger

Substitute **neutral oil** for the olive oil. Add **1 tablespoon minced fresh ginger** along with **the garlic and squid.** Substitute **sliced scallions and lime** for the parsley and lemon. Garnish: **soy sauce.**

Chiles, Celery, and Basil

Use **neutral oil.** Add **1 minced hot chile** along with **the garlic**, then stir in **1 cup thinly sliced celery**, and cook 1 minute. Add **the squid** and, 1 minute later, toss in **a handful of basil** (omit the parsley and lemon zest); continue cooking until squid is done. Garnish: **soy sauce.**

BROILED

Oil and Vinegar

Turn on the broiler. Put a large ovenproof skillet on a rack close to the heat source. When hot, add **2 tablespoons olive oil**, then add the **whole squid.** Drizzle with more oil, and broil until firm but not rubbery, 2 to 3 minutes. Sprinkle with **sherry vinegar.** Garnish: **fresh parsley.**

Bread Crumbs and Parmesan

Sprinkle **the squid** with roughly **½ cup each coarse bread crumbs** (preferably homemade) and **grated Parmesan**; drizzle with **olive oil** before broiling. Be careful not to burn the bread crumbs. Garnish: **fresh parsley and lemon wedges.**

Deviled

Rub **the squid** with a mixture of **2 tablespoons Dijon mustard** and **2 teaspoons Worcestershire sauce.** Scatter with **coarse bread crumbs** (preferably homemade) and **olive oil** before broiling. Be careful not to burn the bread crumbs. Garnish: **chopped fresh chives.**

STEWED

Tomatoes, Garlic, and Anchovies

Cut the **squid** into chunks. Heat **3 tablespoons olive** oil in a large skillet. Add **2 tablespoons chopped garlic** and **3 minced anchovies**; cook for 30 seconds. Add **½ cup white wine, 4 cups chopped tomatoes, 2 thyme sprigs**, and **squid**; simmer until tender, 45 minutes. Garnish: **basil.**

Pimentón and Saffron

Substitute **1 teaspoon pimentón** (smoked paprika) and **a pinch of saffron** for the anchovies, **red wine** for the white, and a **squeeze of lemon juice** for the thyme. Garnish: **fresh parsley.**

Ginger, Chiles, and Coconut Milk

Substitute **neutral oil** for the olive oil, **1 tablespoon minced fresh ginger** and **1 minced fresh hot chile** for the anchovies, **1 cup coconut milk** for the wine, and a **3-inch piece of lemongrass** for the thyme. Use only **2 cups of tomatoes.** Garnish: **fresh mint or cilantro.**

FRIED

Classic Fried

Put **1½ to 2 inches neutral oil** in a deep pan over medium-high heat. When the oil is hot, toss **¼ of the squid rings and tentacles** in a strainer **with flour** and fry until golden, about 2 minutes. Drain on paper towels; eat with **lemon quarters** while you cook the remaining batches.

Fried Calamari Salad

Prepare and fry **the squid** as above. Keep warm while you cook the remaining batches. Toss with **arugula, shaved Parmesan, olive oil, lemon juice**, and **pepper.**

Batter-Fried with Pepperoncino and Lemon

Dip the **squid**, plus whole **pepperoncino** and **half-moon slivers of lemon** (ditch the seeds) in a mixture of **1 cup flour, 1 large egg**, and **1 cup ice water.** Fry in batches as directed.

SURF AND TURF
+4 WAYS

Chicken
with Clams

Even the best foods can become tiresome, which is the only reason you would ever do anything with oysters other than opening and swallowing them. For something almost as primitive, the people of western France, where some of the world's best oysters are grown, perfected the idea of teaming them with sausage.

It's not exactly a recipe—grill some sausage, open some oysters, slice some lemons, and serve—but it did make me think of other beloved combinations of meat and seafood. Our U.S. contribution to this world—a filet mignon with a lobster—is pathetic: the foods don't play well together, and I suspect the dish was originally a conceit born of an

urban desire to showcase abundance and wealth.

Not so the more traditional versions. If you steam mussels with chorizo—or any other sausage—all you're doing is adding a big shot of flavor for very little effort. It's similar if you steam clams with prosciutto or some other cured meat—you get the idea.

Then there's my liberal interpretation of the classic Portuguese pork with clams (usually called *à alentejana* because it's from Alentejo), a magnificent expression of surf and turf, with the brininess of the clams almost overwhelmingly flavoring the pork. Over the years, I've come to prefer this with chicken, which is more reliably tender and marries equally well with the clam juice.

Chicken with Clams

SERVES: 4

2	tablespoons neutral oil	24	littleneck clams, rinsed and drained
4	chicken drumsticks or thighs, skin on, bone in	1	bunch of scallions, white and green parts chopped and separated
	Salt and black pepper		
2	tablespoons chopped garlic	¼	cup fresh cilantro stems, chopped
2	tablespoons chopped fresh ginger	½	cup fresh cilantro leaves, chopped

1. Heat the oil over medium-high heat in a large, deep skillet or broad pot that can later be covered. When the oil is hot, season the chicken pieces with salt and pepper, and add them to the oil. Regulate the heat so that the meat browns evenly, turning as needed. (Drumsticks have 4 sides, really; thighs only 2, so timing is variable.) When the chicken is well browned, it will be almost done.

2. Add the garlic and ginger and cook for 1 minute, just until they soften a bit. Add the clams and sprinkle them with the scallion whites and the cilantro stems. Cover and cook until all the clams open, about 10 minutes; they will generate a good deal of liquid.

3. Remove the top and cook that liquid down as desired. (Perhaps not all, perhaps until syrupy—your call.) Serve over rice, or with crispy potatoes or bread, sprinkled with the scallion greens and cilantro leaves.

Clams with Prosciutto

SERVES: 4

2	tablespoons olive oil	¼	cup dry white wine
1	tablespoon chopped garlic	48	littleneck clams, rinsed and drained
⅛	to ¼ pound prosciutto or other dry-cured ham, chopped		Chopped fresh parsley, for garnish

1. Put the olive oil over medium heat in a large pot that can be covered. Add the garlic and prosciutto and stir. Add the wine and clams.

2. Cover and cook, shaking the pot occasionally, until the clams open, about 10 minutes. Sprinkle with the parsley, and serve.

Oysters with Sausage

SERVES: 4 to 6

1	coil of thin sausage (about 1 pound)	24	oysters, shucked
			Lemon wedges

Cook the sausage in a skillet until nicely browned on both sides. Place it in the center of a platter, and arrange the oysters around it. Serve with lemon wedges.

Mussels with Chorizo

SERVES: 4

2	tablespoons olive oil	4	pounds mussels, rinsed and debearded
1	medium onion, chopped	¼	cup white wine (optional)
¼	pound chorizo or linguiça, chopped		Chopped fresh parsley, for garnish

1. Put the olive oil in a large pot that can later be covered, and turn the heat to medium. Cook the onion and chorizo, stirring occasionally, until the onion softens, about 5 minutes.

2. Put the mussels in the pot; cover and cook, shaking the pot occasionally, until mussels open, about 10 minutes. If they have not generated enough broth for you, add the wine and cook, uncovered, another 5 minutes. Sprinkle with parsley, and serve.

PAELLA
+RECIPE GENERATOR

I was once accused by Catalans near Valencia—which is the home of paella—of knowing nothing whatsoever about paella, and of making at best what they called *arroz con cosas*, or "rice with things." Well, paella really *is* just rice with things, but there's a technique to it. By applying that technique to a variety of ingredients in a variety of ways, you can make something that really approaches great paella, even if a Catalan might scoff at it.

Only a few elements are fixed: you need rice (it should be short-grain, like the kind you use for risotto, though to be authentic it should come from Spain, of course); you need olive oil; you need some vegetables. A few things are optional, and among those are sausage, lobster, shellfish, and chicken.

Water is the most often used liquid in "authentic" paella, but stock is in many cases better. Chicken stock is all-purpose, while a not-too-strong meat stock will work nicely, too. Fish stock is fine as long as you're including fish, and a quickly made shrimp stock might be your best alternative. Or try one of the Quick Stock recipes on pages 36–37. You can also use tomato juice, clam juice, red or white wine, or a combination of these.

The routine is pretty simple. But there are two unusual features. One is that paella is not stirred, or hardly at all. The other is that you want the bottom to brown, the browned bottom is called *socarrat*, and should you achieve it, no one will say you've made *arroz con cosas*.

Paella Universal Instructions

1. Put 3 tablespoons olive oil in a 12-inch skillet over medium-high heat. When hot, add about ½ pound of the chosen meat (or a combination of meats), sprinkle with salt and pepper, and cook until nicely browned. Add 1 chopped medium onion and some minced bell pepper at the same time if you like, and cook until soft. (If you want a meatless paella, skip right to the onion.)

2. Add 2 cups rice and (if you have it) a pinch of saffron, and cook, stirring, until shiny. Add 3½ cups of your liquid of choice, heated, and stir until just combined, then stir in the chosen seafood, or lay it on top of the rice. (Again, skip the seafood if you want vegetarian paella.)

3. Cook over medium-high heat, undisturbed. If the pan is too big for your burner, move it around a little; but after that initial stirring, leave it alone. When the mixture starts to dry, begin tasting the rice; if the rice seems quite tough, add another ½ cup or so of liquid. And if you can smell the bottom starting to burn, lower the heat a bit. About halfway through the cooking (about 10 minutes), add any vegetables, adjust the seasonings, and stir gently, just once.

4. The rice is done when it's tender and still a bit moist; if the mixture has stuck to the bottom of the pan, congratulations: you have the *socarrat*, a characteristic of good paella. The paella should be served in the pan, in the middle of the table, and dinner guests—up to six—should fight over it.

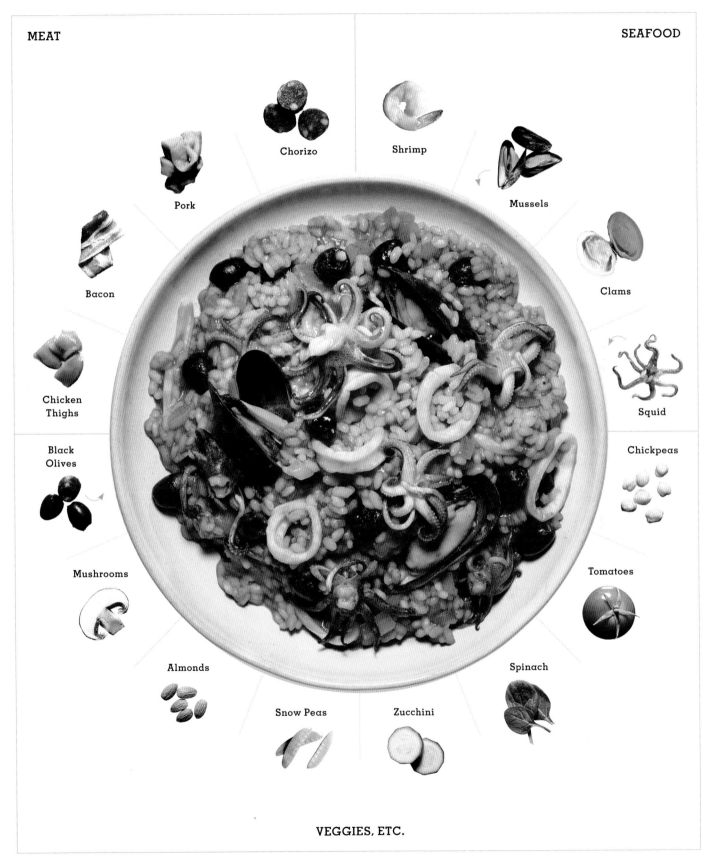

Chorizo

Shrimp

Pork

Mussels

Bacon

Clams

Chicken
Thighs

Squid

Black
Olives

Chickpeas

Mushrooms

Tomatoes

Almonds

Spinach

Snow Peas

Zucchini

VEGGIES, ETC.

SOFT-SHELL CRAB
+12 WAYS

Although fish come and go according to the season, to a large degree seafood has become a global commodity that can be had at any time. The soft-shell crab remains an exception. Starting in May and throughout the summer, the blue crab sheds its shell and starts to form a new one, making its sweet, briny, delicious meat—usually incredibly tough to get at—immediately accessible. When the crab is molting, in fact, practically the whole thing is edible, and the new shell is among the best parts. The combination of tenderness and crunch makes it one of the great delights of eating.

My favorite mode of preparation—and by far the easiest and least messy—is to grill or broil the little guys. But there's no denying that a fried or pan-fried soft-shell is a beautiful thing.

Do not overcook. When the crabs plump up and become firm, they are done, and unless your heat is too low, this won't take more than 8 minutes; if you're deep-frying, 3 or 4 minutes will do. Any of the coatings here—with the possible exception of tempura, which is almost always deep-fried—will work whether you're deep or shallow frying.

The majority of the time I serve soft-shell crabs with just lemon wedges and parsley; there is nothing better. There is, however, different. And some of the best are here. Very few sauces will not work, though I do think the best feature is upfront acidity. Allow one crab per person.

METHODS	COATINGS	SAUCES

Grilled

Heat a charcoal or gas grill, or a broiler, until moderately hot; put the rack at least 4 inches from the heat source. Grill or broil **the crabs** for 3 to 4 minutes per side, basting occasionally with **melted butter** (spike it with **Tabasco** or whatever else you like) or **olive oil** (good with **garlic and herbs**). Finish with **lemon juice** and **chopped fresh herbs**.

Deep-Fried

Put at least **3 inches of neutral oil** in a large, deep saucepan over high heat; you want the oil to be about 350°F. (If you don't have a thermometer, drop in a small cube of bread; when the bread sinks halfway and then bubbles to the surface, the oil is ready.) One at a time, dredge **the crabs** in **the coating mixture** of your choice (dipping them in an egg mixture first, if indicated), then fry (probably in batches) until golden, about 2 minutes total, turning once. Drain on paper towels.

Sautéed

Heat about **¼ inch oil, butter, or a combination** in a skillet. (Even better is clarified butter.) Prepare **a coating**. When the fat is hot (a pinch of flour will sizzle), dredge **the crabs** in **the coating mixture** (dipping them in an egg mixture first, if indicated), and sauté. When the bottoms of the crabs are nicely browned, 3 to 5 minutes, turn, and brown the other side. Drain on paper towels.

Simple Flour or Cornmeal

Put a mound of **all-purpose flour or cornmeal** on a plate (you can add a big **pinch of cayenne** if you like).

Cornmeal Batter

Beat **1 large egg with 1 cup milk** in a bowl. On a large plate, combine **1 cup cornmeal, ½ cup all-purpose flour, and ½ teaspoon cayenne**. Dip the crabs in the egg mixture, then dredge well in the cornmeal mixture.

Ground Oyster Crackers or Saltines

Beat **1 large egg with 1 cup milk** in a bowl. On a large plate, combine **1 cup all-purpose flour** with **½ teaspoon cayenne**. On another plate, put **1½ cups ground oyster crackers or saltines** (a food processor makes short work of this). Dredge the crabs first in the flour, then dip in the egg mixture, then dredge in the crackers.

Tempura Batter

Lightly beat **2 cups ice-cold water** with **3 large egg yolks** and **1½ cups all-purpose flour** in a large bowl. (The batter should be lumpy and thin; don't overmix.) Put about **1 cup of loose flour** on a plate, and one at a time, dredge the crabs in the flour, dip them in the batter, then fry until golden, less than 5 minutes total. Drain on paper towels.

(All coatings are adequate for at least 4 crabs. Add salt and freshly ground black pepper in every case.)

Tomato Sauce

Film a small skillet with **olive oil**; heat and add **1 chopped onion**; stirring occasionally, until soft, 3 minutes. Add **1 pound chopped tomatoes** (along with **fresh oregano or marjoram**, if you have it), and cook until the mixture breaks down, 10 to 15 minutes. Stir in **½ cup chopped parsley or basil**.

Tartar Sauce

In a bowl or food processor, whisk together **1 large egg yolk, 1 tablespoon sherry or white-wine vinegar or lemon juice,** and **2 teaspoons Dijon mustard**. Add **1 cup neutral oil**, a few dribbles at a time, adding more until it's incorporated. When a thick emulsion forms, add the remaining oil a little faster. Stir in **¼ cup chopped shallots or mild onion** and **¼ cup chopped cornichons or pickles**.

Cilantro Pesto

Combine **2 cups loosely packed cilantro, 1 peeled garlic clove,** and **3 tablespoons neutral oil** in a food processor. Pulse several times. Stop, scrape the sides, add **1 table-spoon lime juice,** and blend. Add water as necessary to purée.

Chili Sauce

Combine **2 tablespoons lime juice, 2 table-spoons fish sauce, 1 teaspoon minced garlic, ¼ teaspoon minced hot fresh chile, 2 teaspoons sugar, 1 tablespoon minced dried shrimp** (optional), and **1 tablespoon finely shredded carrot** (optional). Stir until the sugar dissolves.

Ponzu Sauce

Combine **⅔ cup lemon juice, ⅓ cup lime juice, ¼ cup rice vinegar, 1 cup soy sauce,** and **¼ cup mirin** (or **¼ cup sake and 1 tablespoon sugar**) with **one 3-inch piece kelp, ½ cup dried bonito flakes,** and **cayenne**. Let sit for at least 2 hours; strain before serving.

(All recipes make enough sauce for at least 4 crabs. Add salt and pepper, please.)

LOBSTER
+12 WAYS

To fully enjoy cooking and eating a lobster at home, you have to kill it yourself. You can boil or steam it, or plunge a chef's knife behind its head, then boil, steam, or grill it. Here, I'm assuming one 1½-pound Maine lobster per person. To remove the meat from the shell before cooking it fully, just cook the lobster for a couple of minutes, then chill it and remove the meat at your leisure. To make lobster stock, cover the legs and shells (and some onions, carrots, and celery) with water, and simmer for 15 minutes.

BOILED	GRILLED/BROILED

With Melted Butter

Drop **4 lobsters** into a very large pot of salted boiling water. After the water returns to a boil, cook the lobsters for 8 minutes for the first pound plus 3 to 4 minutes for each additional pound. Drain and serve with **melted butter** and **lemon wedges.**

With Olive Oil

Boil **4 lobsters** for 2 to 3 minutes; cool. Heat a grill or broiler with the rack 4 to 6 inches from the flame. Split the lobsters and remove the sand sac. Cook the lobsters for 5 minutes (cut side up), then turn and cook for another 5 minutes. Drizzle with **good olive oil** and serve.

With Curry and Spicy Mayonnaise

Add **2 chopped medium onions,** the juice of **2 limes, 1 teaspoon black pepper,** and **1 tablespoon curry powder** to the water; simmer for 15 minutes; add **the lobsters.** Mix **1 cup mayonnaise, 1 minced fresh hot chile** (like Thai), **1 teaspoon minced fresh ginger,** and **1 teaspoon grated lime zest.** Serve with the mayonnaise for dipping. Garnish: **lime wedges.**

With Seaweed and Soy-Wasabi Dipping Sauce

Instead of salting the water, add **a piece of dried kombu or a handful of fresh seaweed.** Combine ½ cup soy sauce, 2 tablespoons rice vinegar, 2 tablespoons sesame oil, 1 tablespoon sugar, and 2 teaspoons wasabi paste to the dipping sauce.

With Pesto Crumbs

Heat the broiler with the rack 6 to 8 inches from the flame. Split **the parboiled lobsters** down the middle. Remove the tomalley and coral and pulse in a food processor with **2 cups fresh bread crumbs, 1 cup fresh basil, 1 garlic clove, ½ cup olive oil,** and **2 tablespoons pine nuts.** Pack the mixture onto the exposed surface and broil until lobster is opaque and stuffing is browned, 5 to 10 minutes.

Kebabs

Split **the parboiled lobsters,** remove the meat, and thread it onto skewers. Combine ⅓ cup olive oil, 1 tablespoon minced garlic, 1 tablespoon minced fresh rosemary (add a little lavender if you have it), and the **juice of 1 lemon;** brush this all over the meat. Grill, turning and basting, for about 5 minutes.

SOUP	SALAD/SANDWICH

Bisque

In a large pot, cook **1 chopped onion, 1 chopped carrot, 1 chopped celery rib,** and **1 tablespoon minced garlic** in **4 tablespoons butter** for 5 minutes. Add **2 (or more) lobsters** and **a pinch cayenne**; cover and cook for 10 minutes. Add **6 cups lobster or chicken stock** and **1 cup each white wine and chopped tomatoes**; cover and simmer for 30 minutes. Pull out the lobsters; chop the meat. Purée the soup and reheat with **1 cup heavy cream** and the lobster. Garnish: **chopped celery leaves.**

With Tarragon Mayonnaise

Combine **¼ cup good mayonnaise, the juice and zest of 1 lemon, 3 tablespoons minced shallot,** and **1 tablespoon minced fresh tarragon.** Toss with **1 pound cooked lobster meat.** Serve in **toasted hot-dog buns,** or not. Garnish: **more tarragon.**

Chowder with Corn and Potatoes

Skip the wine and tomatoes. Do not purée; instead, add **2 chopped medium potatoes** after you remove the lobsters and cook until tender, 10 to 15 minutes. Add **1 cup corn kernels** and **the chopped lobster meat** in the last 5 minutes of cooking. Add **1 cup milk** along with **the cream.** Garnish: **chopped chives.**

Thai Style

Cook **2 tablespoons minced lemongrass, 3 tablespoons minced ginger, 1 tablespoon minced chile** in **2 tablespoons neutral oil.** Skip the butter, aromatics, cayenne, wine, and tomatoes; use **7 cups of stock.** Don't purée. Add the chopped lobster and use the **juice of 1 lime, 2 tablespoons fish sauce,** and **2 teaspoons sugar** instead of cream. Garnish: **cilantro.**

With Herbs and Lemon-Soy Vinaigrette

Skip the mayonnaise mixture. Combine **⅓ cup neutral oil, 2 tablespoons each lemon juice and soy sauce.** Toss with **the lobster meat, 4 cups torn lettuce leaves,** and **¼ cup each fresh chives, cilantro, mint, and basil.**

With Grapefruit, Avocado, and Spinach

Skip the mayonnaise mixture. Combine **⅓ cup olive oil, 2 tablespoons sherry vinegar, 1 tablespoon minced shallot,** and **1 teaspoon sugar.** Toss with **the lobster meat, 4 cups torn spinach leaves, 1 segmented grapefruit (with its juice),** and **1 chopped avocado.**

CLAMBAKE

Few meals are more beautiful than a well-executed clambake. And because demanding culinary tasks are in vogue, it seems like the right moment for a clambake revival.

Find a suitable beach and start early. (And be sure to check local ordinances regarding what's permitted on the beach.) Do not underestimate your firewood needs: enough to fill a car trunk is not too much, and any less than that might not be enough. If the beach you select doesn't look as if it has enough suitable firewood, bring it.

You also need kindling, newspapers, and plenty of matches or a lighter. Other must-have items that you won't have in the kitchen are a shovel or two to dig the cooking pit, several heavy-duty garbage bags for the seaweed, a bucket for seawater, and a large canvas tarp to cover the fire. (A thick blue plastic tarp will work, but it's not as nice.) Bring flashlights, even if you're planning to eat before sunset.

Don't forget the usual beach and eating equipment, especially insect repellent, drinking water, a colander, potholders, dish towels, more dish towels, tongs, and knives. I use cheesecloth and string to make little packages of shellfish and vegetables, but you can use aluminum foil (easier, cheaper, uglier). Also, remember that lobsters don't crack themselves, though you can smash them on rocks if you forget the nutcrackers.

Lobsters aren't even requisite, of course; some people limit themselves to clams and mussels. Myself, I err on the side of variety: a couple of nice oysters, a huge sea scallop, and a chunk of linguiça make those packages even better.

Three key pieces of advice: Get all the help you can. Try to relax. And don't start drinking too early. Unless you're a veteran, something is likely to go wrong; you can roll with the punches more easily if you're at least partly sober. Trust me.

Ultimate Clambake

SERVES: 8 to 12

3	pounds waxy potatoes	8	to 12 ears fresh corn
	Salt	8	to 12 small lobsters
6	pounds hard-shell clams, preferably littleneck or cherrystone, well scrubbed	1	cup (2 sticks) butter, for serving
6	pounds mussels, well scrubbed		Lemon wedges, for serving

1. Before you leave the house, put the potatoes and a few large pinches of salt in a large pot and add water to cover; bring to a boil and cook until they are about half done, 10 to 15 minutes. Drain and transfer to a container to take with you to the beach.

2. Take all the ingredients to the beach, along with a shovel, a tarp, a few garbage bags, a bucket, some cheesecloth, a box of matches, lots of newspaper, firewood, and kindling. Find a spot above the high-water mark and dig a 4 by 2-foot hole that is 2 feet deep. Build a fire in the hole with newspapers, kindling, and some wood. (Keep everything else upwind of the fire.) Light and feed the fire quickly and steadily with more kindling and wood.

3. Find about 30 longish rocks, each 6 by 4 inches or bigger. Gradually add the rocks to the fire, a few at a time, over the course of about 1 hour, while continuing to feed the fire with wood. While the rocks are heating, gather enough seaweed to half-fill 2 or 3 garbage bags.

4. When the rocks are white-hot (this should take about 1 hour), stop adding wood but let the fire continue to burn. Meanwhile, make 8 to 12 cheesecloth packages, each containing a few of the clams, mussels, and potatoes. Peel back the husks of the corn but don't remove them; remove as much of the silk as you can, then fold the husks back into place.

5. Remove any remaining wood from the fire with a shovel; a bed of coals topped by a layer of white-hot rocks should remain. Immediately dump the seaweed over the rocks, creating a layer at least 2 to 3 inches thick; no rocks should remain exposed or you will burn the food (and maybe the tarp). Sprinkle the seaweed with about 1 gallon of seawater. Put the cheesecloth packages, corn, and lobsters on top of the seaweed in a single layer. Cover the food in an additional layer of seaweed, and then cover the entire pit with the tarp, weighing down the edges with more rocks.

6. Let cook undisturbed for 30 to 40 minutes. Meanwhile, put the butter in a heatproof saucepan. When the seafood is ready, peel back the tarp and put the pan of butter on the seaweed until it melts. Remove the tarp entirely, transfer the food to serving platters, and serve everything with the melted butter, lemon wedges, and more salt.

POULTRY AND EGGS

Americans eat more chicken than any other kind of meat. And why wouldn't we? It's low in fat, mild in flavor, and cheap. This chapter caters wholeheartedly to our obsession with the bird, covering pretty much every part of the animal and every method of cooking it.

There are sections devoted to boneless and skinless breasts, bone-in parts, wings, and pounded cutlets, with recipes that call for frying, braising, and more. If any of this seems like well-worn territory for you, try your hand at something that almost certainly isn't: a chile-smacked one-pot wonder called Spicy Big Tray Chicken (page 190).

You'll also find recipes devoted to a food generally eaten just once a year (turkey) and others based on an ingredient we eat practically every day (eggs). There are twenty different options for what to do with Thanksgiving leftovers (sides included), along with more dishes than you (probably) ever thought to make with hard-boiled eggs, and an egg Recipe Generator that churns out more than 400 possible combinations. If you never tackled a whole duck before, the cassoulet on page 198 is a good place to start.

EGGS+RECIPE GENERATOR

If you can cook an egg, you can cook breakfast, lunch, dinner, snacks—not only for yourself but also for almost anyone else. There are things that turn people off at different times of day, but unless you're a vegan, an egg is not likely to do so.

If you can imagine eggs in slightly out of the ordinary dishes—salad, pasta, grits—you can begin to imagine a world of inexpensive, blazingly fast recipes. Start with a runny egg on a lightly dressed salad, maybe with a little bacon and some croutons. Yes, it's damned good without the egg. But with it, it's transcendent.

Chopped roasted green chiles

Tortillas

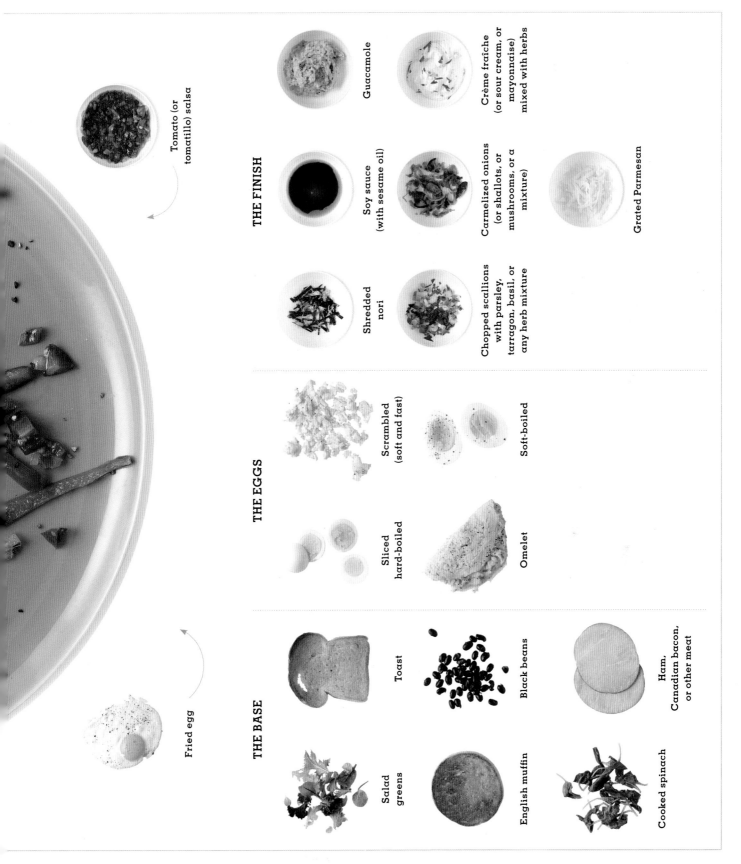

Fried egg

Tomato (or tomatillo) salsa

THE FINISH

Guacamole

Crème fraîche (or sour cream, or mayonnaise) mixed with herbs

Soy sauce (with sesame oil)

Carmelized onions (or shallots, or mushrooms, or a mixture)

Grated Parmesan

Shredded nori

Chopped scallions with parsley, tarragon, basil, or any herb mixture

THE EGGS

Scrambled (soft and fast)

Soft-boiled

Sliced hard-boiled

Omelet

THE BASE

Toast

Black beans

Ham, Canadian bacon, or other meat

Salad greens

English muffin

Cooked spinach

HARD-BOILED EGGS
+12 WAYS

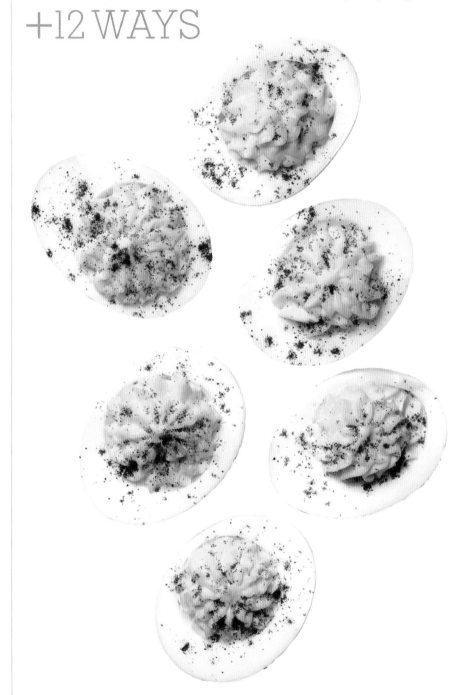

Hard-boiled eggs are worthy food, both as self-contained snacks and as main ingredients in more substantial dishes. The key in either case is cooking them so that the yolks are firm but still creamy rather than chalky, and peeling them without either tearing the egg to shreds or driving yourself mad.

The first part is accomplished easily enough; I've found that 9 minutes in hot water yields the perfect consistency for large to extra-large eggs, but if you prefer your yolks on the softer or firmer side, adjust the timing as needed. If you're going to simmer the eggs in tomato sauce, hard-boil them for only 7½ minutes because they'll continue to cook in the sauce.

There are countless "tricks" to peeling hard-boiled eggs: pricking the shell with a pin before cooking, rolling on a counter to crack every bit of shell, doing a prayer dance. The key, though, is an ice-water bath, followed by cracking them against the countertop and starting to peel from the wider end, where there is usually an air pocket.

Hard-Boiled Eggs Universal Instructions

Choose a pot that will comfortably hold all the eggs you plan to cook. Add the eggs, cover with cold water by 2 inches, and put the pot over medium heat. Bring to a gentle boil, turn off the heat, and cover the pot; the average large to extra-large egg will be ready in 9 minutes. Transfer the eggs to a large ice bath for about 1 minute; then crack, peel, and eat, or refrigerate for up to 1 week.

PICKLED

Classic

Put **6 hard-boiled eggs** in a lidded glass container. In a saucepan, combine 1½ cups apple-cider vinegar; 2 tablespoons each black peppercorns, mustard seeds, and allspice berries; 2 teaspoons salt; 1 tablespoon sugar; and 1½ cups water. Simmer for 10 minutes. Pour over the eggs; let cool. Cover and refrigerate for at least 24 hours.

Beet Pickled

Omit the mustard seeds and allspice. Add **1 grated medium beet** and **2 tablespoons prepared horseradish** to the pot.

Soy Pickled

Omit the peppercorns, mustard seeds, and allspice. Add ¼ cup **soy sauce** and **3 pieces star anise** to the pot, and reduce **the salt to 1 teaspoon.**

DEVILED

Classic

Halve **the eggs** lengthwise and carefully scoop the yolks into a bowl. Mash with **mayonnaise, Dijon mustard,** and **a pinch of cayenne.** Spoon the mixture back into the egg whites, or pipe it in with a pastry bag. Garnish: **paprika** or **chopped fresh parsley.**

Bacon and Deviled

Cook **a few slices of bacon** until crisp. Add some of the rendered fat to **the yolk mixture** instead of the mayonnaise, and crumble the cooked bacon over the top.

Rustic Deviled

Instead of mashing **the yolks,** roughly chop them. Substitute **olive oil** for the mayonnaise, **vinegar** for the mustard, and **chopped capers, shallots, and fresh parsley** for the cayenne. Garnish: **chopped parsley.**

SIMMERED IN TOMATO SAUCE

Curried Tomato Sauce

Put **2 tablespoons neutral oil** in a large skillet over high heat. Add **1 cup chopped scallions,** and cook until soft. Stir in **2 tablespoons curry powder;** add **2 cups chopped canned tomatoes,** and **1 cup coconut milk;** simmer until the sauce thickens, about 20 minutes. Add **hard-boiled eggs,** and heat for 5 minutes. Serve over **rice.** Garnish: **fresh cilantro.**

Classic Tomato Sauce

Substitute **1 medium onion** for the scallions. Omit the curry powder and coconut milk, and increase **the tomatoes to 3 cups (and include their juices).** Serve with **crusty bread.** Garnish: **grated Parmesan.**

Smoky Tomato Sauce

Substitute **1 medium red onion** for the scallions and **1 tablespoon (or more) chopped chipotle in adobo** for the curry powder. Omit the coconut milk, and increase **the tomatoes to 3 cups (and include their juices).** Serve with **tortillas.** Garnish: **crumbled queso fresco.**

EGG SALAD

With Pickles and Dill

Chop **hard-boiled eggs,** and toss them with **chopped gherkins or dill pickles, chopped red onion, mayonnaise, lemon juice,** and **chopped fresh dill.** Garnish: **chopped dill.**

Curried

Substitute **curry powder** for the pickles, **fresh cilantro leaves** for the dill, and **lime juice** for the lemon. Garnish: **a sprinkle of curry powder.**

Waldorf

Substitute **chopped walnuts** for the pickles, **chopped Granny Smith apple** for the red onion, and **chopped celery** for the dill. Garnish: **celery leaves.**

CHICKEN
BREASTS
+9 WAYS

I used to be one of those people who ragged on boneless, skinless chicken breasts for being flavorless and dry. That was until I learned how to not overcook them.

In preparing chicken breasts, remember that they should be cooked only until the last traces of pink have vanished—and no longer. (Use a thin-bladed knife to peek; if you prefer a meat thermometer, measure at the thickest spot and stop cooking at 155°F or a little bit higher.) A thinnish breast subjected to high heat can be done in as little as 6 minutes, or it might take as long as 10 minutes or even a bit more—but never 20 minutes unless you are cooking the thing on a radiator. Overcooking is easy, and the results are predictably undesirable.

Whatever you cook a chicken breast with is going to gain prominence, and whatever cooking method you choose will have plenty of impact. This provides good reason to keep things as simple as possible: a skillfully sautéed chicken breast with lemon juice is a beautiful thing. But gaining that skill takes some practice, and even for veterans, attention must be paid.

For these recipes, each of which serves four, you'll be using four chicken breast halves, about 1½ pounds altogether, not sliced into cutlets or fingers or pounded flat but left as they are, about 1 inch thick at the center. Learn to cook by touch (the meat should yield slightly when pressed) and by sight; with only a little practice, you'll know exactly when the breasts are done.

White Wine, Onions, and Herbs

In a large skillet over medium-high heat, sauté **2 chopped medium onions** in **2 tablespoons butter** until the onions soften, 5 to 10 minutes. Add **the chicken, 1 cup white wine, 2 bay leaves,** and **several fresh thyme and parsley sprigs.** When the liquid boils, lower the heat to a simmer, cover, and cook the chicken for 10 to 15 minutes or until tender and just cooked through. Transfer to a plate and keep warm. Boil the pan mixture until it is reduced by three-fourths; it should be fairly thick. Over low heat, stir in **2 more tablespoons butter,** then return the chicken to the pan to reheat and coat with sauce. Adjust the seasoning. Garnish: **chopped fresh thyme.**

Soy-Poached

Substitute **2 or 3 shallots** for the onions (use butter or oil) and cook until soft, 3 to 5 minutes. Use **2 tablespoons soy sauce, the juice of 1 lemon,** and ¾ cup water instead of the wine. Substitute **1 tablespoon lemon zest, 1 tablespoon sugar,** and **¼ teaspoon cayenne** for the herbs. Reduce the sauce a bit but skip the extra butter. Garnish: **fresh cilantro and lemon juice.**

Coconut-Ginger

Skip the onions, butter, and herbs. Toast **¼ cup shredded coconut** in a dry skillet and set aside for garnish. Put **the chicken** in the pan with **½ cup coconut milk, ½ cup water,** and **1 tablespoon grated fresh ginger.** Reduce the sauce to your liking and skip the additional butter. Garnish: **the toasted coconut.**

| ROASTED | SAUTÉED |

Herb-Roasted

Heat the oven to 425°F. Chop **½ cup fresh parsley, dill, mint, or a combination** (a little minced **garlic** wouldn't hurt, either). Put **4 table-spoons olive oil or butter** in a roasting pan and place in the oven for a couple of minutes, until oil is hot or butter melts. Roll the chicken in the herb mixture, then add it to the pan; return the pan to the oven. Roast, turning once or twice, for 10 to 15 minutes, or until just cooked through. Garnish: **more chopped herbs.**

Mushrooms and Wine

Put a large skillet over medium-high heat for 2 or 3 minutes. Swirl **2 tablespoons olive oil** and **2 tablespoons butter** in the pan. When the butter foam subsides, dredge the chicken in flour, shaking to remove the excess. Cook, turning once, until browned on both sides and nearly cooked through, about 10 minutes total. Transfer to a plate and cover loosely with foil. Add **1 pound sliced fresh mushrooms** to the skillet and cook, undisturbed, until the liquid from the mushrooms evaporates completely. Add **½ cup of any wine** and let it bubble, stirring, until it is reduced by half, about 2 minutes. Add another tablespoon butter and cook until the sauce is thickened; return the chicken to the skillet, turn them in the sauce, and serve. Garnish: **chopped parsley.**

Tomatoes, Capers, and Olives

Skip the herbs. Combine **2 or 3 chopped ripe tomatoes, the juice of ½ lemon, 1 teaspoon drained capers,** and **a handful of olives.** Lightly grease the pan with **olive oil,** then put **the chicken** in the pan and pour the tomato mixture over it. Roast for 10 to 15 minutes, or until just cooked through. Garnish: **chopped fresh basil.**

Deviled

Skip the herbs. Combine **⅓ cup Dijon or coarse mustard, ⅓ cup chopped shallots,** and **¼ teaspoon cayenne.** Spread this mixture over the top of **the chicken** before putting it in the pan. Use any extra mustard mixture to baste the breasts; roast 10 to 15 minutes, or until just cooked through. Garnish: **chopped parsley.**

Florentine

After removing **the chicken** from the pan, substitute **chopped fresh spinach** for the mush-rooms. Use **white wine,** and after you reduce the sauce by half, turn off the heat. Wait 30 sec-onds, then stir in **½ cup heavy cream or sour cream.** Turn the heat to low, stirring, until slightly thickened. Return the chicken to the skillet, turn in the sauce, and serve.

Citrus

Skip the mushrooms. Cut **a large orange in half** and section one half as you would a grapefruit, removing any seeds; set the other half aside. After remov-ing **the chicken** from the pan, instead of wine, add **the juice of the second orange half with the juice of a lime** and **1 tablespoon sugar.** Include the orange sections in the mixture. Finish as above. Garnish: **lime.**

THE NEW AMERICAN CHICKEN DINNER

The appeal of roast chicken is easy to grasp. There remain, however, a few issues with the standard roasting bird. There's the age-old battle of different cooking times: breast versus legs. One or the other is bound to be over- or undercooked. Then there's the carcass, which is normally wasted.

So, here's a dish that uses the whole bird, that accounts for the difference in cooking times between legs and breast, that integrates vegetables, and that can become a reliable and even exciting alternative to roast chicken as the centerpiece of dinner for friends or a relaxed weeknight meal. In other words, a contemporary American chicken dinner.

Braised and Roasted Chicken with Vegetables

SERVES: 4

2 tablespoons chicken fat (or olive oil or butter)

2 skinless chicken legs (drumstick and thigh)

Salt and freshly ground black pepper

1 bone-in, skin-on chicken breast, split to yield 2 halves

3 leeks, trimmed and chopped

4 medium carrots, chopped

6 celery ribs, chopped, leaves reserved for garnish

12 to 16 ounces fresh cremini, shiitake, button, or other mushrooms, trimmed and quartered or sliced

3 to 4 fresh thyme or rosemary sprigs

Meat from 2 chicken wings (see Quick Chicken Stock recipe, below)

About 3 cups Quick Chicken Stock (see below)

1. Heat the oven to 350°F. Put the chicken fat in a roasting pan or Dutch oven over medium heat. Sprinkle the legs with salt and pepper and add them to the pan. Cook, turning and rotating the pieces as necessary, until well browned on both sides, 10 to 12 minutes. Remove, then add the breast halves, skin side down. Brown them well, then flip and cook for just 1 minute or so; remove to a separate plate.

2. Put the leeks, carrots, celery, mushrooms, herb sprigs, and chicken wing meat in the same pan and cook until the vegetables are tender and beginning to brown, 10 to 15 minutes.

3. Nestle the chicken legs among the vegetables, meaty side up. Add enough of the stock to come about halfway up the thighs. (The amount will depend on the breadth of your pan; add a little water if necessary.)

4. Put the pan in the oven and cook, uncovered, for about 1 hour, checking occasionally and stirring the vegetables if they threaten to brown too much. When the thigh meat is tender, raise the heat to 400°F and lay the breast halves on the vegetables, skin side up. Continue cooking until they are done, 20 to 30 minutes longer.

5. Transfer the vegetables to a platter. You can serve one of two ways: slice the breasts and shred the leg meat, and lay the meat on top of the vegetables; or separate the drumsticks from the thighs, cut the breasts in half, and give each person some of each. Garnish with reserved chopped celery leaves.

QUICK CHICKEN STOCK

MAKES: 3 cups

One 3- to 4-pound chicken

½ large onion, roughly chopped (don't bother to peel)

1 large carrot, roughly chopped

1 celery rib, roughly chopped

1 bay leaf

1. Cut the wings off the chicken, then separate the leg portions (drumsticks and thighs) from the carcass. Cut the back away from the breast. Pull the skin off the backbone and legs and put it aside. Leave the skin on the breast. Set aside the legs and the breast. Remove as much meat as you can—without going crazy—from the wings; dice and refrigerate.

2. Combine what's left of the wings with the backbone, onion, carrot, celery, and bay leaf in a large pot with 4 cups water and turn the heat to high.

3. Bring almost to a boil, then lower the heat so the mixture sends up a few bubbles at a time. Cook for 30 minutes, or 1 hour if you have more time.

4. Cool slightly and strain the stock, pressing down on the solids to extract as much liquid as possible; discard the solids.

CHICKEN-SKIN CROUTONS

MAKES: About ½ cup

Chicken skin reserved from backbone and legs of 3- to 4-pound chicken (see Quick Chicken Stock recipe, left)

Salt to taste

1. Heat the oven to 400°F. Lay the skin flat on a rimmed baking sheet, making sure not to let the pieces overlap; sprinkle with salt.

2. Roast for 15 to 20 minutes, or until the skin releases easily from the pan. Flip the pieces and continue to cook for another 10 to 15 minutes or until it's very crisp. Drain the skin on paper towels and transfer the fat to a heatproof bowl. Crumble the chicken skin into a salad or serve as a snack, with more salt if necessary.

CHICKEN PARTS
+12 WAYS

Greek-style chicken parts

If you give a cook a whole chicken, chances are he or she will roast it because, for all its wonderful attributes, a whole bird just isn't that versatile. Other than sticking it in the oven or plunging it into a pot of liquid, there are not a lot of obvious ways to cook it.

Cut that chicken into parts, however, and the possibilities open up, inviting techniques like braising, sautéing, and grilling. And while you have to work pretty hard to get a whole chicken with crisp skin, by using parts you can achieve that result easily and consistently. Bone-in parts also retain their moisture better during cooking.

The highest quality—and tastiest—chickens are usually sold whole, and cutting up a chicken yourself saves money and supplies you with trimmings for making stock. But prepackaged parts come with their own advantages: not only are they convenient (and ubiquitous), but they also let you mix and match your favorite pieces. There's no sadder sight than a devout dark-meat eater having to settle for a breast.

These recipes apply only to bone-in chicken parts, something that no longer goes without saying in a world obsessed with boneless breast. To serve four, start with a 3- to 4-pound cut-up whole chicken or 2 or more pounds of parts. Bone-in breasts remain pretty juicy when cooked in the following recipes, but if you're worried that they'll dry out, just pull them off the heat a few minutes before the dark meat is done. Judge the doneness with an instant-read thermometer (breasts and thighs should fall somewhere in the range of 155–165°F) or visually: when the juices run consistently clear (not pink), the meat is done.

ROASTED	GRILLED

Greek Style

Heat the oven to 450°F. Make a paste of **3 tablespoons minced garlic, 2 teaspoons chopped fresh oregano, the grated zest of 1 lemon,** and **olive oil;** slide your fingers underneath the skin of the breast to loosen it from the meat; slide the paste underneath the skin. Drizzle the chicken with **oil,** scatter **cherry tomatoes** and **black olives** around, and roast, skin side up, basting occasionally with pan drippings, until the juices run clear, about 30 minutes. Sprinkle with **feta** and **oregano.**

Japanese Style

Prepare a grill for indirect grilling. If you're using charcoal, make a fire in one half of the grill; for gas, turn on the burners on only one side. Combine **½ cup soy sauce, ¼ cup sake or white wine, ¼ cup mirin,** and **2 tablespoons each minced garlic and ginger.** Brush **the chicken** with **oil,** and grill over indirect heat, turning occasionally, until most of the fat has been rendered, about 20 minutes. Move directly over the fire and cook, turning and basting with sauce, until browned. Garnish: **scallions.**

Garlic, Rosemary, and Lemon

Substitute **rosemary** for the oregano. Cut **a lemon or two** into quarters and roast alongside **the chicken.** Omit the tomatoes, olives, and feta. Garnish: **minced fresh rosemary or parsley.**

Chinese Style

Substitute **minced fresh ginger** and **a sprinkle of Chinese five-spice powder** for the oregano, and **orange zest** for the lemon. Omit the tomatoes, olives, and feta.

Tandoori Style

For the basting sauce, combine **½ cup yogurt, ¼ cup lemon juice, 1 tablespoon ground cumin, 1 tablespoon paprika, 1 teaspoon ground coriander, a pinch of cayenne, 2 tablespoons minced garlic,** and **1 tablespoon minced fresh ginger.** Garnish: **chopped fresh cilantro leaves.**

Lime Chimichurri

For the basting sauce, combine **2 cups chopped fresh parsley, 3 garlic cloves, 1 tablespoon fresh oregano leaves, 2 tablespoons lime juice,** and **1 teaspoon hot red chile flakes** in a food processor or blender. Process, streaming in **3 tablespoons neutral oil,** until combined. Stir in **2 tablespoons olive oil.** Reserve some sauce for the table before basting.

SAUTÉED	BRAISED

Butter and Tarragon

Use **butter** to brown **the chicken** well in a large skillet. Cover and cook over medium-low heat, turning occasionally, until the internal temperature is 155–165°F, or the juices run clear, 15 to 20 minutes. Transfer to a platter; add **3 tablespoons minced shallots** and **½ cup white wine or chicken stock**. Reduce the sauce over medium-high heat; add **1 or 2 tablespoons chopped tarragon**, pour the sauce over the chicken, and serve.

Chicken and Garlic Stew

Brown **the chicken** in a Dutch oven with **olive oil**. Add at least **2 heads of unpeeled garlic cloves, ½ cup chopped fresh parsley,** and **½ cup white wine or chicken stock**. Bring to a boil, then lower to a steady simmer. Cover and cook until the chicken and garlic are tender, about 45 minutes. Serve, spreading the garlic onto **crusty bread**. Garnish: **chopped fresh parsley**.

Olives, Tomatoes, and Parsley

Use **olive oil** instead of butter. Substitute **½ cup chopped olives, 1 cup chopped ripe tomatoes,** and **1 tablespoon capers** for the shallots, and **parsley** for the tarragon.

Asparagus and Mustard

About 5 minutes before you remove **the chicken,** add **12 ounces chopped raw asparagus** to the pan; leave the asparagus when you remove the chicken. Add **1 tablespoon of mustard** and **a squeeze of lemon juice** to the pan along with **the wine;** if you like, stir in **a splash of heavy cream** before serving.

With Clams

Reduce **the garlic** to 3 cloves and mince them; add **a pinch of hot red chile flakes** and **lemon zest** with the garlic, **parsley,** and **wine**. When **the chicken** is nearly tender, add about **2 dozen littleneck or cherrystone clams**. Raise the heat to medium, cover, and cook until the clams open, about 10 minutes. Garnish: **more parsley**.

With Mushrooms and Peas

Reduce **the garlic** to 6 cloves and peel them. Omit the parsley; add **8 ounces roughly chopped button mushrooms** with **the garlic and wine**. When the chicken is tender, add **1 cup fresh or frozen peas** and **2 tablespoons butter**. Cover, and cook until the peas are tender or heated through.

SPICY BIG TRAY CHICKEN

On the advice of friends, I wandered one day into Spicy Village, in Manhattan's Chinatown, a restaurant that politeness prevents me from describing as anything other than "modest." I ordered, as I'd been instructed, the No. 7: Spicy Big Tray Chicken, which turned out to be a mound of chicken nearly afloat in a bath of dark, spicy sauce that contained star anise, Sichuan peppercorns, chiles, garlic, cilantro, a few mystery ingredients, and . . . potatoes. This was like no other "Chinese" dish I had ever had before.

It's an odd concoction, as I saw when the proprietors, Wendy Lian and her husband, Ren Fu Li, and Wendy's brother, Zeng Xin (who is the restaurant's cook), took me into the kitchen. The chicken is marinated in Budweiser, salt, pepper, and MSG. Over a huge flame in a large wok partly filled with oil, Zeng fried the chicken, stirring it almost constantly. He then drained it, waited a minute, and fried it again.

Zeng stir-fried the quite browned chicken with a mixture of dried spices, spicy bean paste, Fujianese wine, garlic, and ginger. Enormous amounts of black pepper were thrown in at nearly every stage. At some point, half-cooked potatoes were added, and the whole thing was cooked until the potatoes were done and the chicken was beyond tender.

Although there are challenges to re-creating this at home—starting with chopping the chicken legs into portions with a cleaver and continuing with the deep-frying and stir-frying, where it's difficult to get high enough heat—they're surmountable. And not only can you get the technique pretty much right, you also can improve on the ingredients. I didn't use the MSG or the Budweiser (Negra Modelo worked fine), and I made a fast chicken stock with the scraps of the bones, which allowed me to omit the bouillon powder Zeng used. (As for shortcuts, start with boneless thighs; skip the marinating; fry once. It's not quite as good, but it's not a terrible downgrade.)

Spicy Big Tray Chicken

SERVES: At least 4

3	pounds bone-in, skin-on chicken thighs and legs	1	star anise, left whole
2	teaspoons salt, plus more to taste	2	dried chiles, minced
2	teaspoons plus 1 tablespoon black pepper, plus more to taste	1½	tablespoons Sichuan hot bean sauce
12	ounces beer	2	tablespoons dark rice wine (preferably Fujian Cooking Wine)
1	pound new potatoes	3	to 4 cups chicken stock or water
1	to 2 quarts vegetable oil	2	tablespoons sugar
2	tablespoons sliced garlic	¼	cup soy sauce
2	teaspoons cumin seeds		Fresh cilantro, for garnish
2	teaspoons fennel seeds		Noodles or rice, for serving
1	teaspoon Sichuan peppercorns, roughly chopped		

1. With a cleaver, chop the chicken through the bones into 2-inch pieces, and toss with 2 teaspoons salt and 2 teaspoons black pepper. Cover with the beer and marinate it in the refrigerator overnight or for at least a few hours. Cook the potatoes in salted water until nearly done; drain; cut into bite-size pieces unless very small.

2. Heat at least 2 inches of the oil in a wok or tall, narrow pot over high heat. The more oil you use, the more chicken you can cook at one time.

3. When the oil is hot, fry the chicken, in batches if necessary, until slightly brown; depending on your heat, this could take 1 to 5 minutes. Stir frequently. Remove with a spider or slotted spoon and let rest until cool, then fry again—up to 5 minutes depending on your heat—until nicely browned and crisp; remove. (If you like, refrigerate before proceeding, for up to several hours.)

4. Reduce the oil to about 2 tablespoons (reserve the rest for frying or other uses), and turn the heat to high. Add the garlic, and cook a few seconds, then add another tablespoon of oil.

5. Add the cumin seeds, fennel seeds, Sichuan peppercorns, anise and chiles, and stir to combine. Add the bean sauce, and stir; return the chicken to the wok or skillet.

6. Stir in the wine and 2 cups stock or water, and stir to create a sauce. Add 1 tablespoon black pepper, the sugar, and soy sauce; bring to a vigorous boil.

7. Add the potatoes and continue to boil for 10 to 15 minutes, adding more liquid as needed to keep the mixture soupy; you want to wind up with 1 to 2 cups sauce and tender potatoes. Taste and adjust seasoning; add more black pepper if the taste isn't strong enough.

8. Ladle the chicken, potatoes, and broth into bowls. Garnish with cilantro and serve with noodles or rice.

PAILLARDS (CUTLETS)
+10 WAYS

192

There are a number of reasons to madly pound a piece of meat before cooking it, though not all of them make sense. One reason you often hear is that it saves you time—that by flattening the meat first you can cook it that much faster. While that idea is inarguably true, it will take longer to flatten the meat than the extra time required to cook it in the first place.

There are other, better reasons for pounding, however. By broadening the meat's surface area you increase the amount of meat that browns and becomes crisp during cooking. If that is your goal, making a paillard—or, if you like, a cutlet or a scallop—is definitely the way to go. All you need to do is take a boneless cut of meat at least ½ inch thick, slice into it horizontally, and open it up like a book. Then flatten it. Voilà! You have a paillard, a fancy French name for a thinly pounded piece of meat.

The cooking of a paillard is easy and the results are reliable. A sauce is optional, however, because when they are not overcooked, the right cuts of meat (read: relatively fatty cuts) turn out nice and juicy on their own. In the event you do want a sauce, you'll find the fat takes on meaty flavor while the paillards are cooking, which makes it a perfect base for a quick pan sauce; you'll find some examples of this here.

Those "right cuts" include boneless chicken thighs (not breasts), sirloin beef, loin or (perhaps even better) shoulder cuts of pork or lamb. Pork tenderloin will also work, but like the chicken breast, it is susceptible to overcooking.

The final benefit of the paillard is the making of it. This can be very satisfying. Put that piece of meat between two sheets of plastic wrap, grab something heavy—a skillet, a mallet, your shoe—and beat the hell out of it. You will not only end up with a great dish; a few minutes of clobbering paillards is about as good a stress reliever as any day at the spa.

Chicken Scaloppine al Limone

SERVES: 4

About 1½ pounds boneless chicken thighs

Salt and freshly ground black pepper

1 cup all-purpose flour, or more as needed

1½ cups fresh bread crumbs, or more as needed

3 large eggs

2 tablespoons extra-virgin olive oil, plus more as needed

3 tablespoons butter, plus more as needed

¼ cup dry white wine

½ cup chicken or vegetable stock

¼ cup lemon juice

¼ cup chopped fresh parsley, plus more for garnish

Lemon wedges, for serving

1. Heat the oven to 200°F. Slice each chicken thigh open like a book and lay it flat between two sheets of plastic wrap. Using a meat pounder, a wine bottle, or the bottom of a heavy skillet, pound each piece of chicken to ¼-inch thickness. Put two large skillets over medium-high heat for a minute or two. Meanwhile, put the flour and bread crumbs on two plates or in two shallow bowls. Beat the eggs in another shallow bowl. Sprinkle all with salt and pepper.

2. Add 1 tablespoon each oil and butter to each skillet and swirl it around. When it is hot—a pinch of flour will sizzle—dredge a piece of the chicken in the flour, then dip it in the eggs, and finally dredge it in the bread crumbs. Add the chicken piece to one of the pans, then repeat with another piece in the second pan. (You may be able to fit more than one paillard in each pan at a time.)

3. Cook the chicken, rotating occasionally and regulating the heat if necessary so it sizzles constantly but doesn't burn. When the pieces are brown, after about 2 minutes, turn them over.

4. Cook on the second side until the chicken is firm to the touch, 1 to 2 minutes more. (Cut into one with a thin-bladed knife; the center should be white or slightly pink.) Transfer the chicken to a platter and put it in the oven. Wipe out the pan with a paper towel and repeat with the remaining chicken, adding more oil and butter to each skillet as necessary.

5. When all the chicken is cooked, add a tablespoon or two more oil or butter to one of the skillets (remove the other from the heat) and sprinkle the fat with 2 teaspoons of the remaining flour. Cook over medium-high heat, stirring, for 3 to 4 minutes. Add the wine and stir and scrape the pan until the wine has reduced by about half, about 1 minute. Add the stock and lemon juice, and cook, stirring, until the mixture is slightly thickened and a bit syrupy, another 3 to 4 minutes.

6. Add 1 tablespoon of butter and swirl the pan around until it melts. Add any juices that have accumulated around the cooked chicken, along with the ¼ cup parsley. Stir, taste, and adjust the seasoning. Spoon the sauce over the chicken, garnish with parsley, and serve with lemon wedges.

VARIATIONS

Chicken Paillards with Panko and Wasabi-Ginger Pan Sauce

Substitute **panko** for the fresh bread crumbs and **neutral oil** for the olive oil and butter. After removing **the chicken** from the pan, add **1 tablespoon minced fresh ginger** and cook for 1 minute. Substitute more stock for the wine and lemon juice in the pan sauce, and substitute **1 teaspoon wasabi powder dissolved in 1 tablespoon soy sauce** for the parsley.

Chicken Parmigiana Paillards

Substitute **more olive oil** for the butter. After turning **the chicken** in step 3, top each piece with **1 or 2 tomato slices** and **1 or 2 slices of mozzarella cheese.** When the chicken is almost done, put it under the broiler and broil until the cheese is brown and bubbly. Skip the pan sauce. Garnish: **torn basil leaves.**

Beef Paillards with Capers and Watercress

Substitute **sirloin steaks,** sliced open and pounded, for the chicken. Substitute **¼ cup chopped watercress** and **1 tablespoon drained capers** for the parsley. Garnish: **more chopped watercress.**

Beef Paillards, Chicken-Fried-Steak Style

Substitute **flank or sirloin steak,** sliced open and pounded, for the chicken and **more butter** for the olive oil. After removing the last steak from the pan, add **1 chopped small onion** and cook for 5 minutes. Substitute **more stock** for the lemon juice in the pan sauce; after it thickens, add **1 cup heavy cream.** Adjust the heat so it bubbles steadily and cook, stirring, until thickened, 1 to 2 minutes. Skip the lemon wedges.

Pork Paillards with Peanuts and Thai Pan Sauce

Substitute **boneless pork loin chops or tenderloin cutlets,** sliced open and pounded, for the chicken, **ground roasted peanuts** for the bread crumbs (you can grind them in a food processor), and **neutral oil** for the olive oil and butter. Substitute **more stock** for the wine, **lime juice** for the lemon juice, and **fresh cilantro** for the parsley in the pan sauce, and add **1 tablespoon fish sauce** along with **the cilantro.** Garnish: **lime wedges.**

Pork Paillards with Mustard Pan Sauce

Substitute **boneless pork loin chops or tenderloin cutlets,** sliced open and pounded, for the chicken. Add **1 tablespoon mustard seeds** to the bread crumbs. Substitute **more stock** for the lemon juice, and add **1 tablespoon Dijon mustard** along with the butter in step 6. Skip the lemon wedges.

Pork Schnitzel with Sour Cream and Apple Pan Sauce

Substitute **boneless pork loin chops,** sliced open and pounded, for the chicken and **more butter** for the olive oil. After removing the pork from the pan, add **1 chopped medium onion** and cook for 5 minutes. Add **2 chopped apples** and **½ cup white wine,** and cook until the apples are very soft, about another 5 minutes. Turn off the heat, wait 30 seconds, and add **1 cup sour cream.** Garnish: **chopped fresh parsley.**

Pork Paillard Sandwich

Substitute **a whole pork tenderloin** for the chicken; slice it open like a book, cut it into 4 pieces, and pound each of those pieces thin. Add **1 tablespoon Dijon mustard** to **the eggs.** Substitute **more butter** for the olive oil. Skip the pan sauce; serve the paillards on **toasted hamburger buns or hard rolls** with **lettuce, tomato, onion, pickles, mayonnaise,** and **ketchup.**

Lamb Paillards with Olives, Yogurt, and Mint

Substitute **boneless lamb chops,** sliced open and pounded, for the chicken and **more olive oil** for the butter. Substitute **more stock** for the lemon juice in the pan sauce; after it thickens, turn off the heat, wait 30 seconds, and add **1 cup plain yogurt, ½ cup chopped black olives,** and **¼ cup chopped fresh mint.** Garnish: **more chopped mint.**

FRIED CHICKEN

Unless you're a routine visitor to KFC, fried chicken is probably not in your weekly diet. Which is fine: it is, after all, a treat. But even though you can easily find fried chicken that's way better than the fast-food variety, it remains a specialty of home cooking, and one that anyone can handle.

To me, legs make the best fried chicken. You can buy the drumsticks and thighs separately, or portion the pieces yourself: just lay them on a cutting board and wiggle any sharp knife where the drumstick and thigh meet until you find the ligaments that hold them together.

What you season your chicken with is a matter of personal preference (and you need not go beyond salt and pepper if you don't want). I've offered a few spice mixes here; you can use others,

including things as simple as pimentón (smoked paprika) or cumin; and of course, you can use store-bought chili or curry powder instead of making your own. A load of black pepper is also among the best fried-chicken seasonings.

Lard is ideal for frying, though there are other fats that are good, ranging from goose fat to clarified butter to high-quality cooking oil. Getting the fat to 350°F before starting to fry is also important; if you don't have a thermometer, a pinch of flour that sizzles energetically when added to the pan is a pretty reliable indicator that the oil is ready. If you add the chicken gradually but steadily to the fat, the temperature won't fall much, and you'll be able to cover the pan for the first few minutes of frying, when most of the unpleasant spattering occurs.

Fried Chicken Universal Instructions

SERVES: 4

Good-quality lard (preferred) or neutral or peanut oil, for frying	2 cups cornmeal, all-purpose flour, rice flour, or masa harina
4 chicken legs, drumsticks and thighs separated	Lemon wedges, for serving
Salt and freshly ground black pepper to taste	

1. Heat at least ½ inch of fat over medium-high heat in a large, deep skillet, broad saucepan, Dutch oven, or similar vessel with a lid. Do not skimp. Sprinkle the chicken with salt and pepper and whatever seasonings you prefer (see options at right). Put the cornmeal in a large shallow bowl, and roll the chicken pieces in it. Put them on a rack until the fat is ready.

2. When the fat reaches 350°F (a pinch of flour will sizzle in the fat), raise the heat to high and add the chicken pieces one at a time, skin side down. When all have been added, cover the pan, reduce the heat to medium-high, and set a timer for 7 minutes. After 7 minutes, uncover the pan, carefully turn the chicken with tongs, and continue to cook, uncovered, for 7 minutes. If the chicken shows signs of scorching, lower the heat a bit or shift the pieces as necessary.

3. Turn the chicken skin side down again and cook for about 5 minutes more, turning as necessary to ensure both sides are golden brown. As the chicken pieces finish cooking (to check for doneness, remove one piece and cut into it close to the bone; the juices should run clear), remove them from the skillet and drain them on brown paper bags or paper towels. Serve hot, warm, or at room temperature, with lemon wedges or other condiments, if you like.

OPTIONAL SEASONINGS

With Bay Leaves

Flavor **the cooking oil** by adding **10 dried bay leaves** as it heats. When the bay leaves sizzle, add **5 peeled garlic cloves** and cook for 3 to 5 minutes, until they begin to brown; remove and discard the bay leaves and garlic before adding the chicken.

Jerk Seasoning

Mix **½ tablespoon ground allspice**, a pinch of grated **nutmeg**, **½ teaspoon freshly ground black pepper**, **2 teaspoons dried thyme**, **1 teaspoon cayenne**, **1 tablespoon paprika**, **1 tablespoon sugar**, **2 tablespoons salt**, **½ teaspoon powdered garlic**, and **2 teaspoons ground ginger**. Sprinkle liberally onto the chicken before coating.

Garam Masala

Put **seeds from 10 cardamom pods**, a **3-inch cinnamon stick**, **1 teaspoon whole cloves**, **½ teaspoon nutmeg pieces**, **1 tablespoon cumin seeds**, and **1 tablespoon fennel seeds** in a skillet over medium heat; cook until lightly browned and fragrant, just a few minutes. Cool, then grind. Sprinkle liberally onto the chicken before coating.

Chili powder

Put **2 tablespoons ground dried mild chile** (like ancho), **½ teaspoon cayenne** (or to taste), **½ teaspoon black peppercorns**, **2 teaspoons cumin seeds**, **2 teaspoons coriander seeds**, and **1 tablespoon dried Mexican oregano** in a small skillet. Toast over medium heat until fragrant, 3 to 5 minutes. Grind to a powder in a spice grinder. Liberally sprinkle onto the chicken before coating (then wash your hands).

Hot Curry Powder

Put **2 small dried Thai or other hot chiles**, **1 tablespoon black peppercorns**, **1 tablespoon coriander seeds**, **1 teaspoon cumin seeds**, and **1 teaspoon fennel seeds** in a skillet over medium heat and cook until lightly browned and fragrant, just a few minutes; add **1 teaspoon ground fenugreek**, **1 tablespoon ground turmeric**, and **1 tablespoon each ground ginger and cayenne** (optional); cook for 1 minute longer. Cool, then grind to a fine powder. Sprinkle liberally onto the chicken before coating (then wash your hands).

CASSOULET

There are two ways to think of cassoulet. The first is as a canonical recipe from the South of France, in which the beans are tarbais, the confit is goose, the final topping is browned bread crumbs. The second way to think of cassoulet—and if this makes you more inclined to try it, by all means do so—is as simply a glorified version of franks 'n' beans. All that is required aside from time are beans, your seasoning (garlic is essential), your sausage, and whatever other meat you might be able to get your hands on. The confit obviously is traditional, but when making traditional dishes, it's important to remember that the people who "invented" them just used what they had.

This cassoulet recipe is one I've developed over the years, and is one I like. It's not terribly difficult (I promise), so don't be discouraged by the page of instruction that follows. In using a whole duck, this recipe builds on itself. You can choose to make it over the course of two days or four.

There is a clear order of operations. You cut up the duck, remove the skin from the legs, and refrigerate the legs overnight. At this point, you can make the stock or pick up the recipe the next day. You'll use the fat from the stock to make the confit, and you'll use the fat from the confit to brown the meat. But this cassoulet isn't that demanding; it just takes time, and you can do it.

Duck Stock and Confit

MAKES: About 8 cups stock; confit of 2 legs and 2 breasts

1	whole duck, 5 to 7 pounds
	Salt
10	garlic cloves, smashed
10	fresh thyme sprigs
1	shallot, sliced
1	large onion, cut in half (don't peel)

1	large carrot, cut into big chunks
2	celery ribs, cut into big chunks
1	bay leaf
	Several fresh parsley sprigs
	Black pepper
	Olive oil as needed

1. Set the duck breast side up on a cutting board. Using a boning knife, cut along one side of the breastbone; keep the back of your knife flush against that bone and follow the curve, cutting with the tip of your knife and pulling the meat back as you go. (It's actually a kind of natural movement; trust yourself.) When you meet up with the skin from the legs, cut through the skin and detach the breast. Repeat with the other side, releasing the other breast. The legs are now easy to see.

2. One leg (thigh and drumstick) at a time, cut through the skin, pulling the leg back as you go. Bend the leg backward to crack the joint, then cut through the joint (it's easy to see once you've cracked it); detach the leg. Repeat with the other leg. Remove the skin from the legs with your fingers, loosening it with your knife as necessary; reserve. Remove and reserve any fat you encounter.

3. Lightly score the skin of the duck breasts in a diamond pattern; be careful not to cut all the way through to the meat. Sprinkle with salt, cover, and refrigerate until ready to use in the cassoulet.

4. Toss the duck legs with the garlic (use more if your cloves are small), thyme, shallot, and a few pinches of salt. Refrigerate and marinate the duck legs overnight.

5. Heat the oven to 350°F. Put the duck carcass, the onion, carrot, and celery in a roasting pan. Roast, turning every now and then until quite well browned. Take your time; it'll take at least 1 hour.

6. Transfer the contents of the roasting pan to a large pot; pour off the rendered fat and reserve it. Add the bay leaf, parsley, and about 10 cups of water to the pot, and turn the heat to high.

7. Bring just to a boil, then lower the heat so the mixture sends up a few bubbles at a time. Cook, skimming and discarding any foam that accumulates, for at least 60 minutes and up to 2 hours. Cool slightly, then strain. Season with salt and pepper. Refrigerate the stock overnight.

8. The next day, take the stock out of the refrigerator and remove the duck fat from the top; it will have solidified, and you'll be able to scoop it right off. Put the fat in a medium saucepan over medium heat. When the fat melts and reaches about 190°F, add the duck legs along with the garlic and as much olive oil (or duck fat) as necessary to submerge the legs. Discard the thyme and shallot.

9. Cook, never letting the heat exceed 200°F, until the meat is tender and easily pierced with a fork, about 1½ hours. Let cool, then store the duck in the fat in the refrigerator until you're ready to use it in the cassoulet.

Whole-Duck Cassoulet

SERVES: 6 to 8

4	cups dried white beans
½	pound not-too-smoky slab bacon
	Small bunch of fresh parsley, leaves chopped, stems saved
10	fresh thyme sprigs
2	bay leaves
1	teaspoon whole cloves
	Salt and black pepper
1	pound boneless lamb shoulder, cut into 1-inch cubes

	Reserved fat, as needed
2	medium onions, sliced
	Duck Confit (recipe at left)
8	whole garlic cloves, peeled
2	cups duck stock, plus more as needed
4	cups chopped tomatoes
1	tablespoon chopped garlic
¼	teaspoon cayenne
½	pound garlicky sausage, preferably in 1 piece
1	cup bread crumbs
2	boneless duck breasts

1. Boil 5 quarts of water in a large saucepan; add the beans. Remove from the heat and soak for 1 hour.

2. Cut the bacon into 4 large chunks and cover in water in another saucepan; bring to a boil, then simmer gently for 30 minutes.

3. Put the parsley stems, thyme, bay leaves, and cloves in a piece of cheesecloth and tie into a bundle. Add it and the bacon to the beans; bring to a boil, then simmer gently, skimming occasionally, until the beans are just tender, 45 to 90 minutes. (Add water if necessary; the beans should be moist but not swimming when they're done.) Taste and adjust the seasoning.

4. Season the lamb; brown it in a large pot in 3 tablespoons duck fat. Add the onions and cook until soft, 5 or 6 minutes; turn off heat.

5. Scrape the fat from the duck confit; shred the meat. Add the meat, garlic cloves, stock, tomatoes, garlic, and cayenne to the lamb. Bring to a boil, then cover and simmer gently until the lamb is very tender, 1 to 1½ hours. Taste and adjust the seasoning. Cut the fat from the meat and cut the meat into small pieces.

6. Brown the sausage in a skillet in 2 tablespoons duck fat; slice into ¼-inch-thick rounds. Don't wash the pan.

7. Heat the oven to 375°F. Transfer a layer of beans to a large enameled cast-iron pot, leaving behind most of the cooking liquid. Layer half of the sausage and bacon on top, then another layer of beans, then half the duck-lamb mixture; repeat until you have used all the beans and meat.

8. Put the pot over medium heat and bring to a simmer, uncovered, then turn off heat. Cover with bread crumbs and the chopped parsley and bake, uncovered, for 20 minutes.

9. Cook the duck breasts in the sausage skillet, skin-side-down over medium-high heat, until they release easily from the pan, 3 to 5 minutes. Turn and cook until just rare, another minute or two. Remove the breasts, and pour the drippings over the cassoulet; reduce oven heat to 350°F.

10. Bake the cassoulet until it's hot, bubbling, and crusted around the edges, 30 to 40 minutes; add duck stock if it starts to look too dry. Slice the duck breasts and tuck them into the bread crumbs. Cook until the breasts are medium rare, another 5 minutes or so, then serve.

THANKSGIVING
LEFTOVERS
+20 WAYS

Everyone (yes, literally) says that leftovers are "the best part of Thanksgiving," but I'm not especially fond of dry meat on bread with a ton of mayonnaise, or with even that exotic alternative, cranberry sauce.

And yet. There you are with 4 pounds of turkey meat, a pile of meaty bones, cranberry sauce destined to hang around until February, and your grandmother's stuffing, which wasn't easy to make. Oh, and there are the mashed potatoes, an always-challenging leftover.

Fear not. Here are twenty handy-dandy mini-recipes designed to stimulate both your overin-dulged appetite and your tryptophanned-out brain. They're universal enough to accommodate almost whatever kind of Thanksgiving leftovers you're start-ing with (even cranberry sauce in a can), and can be scaled as needed or based on how plentiful your leftovers are.

Turkey-Noodle Soup with Ginger

Cook **chopped onion, carrot, celery, garlic, and ginger** in **neutral oil** until soft, then add **chicken or turkey stock** and bring to a boil. Cook **pasta** in salted water until almost done; drain and stir it into the soup, along with **shredded turkey**; heat through. Garnish: **cilantro.**

Turkey-Lentil Soup

Cook **chopped onion, carrot, and celery in butter** until soft. Add **a sprinkle of curry powder** and cook until fragrant. Add **lentils, a bay leaf, and turkey or other stock** to cover. Bring to a boil; turn the heat to low and cook, stirring occasionally, until the lentils are tender. Stir in **chopped turkey** and heat through. Garnish: **plain yogurt.**

Turkey Salad with Spicy Mayonnaise

Toss **shredded turkey** with **chopped scallions, celery, and cilantro.** Fold in **mayonnaise and pimentón** (smoked paprika) and **chili powder or paprika** to taste. Garnish: **cilantro.**

Turkey Seco Tortillas

Heat oven to 300°F. Spread some **shredded turkey** on a baking sheet. Toss with **olive oil, minced garlic, ground cumin, ground coriander, and/or chili powder.** Bake for 30 minutes, or until dried and crisp, stirring occasionally. Serve with **flour tortillas** and the usual garnishes.

Pulled-Turkey Sandwich

Whisk together **ketchup, a splash of red-wine vinegar, chili powder, minced onion, and garlic**—and **some cranberry sauce,** if you like; add enough water to form a thin sauce. Cook over medium-low heat for 10 minutes, then stir in **shredded turkey** and heat through. Serve on **toasted hamburger buns or rolls.**

Eggs Baked in Stuffing

Heat the oven to 375°F. Pack **a layer of stuffing** into the bottom of a **greased baking dish** or individual ramekins. (If you have time for a layer of caramelized onions, even better.) Make wells in stuffing and crack **eggs** into them. Sprinkle with **Parmesan** and bake until the eggs are just set, 10 to 15 minutes.

Stuffing Cakes

For every **2 cups crumbled stuffing,** stir in **2 beaten large eggs** and **a little flour.** Form into patties and cook in **olive oil or butter** until browned on both sides. Whisk together **equal parts sour cream and cranberry sauce** and dollop on top.

Breakfast Sausage

In a bowl, combine **equal parts stuffing and ground pork or turkey, chopped fresh sage,** and **a sprinkling of fennel seeds.** Form into patties, then cook in **olive oil** until the outsides are crisp and the insides no longer pink. Garnish: **maple syrup, cranberry sauce,** or a mixture of the two.

Stuffing-Stuffed Bell Peppers

Heat the oven to 450°F. Cut the tops off **bell peppers** and remove the seeds and stems. Pack a mixture of **moist stuffing** (add any flavorful liquid, if necessary), **Parmesan,** and **some sautéed ground beef or pork** into the peppers. Drizzle with **olive oil** and roast until the peppers are tender, 30 minutes.

Savory Bread Pudding

Heat the oven to 350°F. Heat **milk** (1 cup per 2 cups of stuffing), **a few tablespoons butter,** and **some chopped fresh herbs** until the butter melts. Beat **eggs** (1 large per 2 cups of stuffing), then slowly whisk in the milk mixture. Pour over the crumbled stuffing, sprinkle **shredded Gruyère** on top, and bake in a baking dish until browned and bubbly, about 50 minutes.

Potato Pierogi

Cook **chopped onion and garlic** in **butter** until soft; stir into **mashed potatoes**. Fill **wonton skins** with a spoonful of the potato mixture (don't overstuff); fold over and seal the edges with a little water. Working in batches, sauté in butter until golden brown. Garnish: **sour cream** and **chopped fresh dill.**

Garlic-Rosemary Potato Fritters

Cook **lots of chopped garlic and rosemary** in **olive oil** until fragrant. Stir into **mashed potatoes** along with **beaten eggs** (1 egg for every 2 cups potatoes) and enough **flour** to bind. Form into patties (chill, if time allows). Dredge in **bread crumbs or flour;** cook in **olive oil** until browned.

Spicy Potato Gratin

Heat the oven to 375°F. Soften **chopped onion, garlic,** and **jalapeños** in **olive oil.** Stir into **mashed potatoes;** pack into a greased baking dish. Sprinkle with **Cheddar, bread crumbs,** and oil. Bake until browned, 15 minutes.

Turkey Shepherd's Pie

Heat the oven to 400°F. Cook **chopped onion and carrot** in **butter** until soft. Stir in **a little tomato paste, chopped cooked turkey, peas or other leftover vegetables,** and **some leftover gravy** (or a spoonful or so of flour and some chicken stock); simmer until thick. Put the mixture in a baking dish, spread **mashed potatoes** over the top, then top with **crumbled stuffing or bread crumbs** and **a drizzle of melted butter.** Bake until golden brown. Garnish: **parsley or sage.**

Mashed Potato and Turkey Croquettes

Stir together **mashed potatoes, chopped cooked turkey, chopped onion, beaten egg** (about 1 egg per cup of the mixture), and enough **all-purpose flour** to bind. (A little **sage** or **thyme** is good, too.) Roll into balls and dredge in **flour,** then in **beaten egg,** then in **bread crumbs.** Cook in **olive oil** until browned all over. Serve with **cranberry or applesauce** and **sour cream.**

Cranberry-Yogurt Parfaits

In individual glasses, alternate layers of **cranberry sauce, plain Greek yogurt, honey,** and **chopped pecans.** Garnish: **fresh mint.**

Cranberry and Gruyère Grilled-Cheese Sandwich

Spread **cranberry sauce** on a slice of bread. Top with some **slices of Gruyère** and **a second slice of bread. Butter** the outside of the sandwich generously. Cook in a skillet over medium heat until the bread is golden brown and the cheese is melted.

Cranberry Negroni

Mix **equal parts gin, Campari, vermouth, and cranberry sauce** in a cocktail shaker with ice. Shake and strain. Garnish: **orange or lemon peel.**

Cranberry-Swirl Quick Bread

Heat the oven to 350°F. Grease a 9-inch loaf pan. Combine **2 cups flour, 1 cup sugar, 1½ teaspoons baking powder, ½ teaspoon baking soda,** and **1 teaspoon salt** in a food processor. Pulse in **4 tablespoons cold butter.** Add **¾ cup buttermilk, 1 tablespoon grated orange zest,** and **1 large egg;** pulse to combine. Pour into loaf pan and swirl in **1 cup cranberry sauce** with a knife. Bake until a toothpick comes out clean, at least 45 minutes

Cranberry-Braised Chicken

Cook **chicken parts in butter,** rotating and turning as necessary, until browned on all sides; remove from the pan. Add **chopped onion, garlic,** and **fresh ginger** and cook until soft. Stir in **cranberry sauce** and a little **chicken or turkey stock or white wine;** add the chicken. Cover and cook over medium-low heat, turning the chicken occasionally until it's cooked through. Garnish: **grated orange zest.**

MEAT

Ten years ago, this chapter would have been a lot bigger than it is now, perhaps even the biggest in the book (that title now goes overwhelmingly to vegetables). The reason meat holds a more modest place today is simply that, to improve my own health and that of the planet, I no longer cook and eat nearly as much of it as I used to. This is not to say that you should cut meat completely out of your diet—I haven't, and likely never will; rather, on the (ideally, rarer) occasions when you do eat meat, treat it like a celebration.

Indeed, there is much in this chapter to celebrate; in fact, I can't name a single dish here that couldn't hold its own at the center of a dinner party (even the salad, which involves slow-roasting confited pork cheek on top of a hunk of bread, is spectacular enough to draw a crowd). Not only are the dishes here impressive, but they cover a wide range of cuisines. There's a Korean barbecue beef and Mexican pork carnitas, a Moroccan leg of lamb and Indian lamb shanks, a Chinese pork stir-fry and Peruvian pork stew, and spare ribs by way of Armenia, Italy, and the American South, plus much more.

In general, the recipes here follow one simple rule: if you're not going to eat meat all the time, it had better be damn good when you do.

STEAK
+3 WAYS

Grilled
spice-
rubbed
tri-tip

When I was growing up in New York City—where outdoor grilling was more or less unheard of— my mom had a rotisserie (essentially a stovetop broiler); strangely enough, it was lousy at spit-roasting meat but, man, did it cook a good steak! If for some reason you do not find yourself in possession of a 1950s rotisserie, have no fear; as it so happens, you can make a perfect steak without one.

There are multiple ways to go about it, three of which are represented here. Which recipe you gravitate to will depend a little on your kitchen setup. If you've got a fairly powerful broiler, the skirt steak recipe is fast and easy. If you don't mind a little smoke, the pan-roasted ribeye is hard to beat. And if you've never slow-cooked a tri-tip—or any other roast-like cut of steak—on the grill, then run, don't walk.

Of course, no technique will seem like a good one if your steak winds up tough and dry. Nailing the doneness on a steak gets easier and easier with experience, to the point where eventually you can tell just by poking it. Until that time comes, though, the best way to ensure your steak is cooked the way you like it is to cut a small slit into it with a paring knife and have a look. For thicker cuts (1½ inches or thicker), you can test the temperature with a meat thermometer: stick it in from the side (not the top) to ensure that the tip of the thermometer is in the center of the steak.

Each of these recipes comes with a simple sauce or spice rub, all of which are delicious and none of which is necessary. A perfectly juicy steak can stand on its own with nothing more than salt and pepper. That's how my mom made it.

Pan-Roasted Ribeye with Herb Butter

SERVES: 2 to 4

2	tablespoons chopped fresh parsley		Juice of ½ lemon
4	tablespoons (½ stick) butter, at room temperature	2	ribeye steaks, about 1½ inches thick
	Salt and freshly ground black pepper		Neutral oil

1. Heat the oven to 500°F. Use a fork to mash the parsley with the butter; add some salt and pepper, and the lemon juice. Put it in the fridge while you cook the steak.

2. Put a large skillet (preferably cast iron) over high heat. When the pan is literally smoking hot, pat the steaks dry with a paper towel, rub them on both sides with a little neutral oil, sprinkle with salt and pepper, and put them in the skillet. Cook until the bottoms are deeply caramelized, 4 to 5 minutes. Turn the steaks, and transfer the skillet to the oven. Cook until the steaks are one shade rarer than you ultimately want them to be, 6 to 8 minutes for medium-rare. To check for doneness, you can peek inside with a sharp knife. Transfer the steaks to a cutting board, and spoon some of the herb butter on top, and let them rest (covered loosely with foil) for 5 to 10 minutes.

3. Slice the steaks thick, or serve them whole, with a little more of the butter on top.

Grilled Spice-Rubbed Tri-Tip

SERVES: 4 to 6

1	tablespoon salt	1	teaspoon ground cumin
1	teaspoon freshly ground black pepper	¼	teaspoon cayenne
1	tablespoon brown sugar	1	tablespoon neutral oil
2	teaspoons sweet paprika	1	whole tri-tip roast (2½ to 3 pounds)
1	teaspoon chili powder		

1. Combine the spices and oil in a small bowl, and stir to form a paste. Rub it all over the roast.

2. Heat a charcoal or gas grill; the fire should be fairly hot, and the rack about 4 inches from the heat. Leave one side of the grill cooler for indirect cooking. Put the steak on the cool side of the grill and cook, turning occasionally, for 20 to 25 minutes.

3. Move the steak to the hot side of the grill and cook, flipping frequently, until charred all over, 6 to 8 minutes (at this point an instant-read thermometer inserted horizontally into the center of the steak should read 120–125°F). Transfer the steak to a cutting board, and let it rest (covered loosely with foil) for 8 to 10 minutes. Slice thin against the grain, and serve.

Seared Skirt Steak with Chimichurri

SERVES: 4

2	pounds skirt steak	1	tablespoon fresh oregano leaves
3	tablespoons neutral oil, plus more for rubbing the steaks	3	garlic cloves
	Salt and freshly ground black pepper	1	teaspoon hot red chile flakes
1½	cups fresh parsley leaves	2	tablespoons red-wine vinegar
½	cup fresh cilantro leaves	3	tablespoons olive oil

1. Heat the broiler as high as it will go. At least 10 minutes before you're ready to cook, position a large cast-iron or other sturdy heatproof skillet on a rack as close to the heating element as you can get it. Cut the steak into pieces as necessary to fit it in the pan, pat dry with a paper towel, and rub it on both sides with a little oil; sprinkle with salt and pepper. Put it in the skillet and cook (no need to flip it) until caramelized on both sides and one shade rarer than you ultimately want it to be, 5 to 8 minutes for medium-rare, depending on the strength of your broiler. To check for doneness, you can peek inside with a sharp knife. Transfer to a platter to rest (covered loosely with foil) for at least 5 minutes.

2. While the steak cooks or rests, put the rest of the ingredients (except for the olive oil) in a food processor along with a sprinkle of salt and pepper. Process until combined, then stir in the olive oil by hand. Taste and adjust the seasoning.

3. Slice the steak thinly against the grain, and serve it with the chimichurri on the side.

BULGOGI

The exoticism and excitement of Korea's take on barbecue—grilled beef served with the assortment of tidbits known collectively as banchan—derives from both the ingredients and the techniques used to prepare it.

I will not (and cannot) claim that every element of this menu is legitimately Korean. In fact, one recipe—the Plum and Wine Herb Cocktail—is plain made up: a sangria-like concoction of white wine, gin, rosemary-infused simple syrup, and fresh plums. I see it as a tribute to the sweet plum wine so often served in Korean restaurants. (If you want to be authentic, drink soju—a less powerful cousin of vodka—or beer.) But if my cocktail isn't authentic, it is good and, like the rest of the menu, very potent.

Beef Bulgogi

SERVES: 4 to 6

1	bunch of scallions, roughly chopped	2	pounds sirloin, ribeye, or skirt steak, thinly sliced, or 3 to 4 pounds beef short ribs, boned and thinly sliced
8	or more garlic cloves, peeled and roughly chopped		Boston or bibb lettuce leaves, for serving
1	tablespoon sugar or honey		Gochujang (Korean chile-bean paste), for serving
½	teaspoon black pepper		
½	cup soy sauce		
1	tablespoon sesame oil		

1. Combine the scallions, garlic, sugar, pepper, soy sauce, and sesame oil in a blender and purée, adding water as needed to form a smooth mixture. Toss the meat with the soy mixture and marinate for 15 minutes to 2 hours. Heat a grill with the rack 4 to 6 inches from the flame; the fire should be as hot as possible.

2. Remove the meat from the marinade, and grill until browned outside but still rare inside—no more than a couple of minutes per side. Serve wrapped in lettuce leaves, with gochujang for dipping.

Sesame Spinach and Tofu

Cook **1 tablespoon minced garlic** in **2 tablespoons sesame oil** over medium-high heat for 1 minute; add **1 pound chopped fresh spinach** and cook, stirring occasionally, until it begins to wilt. Crumble in **½ pound extra-firm tofu** and stir until warmed through. Stir in **1 tablespoon soy sauce**, **a pinch of sugar**, and **1 tablespoon sesame seeds**. Serve hot or warm.

Korean Potato Salad

Cook **1 pound julienned or shredded potatoes** and **½ pound julienned or shredded carrots** in salted boiling water until barely tender, about 5 minutes; add **½ cup fresh or frozen peas** in the last minute. Drain and rinse. Whisk together **½ cup mayonnaise** and **3 tablespoons rice vinegar**; toss with the vegetables, **½ cup chopped fresh chives**, and **¼ cup chopped scallions**. Garnish with **chopped scallions and chives**, season with **salt** and **pepper**, and serve.

Grilled Scallion Salad

Brush **1 pound untrimmed scallions** with **1 tablespoon sesame oil**; grill over moderately high heat, turning once, until charred and tender, 5 to 10 minutes. Roughly chop and toss with **⅓ cup rice vinegar**, **1 to 2 tablespoons gochugaro** (Korean chile powder; or less if using hot red chile flakes), **1 tablespoon sesame seeds**, and **2 teaspoons sugar**. Serve immediately.

Kimchi

Layer **1 small green or white cabbage** (leaves separated) and **1 small daikon radish** (cut into 1-inch cubes) with **½ cup salt** in a large bowl. Let cabbage wilt for 2 hours, massaging it to help soften. Rinse and dry. Roughly chop; toss with **20 chopped scallions**, **¼ cup fish (or soy) sauce**, **¼ cup minced garlic**, **3 tablespoons sugar**, and **2 tablespoons each minced ginger and gochugaro** (Korean chile powder). Serve, or refrigerate for up to 1 week.

Fried Hijiki

Soak **1 ounce dried hijiki** in 2 cups hot water. When it's tender, about 5 minutes later, drain, squeeze dry, remove any hard bits, and chop. Cook **1 tablespoon minced garlic** and **¼ cup chopped scallions** in **1 tablespoon neutral oil** and **1 tablespoon sesame oil** over medium-high heat for 1 minute; add the hijiki and cook until browned and beginning to shrivel, 5 to 7 minutes. Stir in **1 tablespoon each soy sauce and sesame seeds** and **a pinch of sugar**. Serve hot or warm.

Plum and Herb Wine Cocktail

Cook **⅓ cup sugar**, **⅓ cup water**, and **1 fresh rosemary or thyme sprig** over medium-low heat until the sugar dissolves; cool and remove the herb. Combine **1 (750ml) bottle of not too dry white wine** (like Riesling), **¼ cup gin**, the juice of **1 lemon**, **2 to 4 chopped ripe plums**, and **¼ cup of the herb syrup**. Chill for at least 2 hours, taste, and add more herb syrup if you like, and serve.

PORK RIBS
+9 WAYS

You cannot argue that ribs are seasonal. If you're a fan, you want them as badly in January as you do in August. In fact, regardless of when "now" is, it's as good a time as any to be cooking ribs.

You'll find a range of options here. The standard, most straightforward method is two-step grilling with little more than salt and pepper; I offer more elaborate, though hardly difficult, variations. The most complicated recipe, which uses two cooking methods, is also by far the most time-consuming, but it could also be the most rewarding, at least for classicists. You smoke the ribs over indirect heat with sage and ginger (or other spices; see the variations). This can be done in advance, and it can be done while simultaneously direct-grilling something else, or even as the heat is dying down from a big fire. If there is a revelation to be found here, it is in the lightest and probably easiest recipe: ribs braised with anchovies and white wine. This is a dish in which the ribs can be eaten neatly, with knife and fork (and the sauce used to dress pasta or rice, or as a bread-soaker).

I've specified in each recipe whether to use baby back (loin) or spare (belly) ribs, though they're pretty much interchangeable except in the case of grilling. Spare ribs will not become tender if you grill them quickly and at high heat; they need the low-and-slow treatment.

Braised Spare Ribs with White Wine, Garlic, and Anchovies

SERVES: 4

1 tablespoon olive oil	4 garlic cloves, peeled and crushed
3 to 4 pounds pork spare ribs, cut into individual ribs	3 or 4 anchovy fillets, chopped
Salt and freshly ground black pepper	1 cup dry white wine
	Chopped fresh parsley, for garnish

1. Put the olive oil in a large, deep skillet or Dutch oven over medium-high heat. When the oil is hot, add the ribs, meatier side down; sprinkle with salt and pepper. Cook, more or less undisturbed, until the meat browns nicely, 5 to 10 minutes, then turn and brown some more. You can brown the ribs in batches, but perfection is not imperative.

2. If there's too much fat, spoon some off; add the garlic and anchovies, and stir a minute. Add the wine, scraping up any browned bits from the bottom of the pan; bring to a simmer, then cover and cook, adding more wine if the pot gets too dry, until the ribs are tender, about 1 hour. If the mixture is soupy (unlikely), turn the heat to high, and cook until some of the liquid boils off. Serve, garnished with the chopped parsley.

Braised Spare Ribs with Lemon, Olives, and Rosemary

Omit the anchovies, if you like. Add **3 fresh rosemary sprigs** along with **the garlic.** Before covering the pot, add **1 cup black olives** (oil-cured are the best) and **a lemon,** washed and sliced as thin as possible.

Pasta with Pork Ribs

Use **6 or 8 meaty spare ribs.** Omit the anchovies, and add a pinch of **hot red chile flakes** along with **the garlic.** Substitute one **28-ounce can of tomatoes** (lightly crushed) for the wine, and cook until tender. Serve over any cut pasta, giving a rib or two to each diner. Sprinkle with **grated Parmesan.**

Salt and Pepper–Grilled Baby Back Ribs

SERVES: 4

3 to 4 pounds baby back ribs	Lemon wedges, for garnish
Salt and freshly ground black pepper	

1. Prepare a grill for indirect grilling. If you're using charcoal, make a fire in one half of the grill; for gas, turn on the burners on only one side. Rub the ribs with salt and a lot of pepper, and put them on the cool side of the grill. Cover the grill, open the vent slightly, and cook until some fat has rendered and the ribs are no longer raw, about 30 minutes.

2. Uncover, and move the ribs directly over the fire. Cook, turning frequently, until the ribs are nicely browned all over, 10 to 15 minutes. Cut the racks into individual ribs, and serve with lemon wedges.

Teriyaki-Grilled Baby Back Ribs

Combine **½ cup soy sauce** and **½ cup mirin** in a small saucepan over medium-low heat. Cook until it bubbles, then turn off the heat. Once you move the ribs over the fire, baste with the sauce; the goal is to caramelize the sauce without letting it burn. Instead of lemon wedges, garnish with **sliced scallions** and **sesame seeds.**

Grilled Baby Back Ribs with Charred Salsa Roja

Cut **½ pound ripe tomatoes** and **1 small onion** into rounds; halve and seed **a small jalapeño.** Rub the vegetables with **neutral oil.** While **the ribs** are cooking on the cool side of the grill, put **the vegetables** on the hot side; cook, keeping the grill covered and turning the vegetables just once, until they are charred, about 10 minutes. Transfer the vegetables to a blender with **1 small garlic clove, 1 tablespoon neutral oil, 1 teaspoon honey or sugar,** and **2 tablespoons lime juice.** Blend, adding a splash of water if necessary, until smooth. Once you move the ribs over the fire, baste with the sauce; don't let it burn. Garnish with **fresh cilantro** instead of lemon wedges.

Smoked and Roasted Spare Ribs

SERVES: 4

2 tablespoons paprika	1 tablespoon salt
1 tablespoon chili powder	1 tablespoon freshly ground black pepper
1 tablespoon ground cumin	3 to 4 pounds spare ribs
2 tablespoons brown sugar	

1. Prepare a grill for indirect cooking. If you're using charcoal, make a medium fire in one half of the grill, and let it die down to orange embers; for gas, turn on the burners on only one side. While the fire heats, combine all the seasonings, and rub the mixture all over the ribs.

2. If you're using charcoal, put a few heaping handfuls of soaked wood chips directly onto the coals; if you're using gas, put unsoaked wood chips in a tinfoil pan set on the grate over the burners. Put the ribs on the cool side of the grill, cover the grill, and open the vent slightly. Cook, adding another handful of wood chips if the smoke subsides, for an hour or so, long enough to flavor the meat with smoke.

3. Heat the oven to 250°F. Wrap the ribs in aluminum foil, put them on a baking sheet, and bake until very tender, 2½ to 3 hours. If you like, unwrap the ribs and cook them under the broiler or on the grill until browned and crisp.

Pastrami-Spiced Spare Ribs

Instead of the barbecue rub, coat the ribs with a mixture of **1 tablespoon each toasted and coarsely ground peppercorns, coriander seeds,** and **mustard seeds;** add **2 teaspoons salt.**

Smoked and Roasted Spare Ribs with Sage and Ginger

Instead of the barbecue rub, coat the ribs with a paste of **3 tablespoons chopped fresh sage, 2 tablespoons minced fresh ginger, 2 tablespoons grated orange zest, 3 tablespoons olive oil, a pinch of hot red chile flakes,** and **salt** and **black pepper.**

ARMENIAN RIB AND CHICKEN KEBABS

Greater Los Angeles is a collection of not just smaller cities but also exotic populations. Among those cities is Glendale, home to one of the world's largest Armenian populations outside Armenia.

Edward Khechemyan, chef of Glendale's restaurant Adana, left Armenia at age seventeen, and his menu boasts intriguing salads and dishes of beans and of rice, as well as innumerable kebabs. His grilling technique is unusual: he grills slowly (over briquettes fired with gas, by the way) until gorgeously browned. The fire is not superhot, but it's even—gas is good for that—and he keeps the grill grate a good 6 inches above the fire.

Baby Back Rib Kebabs

SERVES: 4

2 to 2½ pounds baby back ribs

1 medium white onion, sliced

1 teaspoon paprika

½ teaspoon mild red chile powder (like gochugaro)

1 teaspoon salt

½ teaspoon black pepper

¼ cup olive oil

1. Cut the racks into individual ribs. Put them in a nonreactive dish (or a resealable plastic bag), and add the rest of the ingredients. Marinate overnight in the refrigerator.

2. Heat a charcoal or gas grill; the flame should be fairly low and the rack about 6 inches from the heat. Once the ribs have marinated, discard the onion (or grill on the side in a grill basket, or sauté on the stovetop, if you like). To thread the meat onto skewers, orient the ribs so the undersides are facing the same direction (the ribs should look like frowns). Pierce the meat with the skewers either right above or below the bone, and run the skewer through to the other side. Wide metal skewers are best; if you're using wooden skewers, use two per kebab so the ribs are stable. Leave a little space between each rib so they brown all over.

3. Grill the ribs slowly, turning as necessary and basting with any leftover marinade, until they're beautifully browned all over, 15 to 20 minutes.

Chicken-Thigh Kebabs

SERVES: 4

2 pounds boneless, skinless chicken thighs, cut into 1½-inch chunks

1 medium white onion, sliced

½ teaspoon mild red chile powder (like gochugaro)

½ teaspoon ground turmeric

1 teaspoon garlic powder

1 tablespoon salt

1 teaspoon black pepper

Pinch of saffron

¼ cup lemon juice

¼ cup olive oil

1. Combine all the ingredients in a nonreactive dish (or resealable plastic bag), and marinate in the refrigerator between 3 and 12 hours.

2. Heat a charcoal or gas grill; the flame should be fairly low and the rack about 6 inches from the heat. Once the chicken has marinated, discard the onion (or grill on the side in a grill basket, or sauté on the stovetop, if you like), and thread the chicken onto skewers.

3. Grill the chicken slowly, turning as necessary and basting with any leftover marinade, until it's browned all over, 15 to 20 minutes.

Baghali Polo

SERVES: 4

2 cups extra-long basmati rice (called sella)

2 teaspoons salt

2 tablespoons olive oil

1 cup chopped fresh dill, or ¼ cup dried dill

½ teaspoon garlic powder

2 cups cooked and peeled fava beans or lima beans (frozen are fine)

2 tablespoons butter

1. Combine the rice, salt, olive oil, and 3 cups water in a medium pot with a lid over high heat. Bring to a boil, and let it bubble, uncovered, until the water evaporates. When the water is gone, the rice should be about half-cooked.

2. Turn the heat to low. Add the dill and garlic powder, and stir with a fork. Spread the beans out over the top of the rice, cover the pot, and cook, until the rice is tender, about 15 minutes.

3. Turn off the heat, add the butter, cover the pot again, and let sit for 2 to 3 minutes, or until the butter melts. Taste and adjust the seasoning, and serve.

Persian Salad

SERVES: 4

4 ripe tomatoes, chopped

4 Persian cucumbers, chopped

½ small white onion, chopped

2 tablespoons chopped fresh purple or green basil

1 tablespoon chopped fresh cilantro

½ teaspoon dried mint

½ teaspoon mild red chile powder (like gochugaro)

½ teaspoon salt

2 tablespoons lemon juice

1 tablespoon olive oil

Combine all the ingredients in a bowl; toss, and serve.

PORK AND APPLES
+3 WAYS

This classic—really, killer—combination of pork and apples is one most people don't play around with much. (Chops with applesauce or maybe the occasional apple-sage sausage is as far as we usually get.) Once I started to think about it, though, the possibilities for pork and apples seemed myriad. The recipes here represent just the tiniest tip of the iceberg: A pork loin stuffed with apples, a Peruvian pork stew with apple-sweetness and chile heat, and an updated version of the classic (and still wonderful) quiche Lorraine, with grated apples to cut through the salty bacon and cheese.

Apple-Stuffed Pork Loin with Moroccan Spices

SERVES: 6 to 8

2	tablespoons butter
2	medium apples, peeled, cored, and thinly sliced
1	large onion, chopped
1	teaspoon ground coriander
1	teaspoon ground cumin
1	teaspoon ground cinnamon
1	teaspoon ground ginger

1	teaspoon paprika
½	teaspoon ground turmeric
1	teaspoon salt, or to taste
1	tablespoon freshly ground black pepper
1	boneless pork loin roast (2 to 3 pounds)
1	cup or more apple juice

1. Heat oven to 450°F. Melt the butter in a large skillet over medium heat; add the apples, onion, spices, salt and pepper, and cook until soft, 10 to 15 minutes.

2. Wriggle a thin, sharp knife into each end of the meat, making a pilot hole. Then use the handle of a wooden spoon to widen the hole all the way through. Stuff with the apple-onion mixture; sprinkle with salt and pepper.

3. Roast for 15 minutes, then lower the heat to 325°F. Continue to roast, basting with apple juice about every 15 minutes. Start checking the roast after 45 minutes of total cooking time. When it's done, a thermometer inserted into the center of the meat (not the stuffing) will register 145°F. Transfer the roast to a platter.

4. Put the pan on over medium-high heat. Reduce the liquid to ¾ cup, or, if the pan is dry, add 1 cup apple juice and reduce. Stir in 2 tablespoons butter, if you like. Spoon the sauce over the roast, slice, and serve.

Peruvian Pork Stew with Chiles and Apples

SERVES: At least 8

2	tablespoons olive oil
3	to 4 pounds trimmed boneless pork shoulder, cut into 2-inch pieces
2	large white onions, chopped
4	large apples, peeled, cored, and roughly chopped

3	snipped and seeded ancho or other dried mild chiles
3	bay leaves
	Pinch of ground cloves
¼	cup lime juice
4	cups chicken stock
	Steamed rice, for serving
¼	cup chopped fresh cilantro

1. Heat the olive oil in a skillet and brown the pork on all sides; you may have to do this in batches for the most efficient browning. Meanwhile, sauté the onions and apples in a pan with the chiles, bay leaves, and cloves until the onions are tender, about 10 minutes.

2. Combine the pork, apple mixture, lime juice, and stock in a saucepan, Dutch oven, or slow cooker. Bring to a boil, then adjust the heat so the mixture bubbles steadily but not vigorously. (If you're using a slow cooker, turn it to high and walk away for 4 or 6 hours.)

3. Cook, stirring every 30 minutes or so, until the meat is very tender and just about falling apart, at least 1 hour. Taste and adjust the seasoning, then lower the heat (this will keep well for at least 1 hour before serving). If you like, remove the meat and reduce the broth to thicken it. Serve over steamed rice, garnished with cilantro.

Bacon and Apple Quiche with Flaky Pie Crust

SERVES: 6 to 8

1	cup plus 2 tablespoons all-purpose flour
½	teaspoon salt
6	tablespoons cold unsalted butter, cut into about 8 pieces
	About 3 tablespoons ice water
8	to 10 slices of good bacon
2	large apples, peeled, cored, and grated or chopped

	Salt and freshly ground black pepper
1	teaspoon minced fresh rosemary
¼	cup crumbled blue cheese, like Roquefort
4	large eggs at room temperature
1⅓	cups heavy cream

1. Combine the flour and salt in a food processor and pulse once or twice. Add the butter and process until the mixture looks like cornmeal. Put the mixture in a bowl and add the ice water; mix with your hands until you can form the dough into a ball, adding another tablespoon of ice water if necessary. Wrap the ball in plastic and freeze for 10 minutes (or refrigerate for at least 30 minutes, or up to a couple days).

2. Sprinkle a countertop with some flour and put the dough on it, sprinkling more flour on top. Use a rolling pin to roll with light pressure from the center out. If the dough is hard, let it rest for a few minutes; if it's sticky, add a little more flour. Roll, adding flour and rotating and turning the dough as needed; use ragged edges of dough to repair any tears, adding a drop of water when you press a patch in place.

3. When the diameter of the dough is about 2 inches greater than that of a 9-inch tart pan, drape the dough over the rolling pin and transfer it to the tart pan. Press the dough firmly into place. Trim as necessary; freeze for 10 minutes or refrigerate for 30 minutes or so.

4. Heat the oven to 425°F and set the rack in the middle. Prick the pie crust with a fork all over, then bake for 10 to 12 minutes, or until beginning to brown; remove and turn the oven down to 375°F. Meanwhile, fry the bacon in a large, deep skillet over medium heat, then remove from pan with a slotted spoon; cool and chop.

5. Pour out all but 1 tablespoon of bacon fat and use the same pan to fry the apples. Add salt, pepper, and rosemary. Turn the heat up to medium-high and cook, stirring frequently, until the apple is soft and lightly browned, at least 15 minutes. Adjust the heat so it doesn't brown too much or crisp up. Turn off the heat and spread the apples in the crust; then sprinkle with the bacon and the cheese.

6. In a mixing bowl, whisk together the eggs and cream. Put the tart shell on a baking sheet and pour in the egg mixture. Bake for 30 to 40 minutes, or until almost firm (it should still jiggle just a little in the middle) and lightly browned on top; reduce the oven heat if the shell's edges are darkening too quickly. Cook on a rack; serve warm.

CRISP PORK
CHEEK SALAD

Since its opening more than twenty years ago, St. John, Fergus Henderson's famous nose-to-tail restaurant in London, has developed a justifiable reputation for using underappreciated parts of many different types of animals (rolled pig's spleen, anyone?). Crispy pig's cheek with dandelions is about as representative a dish as the restaurant offers. It is sensational: crunchy fat-drenched croutons, hard crackling, moist salty meat, and super-bitter greens with a powerful caper-laden dressing. When I asked Fergus how to re-create it at home, this was his reply:

Hi Mark,

Take a fatty pig's cheek with skin on, confit, place on a piece of bread and pop it in the oven to crisp up. The bread will sup up the fat. Then chop up cheek and toast, mix with bitter dandelion leaves and dress with a mustardy vinaigrette and capers. As easy as that.

Best,
Fergus

As it turns out, preparing this dish pretty much *is* "as easy as that"—except for the shopping. The challenge is procuring a skin-on pig cheek and some lard. (Lard can always be replaced with duck fat—though that can be expensive—or good oil.) I ultimately got both from Flying Pigs Farm (they do mail order) in upstate New York.

Nevertheless, the cooking is straightforward, if time-consuming, and even when made by amateurs, the dish is impressive. I have also discovered that it can be tweaked, substituting turkey thighs, or even pork belly, for the more difficult to find and expensive pork cheek. Either way, this recipe is a beauty.

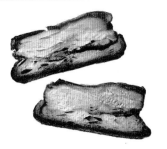

Crispy Pork Cheek or Belly (or Turkey Thigh) Salad

SERVES: 6 to 8

One 2½- or 3-pound pig cheek or piece of pork belly (or 2 turkey thighs), with skin	2 tablespoons olive oil, plus more as needed for drizzling
Salt and freshly ground black pepper	2 tablespoons red-wine or sherry vinegar
6 to 8 cups lard, duck fat, or oil (or a mixture)	1 tablespoon Dijon mustard
1 large slice of good bread, 1 inch thick (about the same size as the cooked meat)	2 teaspoons chopped drained capers
	8 cups dandelion or other bitter greens, like frisée (3 or 4 heads)

1. Sprinkle the meat liberally with salt and pepper. Refrigerate overnight, uncovered.

2. If using the oven, heat to 300°F. Rinse the meat in cold water. Put the fat in a pot that will allow you to submerge the meat, or nearly so. If you're using lard or duck fat, heat it in the oven until melted; if you're using oil, warm it. Submerge the meat in the fat, put a piece of parchment paper directly on top, and weight the paper down with something (I used a wooden spoon) to keep it in place.

3. Cook the meat slowly in the oven or on top of the stove, adjusting the heat as necessary so the fat bubbles gently—not rapidly—and turning the meat once or twice if it is not completely submerged. (You may wind up adjusting the oven to as low as 250°F to keep it cooking slowly.) The meat is done when you can easily pierce it with a skewer, 2 hours or longer (1 hour for the turkey).

4. Remove the meat from the fat. (At this point you can refrigerate the meat, lightly covered, for a day or two.) Increase the oven to 350°F. Put the bread slice on a roasting rack. (If you're using turkey, drizzle the bread first with olive oil.) Place the meat skin side up directly on top of the bread; the meat should cover the bread; any bread that's exposed may burn. Place the roasting rack on a rimmed baking sheet and roast the meat, checking occasionally and adjusting the heat as necessary, until the skin becomes quite crisp, 45 minutes or longer.

5. Meanwhile, whisk together the olive oil, vinegar, mustard, capers, and salt and pepper; the dressing should be quite sharp.

6. Wash and dry the greens. With the meat still on top of the bread, chop the meat and bread into bite-size pieces; it doesn't matter if it crumbles a bit. (If you're using turkey, pull out the thigh bones.) Toss the meat and bread with the greens and the dressing, and serve.

CARNITAS

Cooking with beer makes sense: not only is it more flavorful than water, but it's also more flavorful than any store-bought chicken stock. And unlike wine or liquor, you can substitute beer cup-for-cup for stock or water when you're braising or making soup.

In fact, beer's flavors are arguably more varied and complex than any ready-made liquid besides wine. And like bread, to which it's closely related, beer loves to team up with meat, cheese, and strong flavors like onions, garlic, and spices.

I had made carnitas—those irresistible Mexican pork shoulder chunks braised for hours with spices, then fried in their own fat until crisp—with beer as the braising liquid. After consulting Garrett Oliver, editor-in-chief of the *Oxford Companion to Beer*, I tried making it with Belgian wheat beer because, he said, these beers are often spiced with coriander and bitter orange, akin to Mexican-style braised meat; they are also a little sour, which lends the meat a nice complexity. The result was delicious, but frankly, you can use any full-bodied, full-flavored beer that you like to drink.

Carnitas Braised in Witbier

SERVES: 4 to 6

2	pounds boneless pork shoulder, cut into 1-inch chunks		Salt and freshly ground black pepper
1	large onion, quartered		Two 12-ounce bottles Allagash White, or another wheat beer in the Belgian Witbier style, like Hoegaarden
5	garlic cloves, lightly crushed		
2	bay leaves		
1	tablespoon cumin seeds		
1	tablespoon coriander seeds		Neutral oil if needed
1	cinnamon stick		Lime wedges, for serving
1	ancho or other mild dried chile		

1. Put the pork, onion, garlic, bay leaves, cumin, coriander, cinnamon, chile, and some salt and pepper in a large pot with a lid or a Dutch oven. Add the beer; top with water, if needed, to cover. Turn the heat to high, bring to a boil, and skim any foam that comes to the surface. Partly cover and adjust the heat so the mixture bubbles steadily. Cook until the meat is quite tender, about 1 hour, then cool.

2. Remove the bay leaves, spices, and chile with a slotted spoon and discard. Break or roughly chop the meat into bite-size pieces, return it to the pan, and cook uncovered until all the liquid has evaporated. Continue to cook the meat in the remaining fat until it's crisped and browned; add a little oil if it sticks or becomes dry. Serve hot, warm, or at room temperature with the lime wedges, or cover and refrigerate for up to 2 days.

Thyme, allspice, chiles (jerk rub)

Bell peppers, jalapeños, shishito chiles

KEBABS
+RECIPE GENERATOR

Sausage

Pearl onions, garlic

KITCHEN MATRIX

THE MAIN INGREDIENT

FRUITS AND VEGETABLES

THE FLAVORINGS

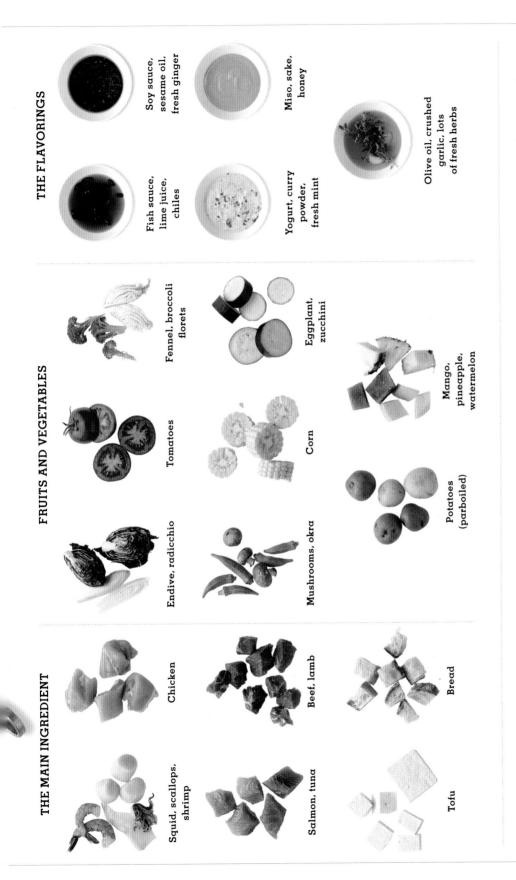

Squid, scallops, shrimp

Chicken

Salmon, tuna

Beef, lamb

Tofu

Bread

Endive, radicchio

Tomatoes

Fennel, broccoli florets

Mushrooms, okra

Corn

Eggplant, zucchini

Potatoes (parboiled)

Mango, pineapple, watermelon

Fish sauce, lime juice, chiles

Soy sauce, sesame oil, fresh ginger

Yogurt, curry powder, fresh mint

Miso, sake, honey

Olive oil, crushed garlic, lots of fresh herbs

While I was vacationing in Istanbul, my daily travels took me past a corner where a vendor parked his glass-enclosed grill cart, which measured about 12 square feet. He lovingly tended, over a bed of charcoal, his lamb-onion-pepper-and-tomato kebabs, which were beautiful. What they were not, however, was varied. His customers expected lamb kebabs, and that's what he gave them.

He had no choice. But you do. In fact, with this kebab Recipe Generator, a little patience, and a few bowls, you can arrange a customizable grilling station where anyone can create a personalized skewer.

You can use metal or wooden skewers, but if you opt for wood, soak them in water first to keep them from catching fire. You might also use two sticks per kebab, to make turning easier. Assemble the kebabs right before grilling, or let your kebabs marinate, refrigerated, up to a few hours.

Figure on ⅓ to ½ pound of meat, poultry, or fish, cut into chunks, per person. The chunks should be uniform in size—1½-inch cubes at least—and cooked according to the degree of doneness you're looking for: a total of 4 or 5 minutes (that will get you pretty rare) to 8 to 10 minutes for well done. The grill heat should be moderate; you don't need to incinerate these.

LAMB SHANKS
+4 WAYS

Slow-braised
lamb shank

A gleaming, massive lamb shank, impressive though it may be, is not the most effective way to serve what amounts to the shin and ankle of a lamb.

It's glorious, for sure, but it has a number of disadvantages, the first of which is that a small to moderate lamb shank weighs in at more than a pound, a nice serving size in the 1970s (or the Middle Ages), but a bit macho for most of us these days. The second is that it's difficult to cook; the size alone makes it awkward, and penetration of flavors is an issue. It's difficult to eat.

Besides, I've slowly begun to realize that my most successful lamb dishes are made from what was left over from a meal of lamb shanks. It makes sense, after all: get that initial, long, slow braising done leisurely and in advance, and then have two wonderful ingredients:, the meat itself, and its barely seasoned juices—dark, natural, laden with fat with which to build other dishes.

It took me something like thirty years of cooking lamb shanks to arrive at that idea, and it took two hours to execute (the technique is detailed in the first recipe). The three recipes that follow then show how to use that initial preparation to make dinner quickly and easily.

Slow-Braised Lamb Shanks

SERVES: 4 to 6

2	lamb shanks, a little over 1 pound each		Salt and freshly ground black pepper
2	tablespoons olive oil	½	cup good white wine or chicken stock

1. In a large skillet, brown the shanks well in the oil; this will take as long as 30 minutes (you can cover the pan to avoid spattering). Sprinkle with salt and pepper as they cook. (If you have an oven that gets really hot—say, 550°F—and you have a pizza stone in there to put the pan on, you can preheat it for 30 minutes or so and do the browning in the oven.)

2. Lower the heat, pour off the excess fat, and add the wine or stock. Simmer over low heat for 1½ to 2 hours, covered, turning and adding water, about ¼ cup at a time, as necessary, until the meat is falling off the bone.

3. Cool. Take meat off the bone and reserve the liquid. When the liquid is cool, skim the fat and reserve the juice. Use the meat and juice in the following recipes.

Indian Lamb Curry with Basmati Rice

SERVES: 6

2	large onions, roughly chopped	½	cup lamb juice, from Slow-Braised Lamb Shanks (see left)
1	tablespoon minced garlic		Lamb from Slow-Braised Lamb Shanks (see left)
1	tablespoon minced fresh chile, or hot red chile flakes to taste	2	teaspoons garam masala or curry powder
1	tablespoon minced fresh ginger		Salt and freshly ground black pepper
2	cups chopped canned tomatoes, with their liquid	½	cup chopped raw cashews
1	cup coconut milk	2	cups cooked basmati rice
			Chopped fresh cilantro, for garnish

1. Put the onions, garlic, chile, ginger, tomatoes, coconut milk, lamb juice, meat, and spices in a large pot that can later be covered over medium-high heat.

2. Bring the mixture just to a boil; cover, reduce the heat, and simmer, stirring occasionally, until the onions are very tender, about 30 minutes.

3. Stir in the cashews, then uncover and simmer steadily until reduced to desired consistency. Serve over rice, garnished with the cilantro.

Tomato Sauce with Lamb and Pasta

SERVES: 6

2	large onions, roughly chopped	1	28-ounce can chopped or crushed tomatoes, with their liquid
¼	cup olive oil		Lamb from Slow-Braised Lamb Shanks (see above)
1	tablespoon fresh thyme leaves		Salt and freshly ground black pepper
2	teaspoons minced garlic	1	pound pasta, like pappardelle
	Pinch of hot red chile flakes (optional)		Shaved pecorino romano cheese (optional)
½	cup lamb juice, from Slow-Braised Lamb Shanks (see above)		

1. Cook the onions in the oil over medium heat, stirring until very soft, about 20 minutes. Add the thyme, garlic, red chile flakes, lamb juice, and tomatoes; cook, stirring, until saucy, about 20 minutes.

2. Stir in the meat and continue to cook, seasoning as necessary, until the flavors meld, at least 15 minutes. Cook the pasta and serve with the sauce; garnish with the cheese.

Chinese Braised Lamb Shanks

SERVES: 6

	Juice from Slow-Braised Lamb Shanks (see above left), plus water or stock to make 1 cup	2	teaspoons five-spice powder
	Lamb from Slow-Braised Lamb Shanks (see above left)	3	bay leaves
2	tablespoons soy sauce		Salt and freshly ground black pepper
2	tablespoons minced garlic	2	cups chopped bok choy, in bite-size pieces
2	tablespoons minced fresh ginger	2	tablespoons neutral oil
1	tablespoon mirin or honey	2	cups cooked rice
			Chopped scallions, for garnish

1. Combine the lamb juice and meat, soy sauce, garlic, ginger, honey, five-spice powder, bay leaves, and salt and pepper in a large pot that can later be covered; bring to a boil and simmer, covered, until the flavors have melded, about 15 minutes.

2. Separately, sauté the bok choy in a skillet in the oil over high heat until tender, 3 to 5 minutes; stir it into the stew at the last minute and serve over the rice, garnished with the scallions.

LEG OF LAMB
+3 WAYS

Leg of lamb
with Moroccan
spices

Whole leg of lamb has advantages that few other cuts of meat can offer: the roasting is pretty much labor free and, thanks to the leg's conical shape, you'll end up with some very rare meat at the thickest part (what you might call the upper thigh), some medium-rare meat below that, and some medium-well meat at the narrowest part and, obviously, in the extreme edges. In other words, there's something for everyone (except, of course, vegetarians).

The three lamb recipes I include here are all roasted legs of lamb in a Mediterranean mode, but they're quite distinct in terms of flavor and technique: one is dry-roasted with a simple if exotic-tasting Moroccan spice spice rub; one is slathered with a yogurt-based marinade laced with fresh mint, orange zest, and cardamom; and the third is smeared with an herb paste not unlike classic pesto. Something for everyone, indeed.

Leg of Lamb with Moroccan Spices

SERVES: 6 to 8

One 5- to 7-pound leg of lamb, preferably at room temperature

2 teaspoons ground coriander

2 teaspoons ground cumin

1 teaspoon ground cinnamon

1 teaspoon ground ginger

1 teaspoon paprika

½ teaspoon ground turmeric

1 teaspoon salt, or to taste

1 tablespoon freshly ground black pepper

1. Heat the oven to 425°F. Remove as much of the surface fat as is practical from the lamb. Mix the spices with the salt and pepper; rub the meat all over with the spice mixture.

2. Put the lamb on a rack in a roasting pan. (You might line the pan first with aluminum foil to make cleanup easier.) Roast for 30 minutes, then check. If the lamb threatens to burn, turn the heat down to 350°F; otherwise leave it at 425°F.

3. After about 1 hour of roasting, check the internal temperature of the lamb with an instant-read thermometer. Continue to check every 10 minutes; when it reaches 130°F for medium-rare (125°F for very rare) in its thickest part (check it in several places), it's done. The total cooking time will be less than 1½ hours. Let it rest for a few minutes before carving and serving.

Yogurt-Marinated Leg of Lamb with Cardamom and Orange

SERVES: 6 to 8

One 5- to 7-pound leg of lamb, preferably at room temperature

½ cup full-fat yogurt

¼ cup chopped fresh mint, plus more for garnish

2 tablespoons grated orange zest

2 teaspoons ground cardamom

1 teaspoon salt, or to taste

2 teaspoons freshly ground black pepper

1. Heat the oven to 425°F. Remove as much of the surface fat as is practical from the lamb. Mix the yogurt, mint, orange zest, cardamom, salt, and pepper; rub the meat all over with the yogurt mixture. If you have time, let the lamb sit for an hour or more (refrigerate if it will be longer than an hour).

2. Put the lamb on a rack in a roasting pan. (You might line the pan first with aluminum foil to make cleanup easier.) Roast for 30 minutes, then check; if the lamb threatens to burn, turn the heat down to 350°F; otherwise leave it at 425°F.

3. After about 1 hour (total) of roasting, check the internal temperature of the lamb with an instant-read thermometer. Continue to check every 10 minutes; when it reaches 130°F for medium-rare (125°F for very rare) in its thickest part (check it in several places), it's done. The total cooking time will be less than 1½ hours. Let it rest for a few minutes before carving. Serve garnished with more chopped mint.

Lamb with Herb Paste and Spinach

SERVES: 6 to 8

One 5- to 7-pound leg of lamb, preferably at room temperature

½ cup chopped fresh parsley

½ cup chopped fresh dill

3 tablespoons extra-virgin olive oil

4 anchovies (optional)

2 garlic cloves, peeled

2 cups coarse bread crumbs, preferably fresh

Salt

Freshly ground black pepper

2 tablespoons pine nuts

2 tablespoons raisins or currants

1 pound fresh spinach, chopped

1. Heat the oven to 425°F. Remove as much of the surface fat as is practical from the lamb. Combine the parsley, dill, oil, anchovies (if using), and garlic in a food processor (if you're not using the anchovies, add some salt). Purée, adding a little water, if necessary. Rub the lamb with this mixture.

2. Put the lamb on a rack in a roasting pan with about ½ cup water. Roast for 30 minutes, then check; if the lamb threatens to burn, turn the heat down to 350°F; otherwise leave it at 425°F. If the bottom dries out (the rendering lamb fat should keep it moist), add a little more water. After about 1 hour of roasting, check the internal temperature with an instant-read thermometer. When it reaches 130°F for medium-rare (125°F for very rare) in its thickest part (check it in several places), it's done. The total cooking time will be less than 1½ hours. Remove from the oven and let it rest.

3. Pour off and reserve all but 2 tablespoons of the fat, and put the pan over a burner (or two, if it fits better). Toast the bread crumbs over low heat, stirring and seasoning with salt and pepper until they're lightly browned. Remove; add another couple tablespoons of the fat to the pan. Add the pine nuts, raisins, and spinach and cook over high heat, stirring frequently, until the spinach is very tender and most of the liquid has evaporated. Carve the lamb and serve it on a bed of spinach, sprinkled with the bread crumbs.

CONDIMENTS AND SEASONINGS

I cook at home much more often than I eat out, and on most nights dinner is some variation on the same theme: a simple combination of vegetables and beans or grains, often with seafood, sometimes with a little meat. What keeps this from feeling absurdly monotonous are condiments and seasonings, the culinary miracles (I'm barely exaggerating) that put an entire world of flavors at your fingertips and transform even the blandest foods into meals you'll want to eat over and over again.

With the help of the recipes in this chapter, and some others like them sprinkled elsewhere in the book, you could eat a chicken breast or a bowl of rice every night for a week and not get bored. You'll find much tastier alternatives to ingredients you might otherwise buy at the store, like barbecue sauce and relish; kitchen staples like vinaigrette, tomato sauce, and spice blends, each with loads of variations so you can customize to your taste; and a few out-of-the-box recipes, like miso butterscotch, that are as surprising as they are delicious. There's also a spicy-salty-sweet chile jam (from a Thai restaurant in San Francisco) that I swear could make shoe leather taste good; keep a batch of that in the fridge and you can turn the everyday into the exotic at a moment's notice.

SPICE BLENDS
+10 WAYS

If you spend enough money, you can buy a good spice blend. But you can also produce an almost perfect version in minutes, and not only will you know exactly what's in it but you will also have a staple that will last for months. And, because each spice blend represents a particular style of cooking, having an arsenal of spice blends at the ready allows you to vary nearly any dish by swapping one blend for another.

For grinding spices, a purist would use a mortar and pestle, but I use an old (and cheap; it cost $9) coffee grinder. If you're grinding spices and coffee in the same machine and don't want your coffee to taste like curry, grind some rice to a powder after removing the spices; it will absorb the residual seasonings and leave your grinder ready for its morning duties.

There is no such thing as the "right" proportions for spice blends; there's only what you like. The recipes here yield about ½ cup; reduce or increase the proportions if you like. Once you're comfortable with the process, you can start personalizing these, as experienced home cooks around the world do.

Spice Blends Universal Instructions

Put whole spices (or seeds) in a small or medium skillet over medium heat; cook, shaking the pan occasionally, until they are fragrant, 2 to 5 minutes. Cool for a few minutes, then grind in a spice or coffee grinder until powdery. Store in sealed jars in a dark, preferably cool place; all of these will keep well for weeks or even months.

Pimentón Mix

Combine ¼ cup **pimentón** (smoked paprika), **2 tablespoons granulated garlic**, **2 teaspoons salt**, and **2 teaspoons pepper**. Before using, add some **freshly grated lemon zest**.

Five-Spice

Grind together the following (no need to toast): **2 tablespoons Sichuan peppercorns**, **12 star anise**, **3 teaspoons whole cloves**, **2 3-inch cinnamon sticks**, and **¼ cup fennel seeds**.

Garam Masala

Toast and grind the seeds from **20 cardamom pods**, **2 3-inch cinnamon sticks**, **2 teaspoons whole cloves**, **2 tablespoons cumin seeds**, and **2 tablespoons fennel seeds**. Add **1 teaspoon freshly grated nutmeg**.

Za'atar

Toast and grind **2 tablespoons each cumin seeds** and **sesame seeds**. Combine with **2 tablespoons dried oregano**, **1 tablespoon dried thyme**, **2 tablespoons sumac**, **2 teaspoons salt**, and **2 teaspoons pepper**.

Adobo

Combine **2 tablespoons granulated garlic**, **1 tablespoon salt**, **4 teaspoons dried oregano**, **1 teaspoon ground black pepper**, **1 teaspoon turmeric**, **2 teaspoons ground cumin**, **2 teaspoons onion powder**, and **2 teaspoons ground ancho chile**.

Quatres Épices

Grind together the following (no need to toast): **2 tablespoons each black and white peppercorns**, **1 tablespoon allspice berries**, and **1 teaspoon cloves**. Combine with **1 teaspoon ground ginger** and **1 teaspoon ground nutmeg**.

Jerk

Grind together the following (no need to toast): **2 tablespoons allspice berries**, **½ teaspoon nutmeg pieces**, **2 teaspoons black peppercorns**, and **4 teaspoons dried thyme**. Combine with **2 teaspoons cayenne**, **2 tablespoons paprika**, **2 tablespoons sugar**, and **¼ cup salt**. Before using, add some **minced garlic** and **fresh ginger**.

Nori Spice

Toast **4 nori sheets** (one at a time) in a hot, dry skillet for a few seconds on each side; coarsely grind them. Toast **2 tablespoons sesame seeds** until golden; combine in a bowl with **2 teaspoons coarse salt**, the ground nori, and **cayenne** to taste. (This keeps for only a week or so.)

Ras el Hanout

Toast and grind **4 teaspoons each coriander seeds** and **cumin seeds**. Combine with **2 teaspoons each ground cinnamon, ginger, paprika, turmeric, and salt**; add **2 tablespoons ground black pepper**.

Chili Powder

Toast and grind **4 teaspoons cumin seeds**, **1 teaspoon black peppercorns**, and **4 teaspoons coriander seeds**; stir in **2 tablespoons dried Mexican oregano**, **¼ cup ground ancho chiles**, and **1 teaspoon cayenne**.

CONDIMENTS
+7 WAYS

Why spend time making your own condiments? A legitimate question, even for cooks who make their own salad dressings, salsas, and hummus, all of which could be considered condiments in their own right. But when it comes to ketchup and its brethren—relish, mayonnaise, barbecue sauce, and the like—most of us cave and revert to using the store-bought versions.

Resist that impulse. The reasons to make your own are the same as they are for countless other foods that you can readily grab at the store: the ability to control and customize flavor, and avoid worthless (or harmful) artificial ingredients. Those are enough reasons for me.

My ketchup, for example, is a superior option to the commercial brands laden with high-fructose corn syrup, well worth making now and then, even if you don't rely exclusively on homemade ketchup.

In addition to the classic burger and dog accompaniments, I've included condiments that will find their way onto things other than meat in a bun, like corn-and-tomato relish—a quintessential summer sauce to spoon over simply grilled fish, chicken, or meat—and teriyaki sauce.

None of these can languish in your fridge for months on end, but that's inevitable when you don't load things up with preservatives. The recipes here all yield quantities that you'll use over the course of a few grilling sessions, or at one big party. The exception is chimichurri, the addictive Argentine herb sauce that you'll want to use as soon as you can. But that's okay: you can't buy anything nearly as good at the store.

Ketchup

In a large pot over medium heat, sauté **1 chopped onion** and **1 chopped red bell pepper** in **2 tablespoons neutral oil** until soft, 8 to 10 minutes. Add **1 tablespoon chopped garlic** and **1 tablespoon tomato paste**, and stir until the paste darkens a bit, 2 or 3 minutes. Add **one 28-ounce can whole tomatoes** (roughly chopped, with their juice), **⅓ cup brown sugar**, **¼ cup apple-cider vinegar**, **½ teaspoon dry mustard**, and **⅛ teaspoon each ground allspice**, **ground cloves**, **cayenne**, and **cinnamon**, as well as **a bay leaf**, salt, and **pepper**. Bring to a boil, then simmer, stirring occasionally, until thickened, about 1 hour. Let cool for a few minutes, then purée in a blender until smooth. (For super-smooth ketchup, pass it through a fine-mesh strainer.) Taste, adjust the seasoning, and store in the fridge for up to 3 weeks. Makes about 3 cups.

Chimichurri

In a food processor, combine **1½ cups fresh parsley leaves**, **½ cup fresh cilantro leaves**, **1 tablespoon fresh oregano leaves**, **3 garlic cloves**, **1 teaspoon hot red chile flakes**, **2 tablespoons red-wine vinegar**, **3 tablespoons neutral oil**, **salt**, and **pepper**. Process until combined, then stir in **3 tablespoons olive oil** by hand. Taste, adjust the seasoning, and use as soon as you can (definitely within a day). Makes about 1 cup.

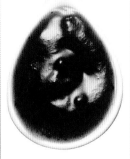

Teriyaki Sauce

Combine ½ cup soy sauce and ½ cup mirin (or ¼ cup honey mixed with ¼ cup water) in a small saucepan over medium-low heat. Cook until the mixture bubbles; turn off the heat, and stir in 1 tablespoon minced fresh ginger, 1 teaspoon minced garlic, and ¼ cup finely chopped scallions. Store in the fridge for up to 2 days. Makes about 1 cup.

Sweet and Hot-Pepper Relish

In a food processor, combine ¼ pound hot red or green chiles (like Fresnos, cherry peppers, Serranos, or a combination), 1 roughly chopped medium onion, and 1 garlic clove. Pulse until finely chopped. Add 1½ pounds roughly chopped bell peppers (some combination of red, orange, and yellow), and pulse until chopped into roughly ⅛-inch pieces. Put ½ cup red-wine vinegar, 1 cup water, ¼ cup sugar, and a big pinch of salt in a saucepan. Bring to a boil, then add the pepper mixture and simmer, stirring occasionally, until the peppers are soft and almost all the liquid has evaporated, 20 to 25 minutes. Taste and adjust the season-ing; cool and store in the fridge for up to 2 weeks. Makes about 2 cups.

Corn and Tomato Relish

Husk 2 ears of corn and strip the kernels off the cobs. Put 1 teaspoon olive oil in a large skillet over high heat. When it's hot, add the corn kernels and cook until lightly browned. Lower the heat to medium, and add 1 large chopped ripe tomato, a pinch of hot red chile flakes, salt, and pepper. Cook for another 30 seconds, then turn off the heat. Store in the fridge for up to a day or two, and serve at room temperature, with some chopped fresh basil stirred in at the last minute. Makes about 2 cups.

Barbecue Sauce

In a small saucepan, combine 2 cups ketchup (the home-made version would be good), 2 teaspoons ground cumin, 2 teaspoons paprika, 1 tablespoon chili powder, ½ cup dry red wine, ¼ cup apple-cider vinegar, 1 tablespoon soy sauce, 1 chopped medium onion, and 1 tablespoon minced garlic. Bring to a boil over medium-high heat, then lower the heat so the mixture bubbles gently but steadily. Cook, stirring occasionally, until the onion softens and the flavors meld, 10 to 20 minutes. Add salt and pepper to taste. For a smooth sauce, purée in the blender. Store in the fridge for up to a week. Makes about 2 cups.

Mayonnaise

Put 1 egg yolk and 2 teaspoons Dijon mustard in a food processor or blender, and turn on the machine. While it's running, start adding 1 cup neutral oil in a very slow, steady stream. Once an emulsion forms, you can start adding the oil a little faster, until it's all incorporated. Season with salt and pepper, and add 1 tablespoon lemon juice or sherry vinegar if you like. Store in the fridge for up to 1 week. Makes about 1 cup.

MISO SAUCES
+4 WAYS

It may surprise you to learn that there is a strong connection between miso and Parmesan cheese. Both of these salty, complex products are made from elemental ingredients: milk, in the case of Parmesan, and soy (sometimes wheat or other grains), in the case of miso, combined with salt and bacteria. The result is intense, uncommonly fine flavors of the umami family. And given my choice in a desert-island situation, I would probably go with miso over Parmesan.

Limiting miso to soup is like limiting Parmesan to pasta. You can dry it and turn it into a condiment (which happens to be reminiscent of Parmesan) to season fish, stir-fries, and dips; you can use it to create a fantastic compound butter (David Chang of Momofuku showed me this eight

years ago); you can stir it into mayonnaise, which is consciousness-expanding. And then there's miso butterscotch, which sounds like dessert—and indeed can be—but is better imagined as a step beyond the caramel sauce you may know from Vietnamese cooking. Talk about umami! All of these can be steered in a variety of directions by combining them with other seasonings.

White misos are milder than red; good miso is generally more expensive than industrially made stuff (the prices and label information usually make that clear). I've noted preferences in these recipes, but it's better to play around than to get hung up on perfect pairings. Refrigerated, miso keeps just about forever, so you can experiment with it at your leisure.

Miso Spice

MAKES: ¼ cup

½   cup miso

1. Heat the oven to 175°F. Line a baking sheet with parchment paper. Smear the miso in an even layer, as thin as possible, over the parchment. It's okay if the miso is ragged around the edges or even a little thick in places.

2. Bake, undisturbed, until large pieces of miso peel easily from the paper, about 3 hours. Turn the pieces and bake on the other side, until the miso crumbles easily, another 3 to 4 hours.

3. Let the miso cool, then crumble it with your fingers or grind until fine in a spice mill or coffee grinder. (It keeps in the fridge in a sealed jar for months.)

POSSIBLE ADDITIONS: Cayenne or other ground chiles; ground kombu or crumbled nori; sesame seeds.

POSSIBLE USES: Season a whole fish, soups, stir-fries, croutons, or bread crumbs; sprinkle the top of bread before baking; warm it in sesame or peanut oil for a bagna-cauda–style dip.

Miso Butter

SERVES: 4 to 8

4   tablespoons (½ stick) butter, at room temperature

2   tablespoons miso
    Freshly ground black pepper (optional)

1. Cream the butter and miso together with a fork, adding black pepper if you like.

2. Use immediately, or roll into a log in plastic wrap and refrigerate or freeze for cutting into slices later.

POSSIBLE ADDITIONS: Chopped scallions or chives; minced garlic, ginger, or chile; lemon, lime, or orange juice or citrus zest.

POSSIBLE USES: Melted onto fish, chicken, or steak (lots of umami); on asparagus, broccoli, or carrots; drizzled on a baked sweet potato (or a regular baked potato).

Miso Butterscotch

MAKES: About 2 cups

¾ cup cream
6 tablespoons (¾ stick) unsalted butter, cut into pieces
¼ cup miso (red miso is a bit salty for truly sweet applications)
¾ cup brown sugar, packed

1. Combine the cream and butter in a small saucepan, and cook over medium-low heat, stirring occasionally, until the butter melts.

2. Stir in the miso and brown sugar and cook, stirring frequently, until the mixture is slightly thickened and shiny, 5 to 10 minutes. Taste and add a little more sugar if you think it's too salty (remember, you'll be using it in savory dishes).

3. Use right away or refrigerate, well covered, for up to 1 week; rewarm before using to loosen it up.

POSSIBLE ADDITIONS: Chopped nuts; some sesame oil instead of butter; honey instead of brown sugar.

POSSIBLE USES: On poached pears or apples; marinade for meat; braising base for sturdy vegetables like cabbage, eggplant, turnips, or new potatoes; sundae sauce, especially over fruit ice creams or sorbets.

Miso Mayonnaise

MAKES: 1 cup

2 tablespoons miso
1 cup mayonnaise

1. Stir the miso into the mayonnaise (homemade, page 231, is best) until smooth.

2. Use immediately, or cover and refrigerate for up to 1 week.

POSSIBLE ADDITIONS: Grated ginger, honey, brown sugar, or agave syrup; chopped pickles (or pickled vegetables); chopped chives or shiso leaves.

POSSIBLE USES: Dip for sweet-potato fries; smeared on croutons to serve with fish soups (like rouille or bouillabaisse); to make a gratinée of simple cooked vegetables with bread crumbs; as an aïoli.

TOMATO SAUCE
+9 WAYS

Thank God for canned tomatoes. They're good, cheap, convenient, and a saving grace during the time of year when fresh supermarket tomatoes are mealy and tasteless. Plus, they are the basis for one of the most useful dishes in all of cooking: tomato sauce. (I'm all for shortcuts in the kitchen, but I don't buy jarred sauce. Even the versions that are good and free from unnecessary ingredients can't hold a candle to what you can make yourself.)

The main recipe here, which makes about 3 cups of sauce, is my go-to: fast, easy, and endlessly variable. I highly recommend making a double or triple batch and stashing some away in the freezer. Just let the finished sauce cool completely, pack it in freezer bags or tightly sealed containers (small quantities are most useful and let you avoid thaw-

ing and refreezing), and store for up to 6 months. You can freeze most of the variations the same way—just avoid adding cheese, seafood, or fresh herbs until you're ready to serve.

As for what to do with the copious amount of sauce that soon will be hanging out in your freezer, pasta and pizza are just the beginning. Stir it into rice, grains, and beans; spoon it over cooked vegetables; braise meat or simmer seafood in it; thin it with water or stock and turn it into soup; or use it as the base for one of the simplest and most satisfying meals of all time: crack a few eggs into the simmering sauce, cover with a tight-fitting lid, and cook until the whites are set and the yolks as firm as you like. Serve with a sprinkling of Parmesan, a drizzle of olive oil, and a hunk of crusty bread.

Tomato Sauce Universal Instructions

Put 3 tablespoons olive oil or butter in a 10- or 12-inch skillet over medium-high heat. When the oil is hot or the butter is melted, add 1 chopped onion and cook, stirring occasionally, until soft, 2 or 3 minutes. Add a 1½- to 2-pound can of tomatoes (drained and chopped) and a sprinkling of salt and pepper. Cook, stirring occasionally, until the tomatoes break down and the mixture comes together and thickens, 10 to 15 minutes. Taste, adjust the seasonings, and serve (or let cool, cover, and refrigerate for up to several days; reheat gently before serving). MAKES: about 3 cups

Fresh Tomato Sauce

A superb option and useful for all the variations here, but only with fresh, in-season tomatoes (I like this very much with butter). Substitute **chopped ripe tomatoes** (preferably peeled and seeded, about 2 cups) for the canned. Cooking time will be about the same. Garnish with **lots of Parmesan or chopped parsley or basil.**

Spicy, Garlicky Tomato Sauce

Omit the onion. Lightly crush and peel **2 to 10 (or even more) garlic cloves;** cook in **the oil** along with **a few dried chiles or a pinch or more of hot red chile flakes** over medium-low heat, turning occasionally, until golden brown, about 5 minutes. Raise the heat, add **the tomatoes,** and cook as directed. Garnish with **parsley or basil.**

Tomato Sauce with Aromatic Vegetables

With **the onion,** add ½ cup **each minced carrot and peeled and minced celery;** cook until tender, about 10 minutes, before adding **the tomatoes.** Especially good puréed. Garnish with **cheese or parsley or basil.**

Tomato Sauce with Fresh Herbs

At the last minute, add ¼ to ½ cup **chopped fresh basil, parsley, dill, mint,** or a combination. Or add smaller amounts of stronger herbs (fresh at the last minute, dried along with the tomatoes): **sage** (10 leaves), **rosemary** (1 teaspoon dried or 1 tablespoon fresh), **thyme** (½ teaspoon dried or 1 teaspoon fresh), **oregano or marjoram** (1 teaspoon dried or 1 tablespoon fresh), or **tarragon** (½ teaspoon fresh or ¼ teaspoon dried). Garnish: **Parmesan or more herbs.**

Cheesy Tomato Sauce

Parmesan is standard but hardly essential, and cheeses can be combined. In a warmed bowl, just before adding pasta and sauce, put in ½ cup or more **ricotta, goat cheese, or mascarpone** for a creamy sauce; **a couple tablespoons of grated Parmesan, grana padano, manchego, or other hard cheese** for a stronger-tasting one; **or up to a cup of grated fresh mozzarella** for a gooey, pizzalike pasta dish. Garnish with **parsley or basil.**

Tomato Sauce with Seafood

When **the sauce** is ready, stir in up to **1 pound peeled shrimp, lump crabmeat, or chopped cleaned squid or scallops.** Reduce the heat so it bubbles gently, cover, and cook until the seafood is warmed or cooked through as necessary, 1 to 5 minutes. Or, add a **6-ounce can of oil-packed tuna** to the pan when you add the tomatoes.

Puttanesca Sauce

(A Roman classic) When you add **the garlic** to **the olive oil,** stir in **a few oil-packed anchovies** (and omit or at least reduce the salt); mash them up a bit as you stir. Then add **2 tablespoons drained capers, some hot red chile flakes** if you like, and ½ cup **pitted black olives** (the wrinkled, oil-cured type, like Moroccan, works best). Then add **the tomatoes.** Garnish with **chopped parsley or basil.**

Meaty Tomato Sauce

Start by cooking up to **1 pound ground beef, pork, lamb, chicken, or turkey** with **the oil and onion** until it browns, 5 to 10 minutes, before adding **the tomatoes.** You can also use sausage; just break it up into chunks as it cooks. Adjust the heat so the meat browns without burning.

VINAIGRETTE
+RECIPE GENERATOR

SEASONING COMBINATIONS

Fish sauce,
Thai chile, mint

Yogurt, curry powder

Mixed herbs

Capers, olives, parsley

Miso, soy sauce, ginger

Egg yolk, anchovies, garlic

Chopped cooked bacon, shallot

Vinaigrette Universal Instructions

Put 3 parts oil and 1 part acid in a jar or mixing bowl. Add a little Dijon mustard (about 1 teaspoon for every ½ cup oil), a sprinkle of salt and pepper, and your seasonings of choice. Screw on the top of the jar and shake until the dressing is thick and creamy, or whisk the dressing in the bowl with a fork, or blend with an immersion blender. Taste and adjust the seasoning. Shake or whisk again and serve right away, or refrigerate for up to 2 weeks; shake or whisk well before every use.

Open my fridge and you will find a jar of vinaigrette. Always. As soon as I run out, I make more. Like salt and pepper, I can't—or really don't want to—cook without it.

That's not just because vinaigrette is useful—I put it on salads, obviously, as well as grains, beans, cooked and raw vegetables, grilled meats and fish—but because it's so ridiculously fast and easy to make from scratch that the preservative-laden stuff in the bottle should be outlawed.

At its simplest, vinaigrette is three parts oil, one part acid, salt, and pepper—whisked, shaken, beaten, or blended together until creamy (or emulsified). But you've got choices to make at every step. The oil: good extra-virgin olive oil is usually the best place to start, but neutral oils, sesame and

nut oils, and more can all play a part. The acid: any kind of vinegar or citrus juice you like. And the seasonings. The ingredient combos listed here are some of my standbys, and just the tip of the iceberg.

Even that golden three-to-one ratio is flexible depending on your taste; and within that ratio you can also play around with combining fats—like olive oil with mayonnaise or tahini—and acids, like balsamic and lemon juice. The texture of the vinaigrette will depend largely on how you mix it; blenders and food processors create the most stable emulsions, giving you thick, creamy dressings; mixing by hand produces something a little looser. You'll be happy to have one or both versions in your fridge at all times.

SALSA
+12 WAYS

Salsa may be the Spanish word for "sauce," but few sauces qualify as salsas. (Conversely, there are, no doubt, many classically trained chefs who balk at the notion that a pile of crudely chopped tomatoes and onions could be called a "sauce.")

Most salsas are served cold or at room temperature, but even that rule isn't defining. Salsas may be raw or cooked, chunky or smooth, spicy or not, and even warm. And while salsas may be hard to define, they're easy to enjoy. There's not a single one of these that wouldn't be just as good spooned over grilled fish, chicken, or meat as it would piled onto a tortilla chip.

Salsas can vary nearly as much in their texture, preparation, and cooking method as they do in their flavors. The most common process is to chop a bunch of raw ingredients and toss them with citrus juice. But you can create a saucier version—and save time—by pulsing everything in the food processor. You can grill and chop, or you can simmer and purée.

Most of the salsas here—starting with Pico de Gallo, the best salsa in the world, as far as I'm concerned—have the flavors we associate with Mexico: tomatoes or tomatillos, onions, chiles, lime, and fruits like mango, peach, or pineapple. I've

taken a few liberties with the other salsa recipes, which veer toward Italy, Spain, and even the Middle East.

Grilled and raw salsas benefit from sitting for 15 minutes once they've been mixed to allow their flavors to develop; even puréed versions are best at room temperature. All will last in the fridge for a few days if need be, but they're best eaten the day they're made. All of these will make about 2 cups of salsa, except the grilled salsas, which yield about 2½ cups.

CHOPPED

Pico de Gallo

Combine **1½ cups chopped ripe tomatoes**, chopped **½ small white onion**, **1 teaspoon minced garlic**, **minced fresh chile** (like jalapeño or Serrano) to taste, **½ cup chopped fresh cilantro**, **2 tablespoons lime juice**, **salt**, and **pepper**. Wait 15 minutes before serving.

Tomatillo, Poblano, and Avocado

Substitute **½ cup each chopped tomatillos, poblanos,** and **avocado** for the tomatoes. Use **red onion** instead of white.

Tabbouleh Style

Omit the garlic and chile. Substitute **2 or 3 chopped scallions** for the onion, **½ cup each chopped fresh parsley and mint** for the cilantro, and **lemon juice** for the lime; stir in **2 tablespoons olive oil**. Serve with **pita chips**.

PULSED

Tomato-Basil

Combine **2 cups roughly chopped ripe tomatoes**, **½ cup fresh basil leaves**, and **1 minced garlic clove** in a food processor with **2 tablespoons olive oil**, **1 tablespoon lemon juice**, **salt**, and **pepper**. Pulse until the mixture comes together but remains a bit chunky.

Radish-Jícama

Substitute **1 cup each chopped radishes** and **roughly chopped jícama** for the tomatoes; **fresh cilantro** for the basil; **1 roughly chopped small white onion** for the garlic; **neutral oil** for the olive oil; and **2 tablespoons lime juice** for the lemon.

Tomato-Strawberry

Substitute **1 cup strawberries** for 1 cup of the tomatoes, **fresh cilantro** for the basil, **1 fresh chile** (like jalapeño or Serrano) for the garlic, **tequila** for the olive oil, and **2 tablespoons lime juice** for the lemon.

COOKED AND PURÉED

Tomato, Chipotle, and Lime

Sauté **1 chopped medium onion** and **1 garlic clove** in **2 tablespoons oil** over medium-high heat until onion softens. Add **1 pound chopped ripe tomatoes**, **1 chipotle**, **2 teaspoons honey**, **salt**, and **pepper**. Simmer until thick, about 20 minutes. Stir in **2 tablespoons chopped fresh cilantro** and **2 tablespoons lime juice**. Cool; purée.

Mango-Habenero

Substitute **mango** for the tomatoes and **1 small habanero** (or a little sliver of one) for the chipotle.

Tomato, Peach, and Sherry Vinegar

Omit the chipotle. Substitute **½ pound peaches** for ½ pound of the tomatoes, **fresh parsley** for the cilantro, and **sherry vinegar** for the lime juice.

GRILLED

Pineapple and Red Onion

Peel and core **a small pineapple**; cut it and **a small red onion** into thick rings. Rub with **oil** and grill over medium-low heat until soft and lightly charred, 8 to 12 minutes. Cool, chop, and combine with **1 teaspoon minced garlic**, **1 minced fresh chile** (like Serrano), **2 cups chopped cilantro**, **2 tablespoons each lime juice and olive oil**, and **salt and pepper**.

Elote Style

Substitute **4 ears husked corn** for the pineapple; strip off the kernels after grilling. Use **chili powder** and **a pinch of cayenne** instead of the fresh chile, and **Mexican crema** (or sour cream) instead of the olive oil. Garnish: **Cotija cheese or queso fresco**.

Pepper and Onion

Substitute **3 bell peppers** (red, yellow, or orange), cut into slabs, for the pineapple, yellow onion for red, **red chile flakes** for fresh chile, **basil** for cilantro, and **balsamic vinegar** for lime juice. Serve with **crostini** or on top of **bruschetta**.

CHILE JAM

This is not your grandmother's jam. Unless, that is, your grandmother is from Thailand.

I learned the recipe from Bangkok-born food-blogger/jam-maker/restaurateur Pim Techamuan-vivit, and have been making it at home ever since. I'm not kidding when I say this is unlike any other jam you've ever had (even other chile versions that tend to use fresh peppers and too much sugar). This one hits on all cylinders: it's spicy (dried chiles), salty (fish sauce), sour (tamarind paste), and sweet (palm sugar), and deep with the flavor of golden-fried garlic and shallots.

At her restaurant in San Francisco, Pim uses it as part of a dressing for a salad of steamed, raw, and fried vegetables (recipe follows), but as some-one who now keeps a jar of this stuff in my fridge or freezer at all times, I can tell you it's good for a whole lot more than that. Toss it with greens or simply cooked (or raw) vegetables, plain noodles, or rice; slather it on grilled whole fish, chicken breasts, pork chops, or tofu; or stir it into soups and stir-fries. Flavor-wise, it's a force of nature capable of transforming mostly anything into pretty much the best Thai food you've ever had.

Nam Prik Pao (Chile Jam)

MAKES: About 1 pint

1   2-inch square of tamarind paste

75 grams (about 2½ ounces) dried Puya chiles

1   cup of rice-bran oil (or any heat-tolerant vegetable oil)

2   heads' worth of garlic cloves, thinly sliced

5   medium shallots, thinly sliced

2   tablespoons Thai shrimp paste, broken into small chunks

½   cup chopped palm sugar

2   to 3 tablespoons fish sauce

1. Combine the tamarind paste with ½ cup very hot water, and break up the paste with a spoon or your fingers; soak for a few minutes, breaking up the paste a few more times if needed. Push the mixture through a mesh strainer with the back of a spoon; set aside the pulp that passes through the strainer, and discard what remains inside the strainer. Stem and seed the chiles.

2. Heat the oil in a wok or large skillet over medium-high heat until hot but not quite smoking. Add the chiles, and cook, stirring, for 15 to 20 seconds, making sure they don't burn. Remove with a slotted spoon, and transfer to a plate.

3. Add the garlic to the oil, and fry, stirring frequently, until just golden brown. (It will continue to brown after it's out of the oil, so don't go too dark now.) Transfer to the plate with the chiles. Fry the shallots until golden brown, and transfer to the plate. Turn off the heat, leaving the oil in the pan. Transfer the chiles, garlic, and shallots to a food processor; pulse, scraping down the sides as necessary, until the mixture turns into a paste (no need to make it totally smooth).

4. Turn the heat under the pan to medium. Add the shrimp paste, and cook, stirring and breaking it up, for about a minute or two. Add the palm sugar, and cook, stirring, until it dissolves. Add the chile, garlic, and shallot mixture, the tamarind pulp, and 2 tablespoons of the fish sauce. Stir to combine, turn the heat to low and cook, stirring occasionally so the bottom of the pan doesn't burn, until it thickens slightly, 2 or 3 minutes. Taste the mixture; if it still needs salt, add more fish sauce, a little at a time.

5. You can store the jam (and the oil) in a jar in the fridge or freezer; use it in stir-fries or soups, spoon it on top of rice or noodles, spread it on toast, or use it as the base for the dressing for Yum Yai Salad.

Yum Yai Salad

SERVES: 4

¼   cup Nam Prik Pao (Chile Jam; see recipe at left)

2   tablespoons lime juice

2   tablespoons fish sauce

2   teaspoons chopped palm sugar

    A pinch of chopped bird's-eye chile (if you like it spicy)

1   medium English cucumber, peeled

1   large carrot, peeled

2   cups vegetable oil, for frying

¾   cup ice-cold water

¾   cup all-purpose flour

1   egg yolk

1½ loosely packed cups whole small green leaves, like baby kale, shiso leaves, pea shoots, or arugula

6   ounces blanched green beans or wax beans

3   radishes, very thinly sliced

2   cups any mixed greens or torn lettuce leaves

1. Whisk together the Nam Prik Pao, lime juice, fish sauce, sugar, and chopped chile if you're using it; set aside. Use a vegetable peeler to slice the cucumber and carrot into long ribbons; set them aside.

2. Put the vegetable oil in a skillet over medium-high heat. While it heats, lightly whisk together the ice water, flour, and egg yolk in a medium bowl; the batter should be lumpy and quite thin. When the oil is ready for frying, start dipping the whole leaves (one at a time) into the batter to coat, and carefully add them to the oil, making sure not to crowd the pan; fingers or chopsticks are the best tools for the job. Fry the leaves in batches, turning once, until golden brown and crisp, just a few minutes. With a slotted spoon, transfer the leaves to paper towels to drain; repeat the process until you have fried all of the leaves.

3. To assemble the salad, start layering all of the ingredients in a large shallow bowl or onto a platter. The beans are best on the bottom because they're the heaviest, and the tempura leaves should go mostly on top so they remain crisp; otherwise, the order is up to you. Drizzle each layer with some of the dressing as you go; serve immediately.

PICKLES
+12 WAYS

I remember when pickles were either something you bought from a barrel on the street or canned in your kitchen. But somehow they've become the emblem of all things hipster-artisanal-twee, as much a joke (we can pickle that!) as they are a food.

The reason so many of us have outsourced our pickle making to the waxed-mustache set is that canning is sufficiently daunting; the thought of boiling jars, with its mysterious science and prospect of imminent disaster, is enough to send most home cooks running to the store. Fortunately, canning is not a prerequisite for pickling. In fact,

as long as you can commit to eating them within a week or two, there are countless pickles that you can make quickly and store in your fridge.

All the recipes here fall into that category. Some (relishes and marinated vegetables) use heat to soften the pickles and infuse the flavor of the brine, while others (miso-smothered and saltwater-soaked) rely on time to do the work. The various brines do double duty, preserving whatever you're pickling while at the same time introducing new flavors and coaxing out inherent ones. Think of the recipes as templates: swap in different vegetables as you like.

WITH MISO

Daikon with White Miso

Peel **1 pound daikon** and slice ¼ inch thick. Spread **2 cups white miso** in a bowl, top with the daikon, and press down; add enough miso to cover completely. Cover, and rest at room temperature for 24 hours, or longer for more intense flavor. Rinse, and refrigerate before serving (save the miso for a second batch).

Eggplant with Miso and Mirin

Cut **1 pound eggplant** into half-moons about ¾ inch thick. Stir **1 tablespoon mirin** into **3 cups of miso,** submerging the pieces, as above. Let stand for 12 hours, then rinse; serve immediately, or refrigerate.

Corn Coins with Yellow Miso

Husk **3 ears of corn** and cut them crosswise into ½-inch-thick slices. Use **yellow miso** instead of white, submerging the pieces, as with the daikon.

MARINATED

Giardiniera

In a pot, boil ½ **cup red-wine vinegar, 1 tablespoon salt, 1 teaspoon dried oregano, 1 bay leaf, 1 peeled and smashed garlic clove, ⅓ cup olive oil,** and 2 cups water. Add **1½ cups broccoli florets**; cook for 1 minute. Add **1 cup each chopped carrot, celery, and bell pepper,** as well as ¼ **cup chopped green olives;** turn off the heat. Cover, let cool, refrigerate.

Bagna Cauda

Use **balsamic vinegar.** Use **6 mashed anchovy fillets** for the salt and ½ **teaspoon chile flakes** for the oregano and bay leaf; use **4 garlic cloves.** Cook **2 pounds mixed vegetables—thin asparagus, green beans, fennel, radishes, parsnips, celery**—in the brine for 1 minute.

Curried Cauliflower

Use **sherry vinegar,** and decrease the **salt to ¼ teaspoon.** Use **2 tablespoons curry powder** in place of the oregano and bay leaf. Cut **1 cauliflower head** into florets; chop **1 small red onion,** then cook in **the brine** until just tender, 3 to 5 minutes. Remove from the heat, cover, and chill.

RELISHES

Chowchow

Finely chop **1½ pounds zucchini, 1 small onion, 1 red bell pepper,** and **1 small hot chile.** Combine **1 cup white balsamic vinegar, 2 tablespoons brown sugar,** and ½ **teaspoon salt,** and bring to a boil. Add the vegetables and cook, stirring occasionally, until slightly reduced, 5 to 10 minutes. Cool in the cooking liquid before serving or refrigerating.

Watermelon Rinds

Peel the green skin off **a small watermelon** and chop the rind. Substitute **apple-cider vinegar** for the balsamic, and increase the brown sugar to ¼ cup; boil with ½ **cup lime juice** and **2 tablespoons minced fresh ginger.** Cook until the rind is tender, 10 to 20 minutes.

Peach Chutney

Peel, pit, and chop **2 pounds peaches.** Use ½ **cup apple-cider vinegar;** substitute ¼ **cup honey** for the brown sugar. Use ¼ **teaspoon salt;** add **4 smashed cardamom pods** and ½ **vanilla bean.** Bring to a boil, add the peaches, and cook, stirring occasionally, until they soften.

SALTWATER

Kosher Cukes

Halve or quarter **2 pounds Kirby cucumbers.** Dissolve ⅓ **cup kosher salt** in 1 cup boiling water; add ice cubes to cool, then the cukes, **5 crushed garlic cloves,** and **1 bunch dill.** Cover with cold water; use a weighted plate to keep cukes submerged. Let sit for 12 to 48 hours—they get saltier over time. When they taste right, refrigerate in the brine.

Carrots with Cumin and Coriander

Peel **2 pounds carrots;** cut them into ½-inch-thick sticks. Omit the garlic. Instead of the dill, toast **2 tablespoons each coriander and cumin seeds,** and add them to the brine. Refrigerate (in the brine) when they taste right.

Sort of Sauerkraut

Trim, core, and thickly shred **2 pounds green cabbage.** Keep the garlic, but swap **2 tablespoons caraway seeds** for the dill. Refrigerate (in the brine) when they taste right.

FRUIT

When people tell me what their favorite food is, more often than you might expect it's a fruit. It makes sense when you think about it: most fruits taste impossibly good for things that are simply plucked off a tree or bush. A perfectly ripe peach, a slice of watermelon that dribbles juice all the way down your arm, an apple that's as sweet as it is tart—all offer immediate gratification and even conjure up some sort of childhood nostalgia.

Whatever it is that you love about fruit, this chapter's got something for you. While there are plenty of recipes that follow a classic approach, like stewed stone fruit and watermelon granita, what's even more exciting (in my opinion) are the ones that take unexpected turns, often into savory territory. Have you ever stir-fried grapefruit with meat, for instance, or pickled cherries? What about lacing a watermelon soup with fish sauce, or putting lemongrass in jam? If you aren't already a fan, the dishes in this chapter (spanning cocktails, appetizers, main courses, and desserts) show just how incredible fruit can be.

STONE FRUIT
+12 WAYS

Stone fruits are summer in your hand. To me, no food is better "unmessed with" than a good, ripe peach. Still, stone fruits can be fun to play around with, and a recipe for one kind is a recipe for almost all. Peaches, nectarines, apricots, plums, mangos (technically not a stone fruit), and cherries all respond similarly to sautéing, poaching, macerating, grilling, roasting, and drying. And once cooked, stone fruits go with just about everything.

These twelve recipes work with most varieties. (Alas, it's not easy to grill cherries.) The length of the cooking time will vary, depending mostly on the quality and ripeness of the fruit. Peel it if you like, or leave the skin on (except for mangos) to retain texture and extra flavor. (Peeled fruit will cook through faster.) To peel, plunge the fruit into boiling water for 10 to 20 seconds to loosen the skin, then slip it off. When you pit the fruit—and you will need to remove the stones for each of these recipes—do so over a bowl to catch the juice, and use the juice instead of water where needed.

Most of these preparations require little more than the simple combining of ingredients and a short cooking time; some take no cooking at all. But one method—drying—is worth singling out. It's a slow process that allows you to control the texture, making the final product as moist or as dry as you like. The drying is best done on a gas grill or in the oven, though if you have the patience to use a wood or charcoal fire, you'll be rewarded with smoky dried fruit. Place the fruit directly on the grill, or line a baking sheet with parchment paper and place the fruit on top.

Don't forget salt and pepper on the savory dishes. Refrigerated, any of these can be stored for up to a week. Dried fruit will keep indefinitely.

Stewed

Combine **1½ pounds chopped fruit, ¼ cup sugar,** and ½ cup water in a skillet and bring to a boil; reduce the heat and simmer until just tender, about 15 minutes, stirring occasionally. Taste; add **more sugar, if needed,** and **lemon juice to taste.** Cool and serve.

Butter-Poached

Combine **2½ cups sugar,** 5 cups water, **½ cup (1 stick) butter,** and the **seeds of 1 vanilla bean** in a saucepan; bring to a boil. Add **1½ pounds halved fruit,** reduce the heat, and cook until tender, 10 to 15 minutes. Remove the fruit from the liquid. Cool slightly and serve.

Mostarda

Use ¾ pound dried fruit. Add **1 minced shallot, 1 tablespoon minced crystallized ginger, ¾ cup white wine, 4½ table-spoons white-wine vinegar,** and **2 to 3 teaspoons each Dijon mustard and butter.** Simmer until jamlike, 15 minutes or more. Skip the lemon juice. Cool and serve.

Chutney

Use **brown sugar** instead of white. When fruit is tender, use **orange juice** for lemon juice, and add **1 tablespoon minced ginger, 1 teaspoon curry powder,** and **a pinch of ground cloves.** Simmer, reducing the mixture to desired thickness. Partly cool, then stir in **¼ cup each raisins and toasted nuts** (like macadamia), and serve.

Jam

Reduce the **sugar to 1½ cups.** Instead of water, use the **juice of ½ orange;** skip the butter and vanilla; use **chopped fruit** and add immediately. When the sugar dissolves, reduce the heat and cook until the liquid is thick and clear; stir frequently until it darkens, 15 to 20 minutes. Cool completely and serve.

Turkish Fruit Butter

Reduce the **sugar to ¾ cup** and the water to 1 cup; skip the butter and vanilla. When the fruit is tender, cool slightly and purée. Return to the pot and cook 2 hours, stirring, until thick. Add **1 tablespoon honey, 1 tea-spoon lemon juice, ¼ teaspoon ground nutmeg,** and **a pinch of ground cloves.** When thick, cool and serve.

Macerated

Mix **2 pounds dried fruit** with **½ pound blanched almonds, 2 table-spoons pine nuts, 2 cups orange juice, 2 cups water, 1 teaspoon ground cinnamon, 1 tablespoon rosewater,** and (optional) **1 tablespoon anise liquor or 2 or 3 star anise.** Cover and stir every few hours for 12 to 24 hours. Serve when fruit is tender.

French Style

Brush **fruit halves** with **melted unsalted butter** and sprinkle with **sugar.** Place on a grill over low heat or in the broiler, with the rack at least 4 inches from the heat source, and grill until soft and glazed, about 10 minutes. Serve.

Minty Fruit Salad

Use **chopped fresh fruit.** Skip the nuts. Use only **¼ cup orange juice,** and skip the water, cinnamon, rosewater, and anise. Add **¼ cup chopped fresh mint leaves** and **1 tablespoon honey.** Stir and serve.

Mexican Style

Use **chopped fresh fruit.** Skip the nuts. Substitute the **juice of 1 lime** for the orange juice and **chili powder** for the cinnamon. Skip the rosewater and anise; add **a pinch of cayenne** (optional), **¼ cup chopped fresh cilantro, 1 tablespoon sugar,** and **½ teaspoon salt.** Toss and serve.

With Asian Spices

Brush **fruit halves** with **unsalted butter** and sprinkle with **sugar** and a mixture of **equal parts ground star anise, cinnamon, and allspice.** Cook until caramelized and fragrant, about 20 minutes. Serve.

Dried

Skip the butter and sugar. Grill or bake (at 200°F) **halved or sliced fruit** until it feels dry and dehydrated but is still soft, about 3 hours, turning every 30 minutes or so. Cool and serve.

CHERRIES
+4 WAYS

When cherries are good—juicy, fleshy, even crisp—even the supermarket variety can be irresistible. I buy them by the sack, mostly for snacks.

To give cherries their due, I've dished up four cherry-based preparations, and one is a boozy cocktail, pretty much rendering the next three enjoyable no matter what.

The cocktail is a riff on a classic old-fashioned that calls for sour cherries—those small, bright red spheres most often found at farmers' markets and the best cherries for pies. They're too tart to eat raw, but they mellow considerably when cooked—or muddled with sugar and bathed in whiskey. If you can't find sour cherries for the drink, use sweet (Bing) cherries and ease off on the sugar.

The rest of the recipes rely on Bing cherries, the sweet, deep red, heart-shaped variety that you see in every supermarket. They are stellar in a cobbler-esque dessert, a worthy companion for grilled pork chops—dare I say better than apples?—and a surprisingly good candidate for pickling.

A cherry-pitter is handy for large quantities, and it works nicely on olives, too. You can also go MacGyver on them with a chopstick, straw, paper clip, or pastry-tube tip. And if you don't care about keeping the cherries intact, which usually makes no difference, just lightly crush them with the flat side of a chef's knife and pull out the pits. Your fingers will drip with juice, but that's hardly a problem.

Frisée with Pickled Cherries, Pistachios, and Brie

SERVES: 4

¾	pound sweet cherries, stemmed and pitted	¼	cup olive oil
1	fresh tarragon sprig		Salt and freshly ground black pepper
3	tablespoons balsamic vinegar	6	cups torn frisée
2	tablespoons red-wine vinegar	4	ounces Brie or other creamy French cheese, cut into slices or bite-size pieces
¼	cup sugar	½	cup shelled pistachios
12	black peppercorns		

1. Put the cherries and tarragon in a glass jar. Put the vinegars, sugar, peppercorns, and ½ cup water in a small saucepan over high heat. Bring the mixture just to a boil so that the sugar dissolves, then turn off the heat and let it cool slightly. Pour it over the cherries (it's fine if they're not completely submerged), and cool completely before capping and refrigerating. The cherries will be ready in a week and will last for a month.

2. Drain the cherries (reserving the liquid) and slice them in half. Whisk together the olive oil, 2 tablespoons of the cherry liquid, and salt and pepper in a small bowl; drizzle it over the frisée. Scatter the cherries, the Brie, and pistachios over the frisée, and serve.

Grilled Pork Chops with Cherry Sauce

SERVES: 4

4	pork loin chops, bone-in and at least 1 inch thick	3	tablespoons butter
1	tablespoon minced fresh rosemary	1	tablespoon minced shallot
	Salt and freshly ground black pepper	1	cup sweet cherries, stemmed, pitted, and halved
1	teaspoon minced garlic	½	cup fruity red wine

1. Pat the chops dry; rub them with a mixture of rosemary, 1 teaspoon salt, ½ teaspoon pepper, and garlic. Marinate for up to 2 hours at room temperature, or overnight in the fridge. Bring back to room temperature.

2. Heat one side of a charcoal or gas grill, and put the rack 4 inches from the heat. Sear the chops over the hottest part, 3 or 4 minutes per side. Move them to the cool part of the grill, cover, and cook until the meat is rosy in the center, or a thermometer registers 135°F, anywhere from 3 to 10 minutes, depending on the heat and the chops' thickness. Transfer to a platter and cover loosely with foil.

3. Put 1 tablespoon of the butter in a skillet over medium-high heat. When the foam subsides, add the shallot and cook until soft, 2 or 3 minutes. Add the cherries, wine, and whatever juices have accumulated around the pork chops; cook until the liquid reduces to a thin syrup, 5 or 6 minutes. Stir in the remaining butter, a little at a time, until incorporated. Season the sauce, pour over the chops, and serve.

Cherry-Cornmeal Slump (or Grunt)

SERVES: 8

2	pounds sweet cherries, stemmed and pitted		Salt
⅓	cup plus 2 tablespoons sugar	½	cup (1 stick) cold unsalted butter, cut into bits
1	tablespoon lemon juice	1	large egg
½	cup all-purpose flour	½	teaspoon vanilla extract
¼	cup cornmeal		Ice cream, whipped cream, or Greek yogurt, for serving
½	teaspoon baking powder		

1. Put the cherries, ⅓ cup sugar, lemon juice, and 2 tablespoons water in a large skillet over medium heat; you can also put the skillet on the grill or over a campfire. Cook, stirring occasionally, until the juices have released, about 10 minutes.

2. Meanwhile, combine the flour, cornmeal, baking powder, a pinch of salt, and the remaining 2 tablespoons sugar in a bowl to combine, or pulse once or twice in a food processor. Add the butter, and process for 10 seconds or until the mixture is well blended. Add the egg and vanilla; mix until combined.

3. When the cherry mixture is thickened slightly, dollop the batter over the top and cover the skillet tightly with a lid or aluminum foil. Cook, undisturbed, until the dumplings are cooked through and their tops are dry (not sticky), 20 to 25 minutes. Serve with ice cream, whipped cream, or yogurt.

Sour-Cherry Old Fashioned

MAKES: 1 cocktail

2	sour cherries, stemmed and pitted	1	sugar cube or ½ teaspoon sugar
	One 2-inch strip orange peel	2	or 3 dashes Angostura bitters
		¼	cup rye whiskey or bourbon

Put the cherries, orange peel, sugar, and bitters in an old-fashioned glass; crush the sugar and cherries with a muddler, spoon, or anything else that will get the job done. Fill the glass with ice, add the whiskey, and stir until the drink is cold, about a dozen times.

PEARS
+10 WAYS

Pear salad
with
spinach
and apples

Pears, for some reason, are always second to apples. Nobody ever goes pear picking. Yet there's nothing you can do with an apple (see page 258) that you can't do with a pear. In fact, pears are more versatile because they're not only good when they're underripe and crisp; they're also fantastic when they're perfectly ripe and creamy. I know that with endless varieties of both apples and pears piled high at the market, you're most likely going to buy more apples. That's just the way it is. But I'm here to persuade you to reconsider the pear.

To make my case, I offer ten salads that can be used with any variety of pear. You'll most commonly find green (and, increasingly, red) Anjou, yellowy green Bartlett, and brownish Boscs; of the common ones, these last are best. But all are sweet and will soften with time, and without special treatment. Just be patient. When the "shoulders" soften, they're ripe.

One thing I like about these salads is that many can be made with pears at any stage of ripeness. A couple of them aren't what you'd traditionally call

Pear salad
with iceberg
and onion

salads—the salsa and the relish—and these are best with crisp, not-quite-ripe pears. The other recipes serve four, but these will go much further. Use the relish as you would chutney; it's great with roasted meat. (In each case, core the pear first.)

Make a simple vinaigrette like the one on page 238 for any of these salads or just drizzle the salads with oil and vinegar or citrus juice (and salt and pepper, of course). In any case, these are salads that should help change your thinking about pears, making them at least the equal of apples.

Spinach and Apples

Thinly slice **2 unripe pears** and **2 crisp apples**; put on a bed of **4 cups fresh spinach**. Sprinkle with **¼ cup raisins** and drizzle with **the dressing**. Dressing variation: add **2 tablespoons chopped fresh rosemary** and **1 tablespoon honey**.

Iceberg and Onion

Caramelize **2 thinly sliced onions** in **3 tablespoons butter or oil**. Cut **1 head iceberg** lettuce into 4 sections. Cut **2 pears** into eighths and divide among the lettuce; add **1 ounce crumbled feta to each**; add the onions and **the dressing**, garnishing with **crumbled bacon**, if desired. Dressing variation: use **balsamic vinegar**.

Boston and Bresaola

Roughly chop **1 head Boston lettuce** and put it on a plate. Top with **2 thinly sliced pears**; 1 peeled, pitted, and quartered avocado; and **½ pound thinly sliced bresaola or prosciutto**. Drizzle with **the dressing**. Dressing variation: use **sherry vinegar**.

Romaine and Stilton

Tear **1 head romaine lettuce** into pieces and put in a bowl; add **2 roughly chopped pears**. Crumble **¼ pound Stilton** on top, add **the dressing**, and toss. Optional: add **¾ cup chopped toasted walnuts**. Dressing variation: skip the vinegar and mustard; add **¼ cup chopped fresh tarragon** and **3 tablespoons lemon juice**.

Fennel

Trim and quarter **2 fennel bulbs**; cut **2 unripe pears** in half. Use a mandoline to thinly slice everything; put in a large bowl. Toss with **the dressing** and garnish with **shaved Parmesan**. Dressing variation: skip the vinegar and mustard; reduce the **oil to ½ cup**; add **3 tablespoons lemon juice** and **2 tablespoons chopped fresh parsley**.

Endive and Goat Cheese

Sauté **2 or 3 chopped shallots** in **2 tablespoons butter** until soft; drain. Tear **4 Belgian endive** into pieces and arrange on a large plate; top with **3 thinly sliced pears**, the drained shallots, and **4 ounces goat cheese**. Dressing variation: use **red-wine vinegar**.

Salsa

Chop **4 unripe pears** and **1 red onion**; seed and mince **1 serrano chile**. Combine in bowl with **¼ cup each chopped fresh cilantro and mint**. Add **the dressing** and stir. Dressing variation: skip the vinegar and mustard; reduce the **oil to ½ cup**, and add **¼ cup lime juice** and **a pinch of sugar**.

Jícama

Halve **3 unripe pears**. Peel and quarter **1 jícama**; use a mandoline to thinly slice the pears and jícama and put in a bowl. Toss with **2 tablespoons chopped mixed fresh herbs** and **the dressing**. Dressing variation: skip the vinegar and mustard; reduce the oil to ½ cup, and add **3 tablespoons lime juice** and **1 tablespoon minced chile**.

Relish

Dice **4 unripe pears**; chop **2 whole scallions** and **¼ cup cashews**; put in a bowl. Add **3 tablespoons minced crystallized ginger** and **¼ cup dried cranberries**. Dress and stir; let marinate 20 minutes. Dressing variation: skip the mustard; use **sherry vinegar** and add **1 tablespoon orange juice** and **a pinch of ground cinnamon, allspice, and cloves**.

Arugula and Orange

Peel **1 small, juicy orange** and divide into sections. Roughly chop **2 pears** into chunks and arrange on a bed of **4 cups arugula**. Add **¼ cup pitted green olives** and the orange sections. Top with **2 tablespoons chopped fresh mint** and **the dressing**. Dressing variation: skip the mustard; use **red-wine vinegar** and add **1 tablespoon chopped fresh cilantro, ¼ teaspoon ground cumin**, and **a pinch of ground coriander**.

APPLES
+12 WAYS

When you transform an apple by cooking, you may make it soft, fluffy, chewy, savory, sweet, or creamy—the potential is enormous. Yes, an apple loses some juiciness and freshness when you cook it, but as an ingredient it's just as versatile as a potato. (You probably know that in French the potato is called *pomme de terre*, or "apple of the earth.")

This matrix explores cooked apples in various forms, at least some of which (I hope) you'll find unexpected. All of the sweet versions are wonderful for either dessert or breakfast, while the savory ones make terrific side dishes for just about anything roasted or pan-cooked. All serve four.

Peeling is always optional—I personally like the texture of apple skins—but coring is not. If you're slicing apples or cutting them into chunks, you can core them the easy way: cut them into quarters, then take out the seeds with a paring knife. If you're halving them, take out the core with a melon baller and trim the rest with a paring knife. And if you want to cut them into rings, dig into the flower (the non-stem) end with a paring knife until you get all the inedible parts out, or use an apple corer.

BAKED

Praline

Halve and core **4 apples.** Put cut side down in a greased baking pan. Drizzle with **1 tablespoon melted butter** and **1 cup apple juice.** Bake at 375°F for 20 minutes. Cook **½ cup brown sugar, ½ cup chopped pecans,** and **3 tablespoons butter** until butter melts; add **½ teaspoon vanilla.** Turn the apples, baste, then top with the praline; bake for 20 minutes.

Blue Cheese and Fig

Use **port, brandy, or Riesling** instead of apple juice. Skip the praline mixture; combine **4 ounces crumbled blue cheese** and **¼ cup chopped dried figs** (or raisins). After turning and basting, fill each cavity with the cheese mixture instead of topping with the praline.

Balsamic-Rosemary

Substitute **olive oil** for the butter and **¼ cup balsamic vinegar** for ¼ cup of the apple juice. Skip the praline mixture; instead, sprinkle the apples with **1 tablespoon chopped fresh rosemary** after turning and basting.

SAUTÉED

Shallot-Thyme

Cook **4 thinly sliced shallots** in ¼ cup olive oil over medium heat, stirring, until soft and brown, 15 to 20 minutes. Add **1½ pounds thinly sliced apples** and **1 teaspoon fresh thyme leaves;** cover, turn the heat to low, and cook for 10 minutes. Uncover, turn the heat to high, and cook, stirring, for another 10 minutes.

Brussels Sprouts and Sage

Substitute **4 tablespoons butter** for the oil and skip the shallots and thyme. When butter melts, add **the apples, ½ pound quartered Brussels sprouts,** and **1 tablespoon chopped sage;** cover and continue as above. Garnish: **Parmesan.**

Cranberry-Orange

Substitute **4 tablespoons butter** for the oil; skip shallots and thyme. When the butter melts, add the **apples** and **1 cup fresh cranberries;** cover and continue as above. After uncovering, stir in **½ cup sugar** and **1 tablespoon orange zest;** keep the heat at medium-high.

FRIED

Tempura with Honey

Heat 2 inches of **neutral oil** in a deep pan to 350°F. Whisk together 2 cups ice water, **1½ cups flour,** and **3 egg yolks.** Put **another 1 cup flour** in a bowl. One piece at a time, dredge **1½ pounds apples,** cut into rings, in the flour, then dip in the batter. Fry each piece until golden, 5 minutes or less. Drain on paper towels. Garnish: **drizzle of honey.**

Cornmeal-Crusted

Skip the batter, flour, and honey. Put **2 cups buttermilk** in a large bowl; combine **1 cup flour, 1 cup cornmeal,** and **¼ teaspoon cayenne** in a separate bowl. Dip the apple rings in buttermilk, then dredge in the cornmeal mixture. Fry as above.

Fritters

Skip the tempura batter, flour, and honey; **grate the apples.** Beat together **1 large egg** and **½ cup grated fontina cheese;** stir in the apples and **½ cup flour.** Shape into walnut-size balls and fry as above. Garnish: **lemon wedges.**

ROASTED

Moroccan Spiced

Heat the oven to 425°F. Toss **2 pounds apples,** cut into chunks, with **2 tablespoons olive oil;** spread on a rimmed baking sheet. Roast for 10 minutes; add **1 tablespoon minced garlic, 1 tablespoon minced fresh ginger, 1 teaspoon ground cumin, ½ teaspoon ground coriander,** and **½ teaspoon ground cinnamon;** toss well to coat. Roast until tender, stirring occasionally, another 10 to 15 minutes.

Cheddar Gratin

Use **melted butter** for the oil; skip the ginger and spices. Combine **½ cup grated Cheddar, ½ cup bread crumbs,** and **2 additional tablespoons melted butter.** When the apples are tender, top with the Cheddar mixture; broil until lightly browned.

Lemon and Poppy Seed

Substitute **melted butter** for the olive oil. Substitute **¼ cup sugar, 1 tablespoon poppy seeds,** and **1 tablespoon lemon zest** for the garlic, ginger, and spices.

WATERMELON
+12 WAYS

Farro
salad

When the weather is clammy and the watermelons are juicy and sweet (and cheap), it makes sense to have them on hand pretty much all the time. And that means there may be instances when your innate creativity (or boredom) might drive you a little further. Luckily, there are many worthy things to do with watermelon that are somewhere between simple slicing and full-blown cooking.

Even in season, bad watermelons do exist, so how can you improve your chances for a ripe, delicious one? The cheater's answer is to buy them at a farmstand or a farmers' market, where not only are they likely to be tastier but there will also be a seasoned pro to help. If you're in the grocery store, put your ear close and slap the side of the watermelon. If it makes a hollow sound, you're in business.

Ice pops

Spicy Thai
soup with
crab

Because all the concoctions here (aside from the salads) involve buzzing the watermelon in a food processor or a blender, you'll probably want to get rid of the seeds first. In the luxurious era of seedless watermelons, of course, this is often taken care of; however, I am not convinced that seedless watermelons are as tasty as some of the older varieties. If you do get a melon with seeds,

cut it lengthwise into quarters, slice off the "heart" of each quarter to expose the row of seeds and remove them with the tines of a fork. Cut the watermelon into chunks, and use the flesh for any of the recipes here, all of which should give you four servings.

Save yourself a few wedges to munch on while you work.

Gin and Basil

Put 1 cup water, **1 cup sugar,** and **a small bunch of fresh basil** in a small saucepan. Boil until the sugar dissolves, then discard the basil and chill the mixture. Peel **1 small watermelon (3 pounds),** and cut the flesh into large chunks. Purée in a blender until smooth. Pour the purée through a fine-mesh strainer and discard the solids. Combine the juice with the chilled basil syrup and about **½ cup gin.** Serve over ice.

Greek Style

In a large bowl, combine **3 cups cubed watermelon; 2 chopped large ripe tomatoes; 1 peeled, seeded, and chopped cucumber; 1 sliced small red onion; ⅓ cup pitted kalamata olives; ⅓ cup crumbled feta;** and some **chopped fresh parsley and mint.** Drizzle with **olive oil** and **red-wine vinegar,** toss, and serve.

Daiquiri

Skip the basil syrup. Blend **the watermelon** with **⅓ cup lime juice** (or more to taste), **1 tablespoon honey, ½ cup rum,** and some ice until cold and smooth. No need to strain. Serve in chilled glasses.

Lemonade

Omit the basil from the syrup (use just water and **sugar**), and use only **half as much watermelon.** Pour the strained watermelon into an ice-cube tray (plastic, not silicon), and freeze until solid. Make **lemonade** (to your specifications), using the simple syrup to sweeten it, adding **vodka** to make it boozy, if you like. Serve in glasses over the watermelon ice cubes.

Farro

Substitute **4 cups cooked and cooled farro** (or wheat berries) for the tomatoes and cucumber. Skip the olives; use **ricotta salata** instead of the feta and **lemon juice** instead of the red-wine vinegar.

Pancetta Vinaigrette

Use **3 large tomatoes.** Skip the cucumber, onion, olives, parsley, and mint. Substitute **little cubes of fresh mozzarella** for the feta. For the vinaigrette, render **4 ounces chopped pancetta in olive oil** until crisp. Add **chopped shallot, sherry vinegar,** and **lots of black pepper.** Toss with **the watermelon** and tomatoes. Garnish: **chopped fresh basil.**

Gazpacho

Peel **1 small watermelon (about 3 pounds)**, and cut the flesh into large chunks. Put them in a food processor along with **2 chopped ripe tomatoes, 1 minced garlic clove,** and **2 tablespoons lemon juice.** Pulse the mixture, adding a few ice cubes, one at a time if necessary, to the machine. Chill in the fridge. Garnish: **chopped fresh basil** and **a drizzle of olive oil.**

Sorbet

Cut **a small watermelon** into small chunks (discarding the rind), and freeze them. When frozen, put them in a food processor with **½ cup yogurt, 2 tablespoons sugar,** and **1 tablespoon lemon juice.** Process until just smooth, being careful not to let it become watery. Transfer to a shallow glass or ceramic dish, and freeze for at least 1 hour.

Spicy Thai with Crab

Substitute **lime juice** for the lemon juice. Add **a minced fresh hot chile** (like Thai or serrano) and **fish sauce,** to taste. After pouring the soup into bowls, top with a small mound of **lump crabmeat.** Garnish: **chopped fresh cilantro.**

Peach and Blue Cheese

Substitute **2 large ripe peaches** for the tomatoes and **sherry vinegar** for the lemon juice. After pouring the soup into bowls, top with **a few crumbles of blue cheese.** Garnish: **chopped fresh tarragon** and **a drizzle of olive oil.**

Ice Pops

Purée **the unfrozen watermelon chunks** in a blender, substituting **2 tablespoons lime juice** for the yogurt and adding enough water (or fruit juice) so that the mixture liquefies. Pour into molds and freeze.

Granita

Use a blender. Use **2 tablespoons lemon juice** and skip the yogurt; blend until the mixture liquefies. Pour the mixture into a shallow glass or ceramic pan, and freeze for about 2 hours, breaking up the ice crystals with a fork every 30 minutes or so. It should be slushy and crunchy.

GRAPEFRUIT
+12 WAYS

Grapefruits are curious. There's a tacit acknowledgment that they're delicious—people eat them plain for breakfast—but most cooks seem to have never used them as an ingredient in anything other than fruit salad. Why a food worthy of its own kind of spoon has been deemed largely unfit for savory cooking is beyond me.

Chopped into chunks or sliced into supremes (more on that in a moment), grapefruit adds an incomparable hit of brightness to salads and raw-fish dishes, while its juice brings an ideal blend of sweetness and acidity to sauces and vinaigrettes.

To prepare a grapefruit for cooking, cut a small slice from each end, and stand it up flat on a cutting board. Cut down around the outside to remove the skin and pith from the flesh. To make supremes (half-moon slices that don't include the membrane), use a paring knife to cut out wedges from between the membranes. If you don't mind including the membranes (I don't, usually), just chop the whole thing into rough chunks. Or you can peel and section it as you would an orange, and then chop.

The recipes serve four.

RAW

Shaved Fennel and Olives

Peel **a grapefruit** and chop the flesh or slice it into supremes. In a bowl, toss with **thinly sliced fennel, chopped pitted green olives,** and **olive oil;** toss to combine. Garnish: **fennel fronds.**

Crudo

Skip the fennel and olives. Thinly slice **raw yellowtail, hamachi, tuna,** or **scallops** and lay the slices on a plate. Place **grape-fruit supremes** on top, then drizzle with **olive oil.** Garnish: **fresh chives.**

Squid Ceviche

Substitute **thin rings of raw squid** for the fennel and **sliced red onion** for the olives. Squeeze in **some extra grapefruit juice** and **a sprinkle of hot red chile flakes.** Let sit for 30 minutes. Garnish: **chopped fresh cilantro.**

BROILED

Brown Sugar and Butter

Halve **a grapefruit** (or more), and run a serrated knife around the inside rim of each half. Sprinkle the cut sides with **brown sugar** and top with **a few dots of butter.** Broil until the sugar caramelizes, 2 to 5 minutes, depending on your broiler.

Olive Oil and Tarragon

Substitute **salt** for the brown sugar and **olive oil** for the butter. Garnish: **chopped fresh tarragon.**

Spicy

Substitute **chili powder, ground cumin,** and **cayenne** for the brown sugar, and **vegetable oil** for the butter. Garnish: **chopped fresh cilantro** (and **queso fresco,** if you like).

STIR-FRIED

Beef, Chiles, and Mint

Heat a skillet on high until nearly smoking, add **2 tablespoons oil** and **1½ pounds sliced sirloin or ribeye.** Cook until it loses its red color. Add **1 tablespoon each minced garlic, ginger,** and **fresh hot green chile.** Cook until fragrant; add **1 chopped grapefruit;** toss. Garnish: **mint.**

Lamb, Curry, and Cilantro

Substitute **lamb shoulder** for the beef, and **curry powder** for the chile. Garnish: **lots of chopped fresh cilantro.**

Pork and Scallion Noodles

Substitute **pork loin or shoulder** for the beef, and **five-spice powder** for the chile. Serve over **Chinese egg noodles or udon.** Garnish: **chopped scallions** and **a drizzle of soy sauce.**

VINAIGRETTES / SAUCES

Grapefruit and Dijon Vinaigrette

Whisk together (or use a blender) **6 tablespoons grapefruit juice, 1 teaspoon Dijon mustard,** and about **½ cup olive oil.** Shallots and/or herbs are good in here, too.

Nuoc Cham

Substitute **1 teaspoon minced garlic, ½ teaspoon minced hot fresh chile,** and **4 teaspoons sugar** for the mustard, and **4 tablespoons fish sauce** for the olive oil.

Butter Sauce with Dill

In a small saucepan, combine **2 tablespoons minced shallots** and **⅓ cup each grapefruit juice** and **white wine.** Reduce to a few tablespoons over medium heat; let cool. Over low heat, whisk in **½ cup (1 stick) butter** bit by bit until creamy. Stir in **chopped dill.**

JAM
+RECIPE GENERATOR

It's hard to argue with the impulse to eat fruit raw in summer. After a while, though, there may be a hankering to do something to it: make a pie, or a crisp, or jam. Jam—which is the whole fruit, sweetened, seasoned, and cooked—does much more justice to summer's bounty than jelly, which is cooked, strained into juice, and thickened, usually with pectin.

Homemade jam is in a category all by itself because, not to put too fine a point on it, it actually reminds you of the fruit from which it's made, rather than melted fruit-flavored sugar, as are most mass-produced jams.

You might be wary of making your own jam, but this isn't the old-fashioned jam we're talking about, with Mason jars, canning tongs, pots of steam, and loads of sweat. It's less about preserving the harvest (that's what freezers are for) and more about making the kind of jam you keep in your fridge for a week or two. All that is needed is delicious fresh fruit and 30 minutes of your time.

Many commercial jams are 50 percent sugar by weight. I think somewhere around 10 percent makes more sense. You don't hear many people complaining about the sourness of good strawberries or peaches, so why load them up with sugar?

Because sugar plays three legitimate roles in jam-making: as a thickener, a sweetener, and a preservative. I am less concerned with the last of these, as we're not making forty-eight jars of jam to last through the winter and spring; mine rarely last a week. I do, however, like a little more body than most fruit gives me when it's cooked (though many berries are naturally loaded with pectin, and don't need any thickening agent), and sometimes I like a little extra sweetness.

If you don't care about either, skip the sugar entirely. If you care only about sweetening, you might try honey or maple syrup. To me, ¼ cup sugar (or honey or syrup) is usually plenty for a pound of fruit, but start with less and taste as you go. It's also fun to play around with different flavorings. In addition to spices and herbs, you'll need to add a couple tablespoons of liquid, which expands the flavor possibilities: citrus juice, port or red wine, balsamic or sherry vinegar, rosewater, and brandy are all suitable.

It is quite possible to make exquisite jam with nothing more than ripe fruit and a saucepan. Provided that you don't eat all the fruit before you begin.

Jam Universal Instructions

Put 1 pound fruit (pitted and chopped, if necessary) in a medium saucepan over medium heat. After a minute or so, add ¼ cup sugar (or to taste), seasonings to taste, and 2 tablespoons juice, vinegar, or whatever liquid you prefer. Adjust the heat so the mixture bubbles steadily, using higher heat if the mixture looks too soupy; lower the heat if it seems dry. Cook, stirring occasionally, until the mixture is thick—10 to 30 minutes. Cool completely and refrigerate; it will thicken more as it cools. Store in the refrigerator, where it will keep for at least a week. If necessary, remove any flavorings (like lemongrass stalks) before serving.

Figs

Cherries

Nectarines

Raspberries

Blackberries

Plums

Apricots

Strawberries

Basil

Rosemary

Cardamom

Vanilla

Cinnamon

Mint

Lavender

Lemongrass

FLAVORINGS

DESSERTS AND BAKING

While I don't have the biggest sweet tooth in the world, I definitely have a soft spot for desserts. The first dish I ever made from a recipe was a chocolate pie in a meringue shell, and I can still remember how satisfying (and surprising, frankly) it was when it came out perfect. Desserts can be simple, sweet fixes that round out a meal, impressively complicated cooking projects that take all day, or anything in between, and though this chapter is far from the longest in the book, it covers an impressive amount of that ground.

On the simple end of the spectrum there are ice pops (perfect for kids, just not the boozy ones), all-purpose cookies, and shortbread doughs that you can spin a hundred different ways, and even pâte à choux, the fancy French cream puff pastry that's a lot easier than you might think. If you're up for something a bit more involved, try the Knafeh à la Crème (page 286, a beautiful shredded phyllo pie from one of my cooking idols, Claudia Roden).

You may get too caught up in the Dessert Bar Recipe Generator to even realize that there are bread recipes, too: all whole wheat, no kneading, tons of flavor. After eating the pungent sourdough rye, you're probably going to want something sweet; fortunately, you've come to the right place.

COOKIES
+12 WAYS

Cookie recipes are just about infinite because almost anything can be shaped into a circle and baked—hence, gluten-free, dairy-free, sugar-free "cookies." But at its most basic a cookie contains three key ingredients: butter, flour, and sugar. That combination has not been bettered, and it can be varied in so many ways that you hardly need another recipe.

This dough can be doubled, tripled, and so on, and refrigerated up to two days in advance (or frozen for longer) and flavored as you like. Then spoon it out and fill it for thumbprints, chill and roll it and frost it, turn it into "sandwiches," or press and spread it into bars. Master those options, and you can create pretty much any cookie you can dream of.

The Basic Dough Universal Instructions

MAKES: 2 to 3 dozen (or half as many sandwich cookies)

½ cup (1 stick) unsalted butter, softened

¾ cup granulated sugar

1 teaspoon vanilla extract

1 large egg

2 cups all-purpose flour

½ teaspoon baking powder

Pinch of salt

¼ cup milk, plus more if needed

1. Heat the oven to 375°F. Use an electric mixer to cream together the butter and sugar; add the vanilla and egg and beat until well blended.

2. Combine the flour, baking powder, and salt in a bowl. Add half the dry ingredients to the dough, beat for a moment, then add the milk. Beat for about 10 seconds, then add the remaining dry ingredients and a little more milk, if necessary, to make a soft dough. Shape and bake using one of the four variations that follow.

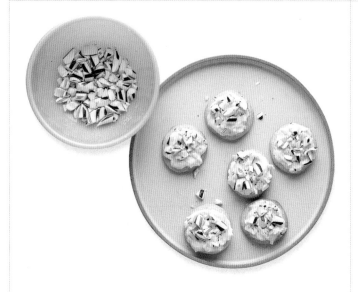

Coconut and Cream Cheese Icing

Roll **the dough** by hand into three logs of equal size and chill for at least 2 hours. Heat the oven. Slice off rounds to create cookies. Bake until the edges are brown, about 10 minutes. Cool for about 2 minutes on baking sheets before using a spatula to transfer the cookies to a rack to finish cooling. Beat together **8 ounces softened cream cheese** and **1 cup confectioners' sugar** until fluffy; beat in **1½ teaspoons vanilla extract** and **¼ cup shredded coconut**. When cookies are completely cooled, cover generously with frosting or icing. After frosting, sprinkle the cookies with **additional shredded coconut**.

Simple Lemon Curd

Roll **the dough** into 1½-inch balls, then press your thumb into the middle and flatten the ball, making an indentation. Arrange on baking sheets and bake until the bottoms are brown, about 10 minutes. Cool on the baking sheets for 2 minutes before transferring the cookies to a rack to cool slightly. Melt **½ cup (1 stick) butter** in a medium saucepan over low heat. Remove from heat and cool slightly. Add the **juice of 3 lemons, 1 cup sugar,** and **5 large egg yolks,** stirring constantly. Return the pan to medium-low heat and cook until the mixture coats the back of a spoon. Strain, then add the **grated zest of 3 lemons.** Cool until thick. (Makes enough lemon curd to fill 2 to 3 dozen thumbprint cookies.) While the cookies are still warm, add teaspoons of lemon curd to the depressions.

Mocha Frosting

Melt **1 ounce unsweetened chocolate** in a microwave or double boiler and set aside. Cream **½ cup (1 stick) butter** and gradually work in 4 cups **confectioners' sugar,** alternating with **4 tablespoons heavy cream** (more if necessary). Stir in the chocolate, **2 tablespoons instant espresso, 2 teaspoons vanilla extract,** and a pinch of **salt**.

Vanilla Frosting

Cream **½ cup (1 stick) butter** and gradually work in **4 cups confectioners' sugar,** alternating with **6 tablespoons heavy cream** (more if necessary). Stir in **2 teaspoons vanilla extract** and **a pinch of salt.** Optional: smash **candy canes** and sprinkle onto frosted cookies.

Dark Chocolate and Sea Salt

Bake the cookies without filling, then let cool slightly. While the cookies are still warm, **place chunks of dark chocolate** into the thumbprints and sprinkle with **sea salt.**

Jam

Drop **1 teaspoon of jam, marmalade, or preserves** into the thumbprints and bake.

Chocolate-Buttercream Frosting

Roll out **the dough** by hand into three logs of equal size, then chill. Slice off rounds to create cookies. Bake until the edges are brown, about 10 minutes. Cool for about 2 minutes on baking sheets, then use a spatula to transfer the cookies to a rack to finish cooling. Melt **2 ounces unsweetened chocolate** over low heat and let cool. In a mixing bowl, cream ½ **cup (1 stick) butter** and gradually beat in **2 cups confectioners' sugar**, alternating with **3 tablespoons heavy cream**. Add the melted chocolate. Add **2 more cups confectioners' sugar**, alternating with **3 more tablespoons cream**. If the frosting is too thick, stir in a little more cream, a teaspoon at a time. Stir in **2 teaspoons vanilla extract** and a pinch of salt. Smear **the frosting** on the bottoms of two cookies and smush them together.

Butterscotch and Cayenne

Spread **the dough** onto the bottom of a deep, well-greased 9 by 13-inch baking pan (or one lined with parchment). Bake for 20 to 25 minutes, until just barely set in the middle. Take the bars out of the oven when the edges are still firming up and the middle is a bit soft; they will cook as they cool. Combine **1 cup heavy cream, 10 tablespoons butter,** and **1½ cups packed brown sugar** in a small saucepan over medium heat, stirring frequently. Adjust the heat so the mixture bubbles gently, and cook, stirring occasionally, until the mixture is shiny and coats the back of a spoon, 10 to 15 minutes. Spread the mixture over the cooled cookie layer and sprinkle with **cayenne.** Refrigerate until set, then cut into squares and serve.

Dulce de Leche Frosting

Combine ⅔ cup whole milk, ⅔ cup granulated sugar, and 1 teaspoon each vanilla and corn syrup in a pan. Cook over medium heat until the sugar dissolves, then whisk in **a pinch of baking soda.** Simmer over low heat until the mixture is dark (about 45 minutes). Pour into a bowl and let cool completely, scraping off any foam that forms on top. Cream **1 stick butter;** gradually work in **2 cups confectioners' sugar,** alternating with **3 tablespoons heavy cream.** Beat in the dulce de leche and **a pinch of salt.** If necessary, refrigerate to solidify.

Orange-Mascarpone Frosting

Beat together **1 cup mascarpone cheese** with **2 tablespoons confectioners' sugar** and the **grated zest of 1 orange.** Keep the frosted cookies refrigerated.

Fig Bars

Place **1 cup bourbon, brandy, or water** in a medium saucepan over high heat. When it steams, stir in **1½ to 2 cups dried figs,** turn off the heat, and cover. Let stand until soft, 10 to 15 minutes. Drain well, reserving a little of the liquid. Transfer the figs to a food processor and add another ½ **cup dried figs.** Pulse until the mixture is puréed and comes together, adding a few drops of the reserved liquid, if necessary, to keep smooth. Spread **8 ounces of softened cream cheese** over the cookie layer, then top with the fig mixture.

Pecan Pie

Melt **8 ounces semisweet chocolate;** pour onto the cookie layer and set aside. Make the caramel: Put **1½ cups granulated sugar** in a heavy saucepan and cook gently over medium heat, shaking the pan occasionally, until the sugar melts. Continue to cook, stirring occasionally and scraping sides with a heatproof spatula, until golden, 4 to 5 minutes. Turn the heat to low and carefully stir in ½ **cup heavy cream** until the mixture is smooth. Fold **1½ cups crushed pecans** into the caramel and turn off the heat. Spread the mixture onto the chocolate-coated cookie base.

SHORTBREAD +12 WAYS

Shortbread cookies are—when correctly made—rich, crumbly, and impossible to resist. In their simplest form they taste mostly of sweet and sweetened butter, so the best butter you can lay your hands on will make a difference here. I like that side-of-the-tongue tingling presence of saltiness, and so I tend to use a little more salt than is strictly necessary, hence the range in the recipe.

You can flavor shortbread cookies in many different ways, and most variations are pretty easy. Citrus is most appealing to me, but I also love shortbread made savory, even with the addition of a bit of olive oil.

These cookies are so easy that kids can make them, but they do require a bit of care; once you add the flour, proceed as gently as possible. You don't want to overdevelop the gluten, which will make the cookies tougher than they might be otherwise. (With this much fat, they'll never be anything but tender, but there are degrees of tenderness.)

You can enlist the help of a cookie cutter to make shapes, or go the easy route, rolling the dough into a log and slicing off rounds. Chilling is crucial. (Conveniently, you can leave the dough in the freezer for up to a few days, if you like, and once chilled, the dough is a dream to work with.)

Shortbread Universal Instructions

MAKES: 1½ to 2½ dozen

1	cup (2 sticks) unsalted butter, at room temperature
¾	cup sugar
1	large egg yolk
1½	cups all-purpose flour
½	cup cornstarch
¼	to ½ teaspoon salt

1. Use an electric mixer on low speed to combine the butter and sugar, about 30 seconds. Keeping the speed on low, beat in the egg yolk, then the flour, cornstarch, and salt until the mixture barely holds together. Don't overbeat.

2. To make shapes, form the dough into a ball, wrap in plastic, and freeze or refrigerate for at least 30 minutes, until firm. Roll it out on a lightly floured surface until it is ¼ inch thick. Cut into any shapes you like, then chill in an ungreased baking sheet for at least 1 hour. Alternatively, shape the dough into a log and refrigerate or freeze until firm, at least 30 minutes. Slice ¼-inch cookies and put on an ungreased baking sheet.

3. Heat the oven to 275°F. Bake the cookies until just firm but still quite tender and not at all brown, about 30 minutes. Cool for 1 minute on the sheet before using a spatula to transfer the cookies to a rack to finish cooling.

Espresso-Chocolate

Melt **1 ounce bittersweet chocolate** in a double boiler or microwave and let it cool a bit. Beat the chocolate into **the butter and sugar** before adding **the egg yolk.** Add **1 tablespoon instant espresso powder** with **the dry ingredients.**

Chocolate-Dipped

Melt about **1 cup semisweet chocolate** in a double boiler or microwave; stir until smooth. Dip **the baked shortbread** into the chocolate and put on wax paper to dry and harden.

Vanilla or Almond

Add **1 teaspoon vanilla or almond extract** along with **the egg yolk.**

Orange

Add **2 tablespoons grated orange rind** with the egg yolk.

Lemon-Poppy Seed

Reduce the **butter to 14 table-spoons** (not quite 2 sticks). Add **2 tablespoons lemon juice** and **1 tablespoon lemon zest** with the egg yolk. Add **1 tablespoon poppy seeds** with **the dry ingredients.**

Coconut-Lime

Heat the oven to 325°F. Spread **½ cup shredded unsweetened coconut** on a rimmed baking sheet and bake until toasted, about 3 minutes; cool slightly. Add **2 tablespoons lime zest** with **the egg yolk;** add the **toasted coconut** with **the dry ingredients** and bake at 275°F.

Crystallized Ginger

Reduce the **sugar to ½ cup** and add **½ cup finely chopped crystallized ginger.**

Cinnamon Sugar

Reduce the **sugar to ½ cup** and add **¼ cup packed brown sugar.** Add **1 teaspoon ground cinnamon** with **the dry ingredients.**

Nuts

Add **½ cup chopped pecans, pistachios, or almonds** and **1 teaspoon ground cinnamon,** if you like.

Rosemary and Olive Oil

Reduce the **butter to 12 tablespoons** and add **¼ cup olive oil.** Add **1 teaspoon minced fresh rosemary** with **the dry ingredients.**

Parmesan

Add **½ cup grated Parmesan** with **the dry ingredients.**

Black Pepper

Add **½ teaspoon freshly ground black pepper** with **the dry ingredients.**

DESSERT BAR
+RECIPE GENERATOR

Cacao nibs

Blackberry mousse (or chocolate)

Brownies

THE BASE

Biscotti

Ladyfingers

Shortbread

Mini pie crusts or tartlet shells

Meringues (coffee-flavored, vanilla, chocolate)

Any kind of cookies (chocolate crinkle, chocolate chip, plain sugar)

THE FILLING

Whipped cream

Lemon pudding

Thinned raspberry jam

Ricotta whipped with honey

Ice cream or sorbet (strawberry, mango)

THE TOPPING

Caramel popcorn

Toasted, shredded coconut

Almond brittle

Butterscotch or caramel sauce

Chocolate Sauce (page 281) topped with flecks of cayenne

Macerated strawberries, blueberries, and raspberries

Sliced kiwi, banana, or other fresh fruit

Fruit sauce: cooked peaches

While DIY dessert bars most immediately call to mind those first-grade birthday parties where kids get to build their own sundaes, they should by no means be off limits to adults (and can actually lead to some rather sophisticated plated sweets).

Many of these ingredients can be store-bought, and most keep well enough so that you can have them around to put something like this together on short notice. (I'm not suggesting that you put all of them out at once, but you could; just three or four of each make for terrific possibilities.)

Some ideas for the base are mini pie crusts, ladyfingers, shortbread, brownies, cookies, little pancakes. For the filling, try pudding or custard, ice cream or sorbet, yogurt with sugar or ricotta with honey or cream cheese with confectioners' sugar and vanilla. Thinned jam (just warm it) is also really nice.

Toppings, as with sundaes, can be simple or sophisticated: add a pinch of cayenne to chocolate sauce, or chop cashews or pecans. To make caramel sauce, simply melt a few tablespoons of butter in a saucepan on low heat, then add ½ cup sugar and ¼ cup heavy cream and stir until the mixture is smooth. Fresh fruit will become more of a treat as summer arrives: macerate blueberries or strawberries, poach some pears, slice some kiwi.

So fill a pie crust with chocolate mousse and add some caramel corn (why not?). Or try a slice of shortbread with lemon pudding and peaches. The seven-year-old in you would have put the caramel corn and the peaches on the mousse, and that's okay, too. The animating spirit behind the dessert bar is endless variety. There are almost 800 variations here alone.

DOUGHNUTS
+4 WAYS

Here's something I've never quite understood. Places that serve fried food—french fries, fried chicken, tempura, you name it—either serve it straight from the fryer, at its peak, or they find some way, often a heat lamp, to keep it as crisp as possible. So why don't doughnuts get the same love? Most are so far removed from that bubbling bath of oil by the time you eat them that they've almost entirely lost their fresh-fried luster.

That's why, I'm sorry to say, if you want a truly great, hot, crisp doughnut, chances are you're going to have to make it yourself. Like anything involving deep-frying, DIY doughnuts are a bit of a

project, but they're less work than you might think. And once you've mastered the basic recipe—this one is for fluffy yeasted doughnuts, as opposed to the denser cake variety—you can geek out to your heart's content on the glazes, toppings, and fillings.

The recipes here are just the beginning. Roll plain doughnuts in sugar mixed with cinnamon, lemon zest, or ground nuts. Make the glaze with citrus juice—or alcohol—instead of milk. Fill doughnuts with whipped cream and roll them in pulverized bacon, if that's your thing. Just don't let them sit around too long before you eat them. They'll keep, but a doughnut deserves better.

Raised Doughnuts

MAKES: About 1 dozen

1¼	cups milk	1	teaspoon salt
2¼	teaspoons (1 package) active dry yeast	4¼	cups all-purpose flour, plus more as needed for dusting
2	large eggs	2	quarts neutral oil, for greasing and frying
½	cup (1 stick) butter, melted and cooled		
¼	cup granulated sugar		

1. Heat the milk until it is warm but not hot, about 90°F. In a large bowl, combine it with the yeast. Stir lightly, and let sit until the mixture is foamy, about 5 minutes.

2. Using an electric mixer or a stand mixer fitted with a dough hook, beat the eggs, butter, sugar, and salt into the yeast mixture. Add half the flour (2 cups plus 2 tablespoons), and mix until combined, then mix in the rest of the flour until the dough pulls away from the sides of the bowl. Add more flour, about 2 tablespoons at a time, if the dough is too wet. If you're using an electric mixer, the dough will probably become too thick to beat; when it does, transfer it to a floured surface, and gently knead it until smooth. Grease a large bowl with a little oil. Transfer the dough to the bowl, and cover. Let rise at room temperature until it doubles in size, about 1 hour.

3. Turn the dough out onto a well-floured surface, and roll it to a ½-inch thickness. If making doughnuts with holes, cut out the doughnuts with a doughnut cutter, concentric cookie cutters, or a drinking glass and a shot glass (the larger one should be about 3 inches in diameter), flouring the cutters as you go. Reserve the doughnut holes. If you're making filled doughnuts, don't cut out the middle. Knead any scraps together, being careful not to overwork, and let rest for a few minutes before repeating the process.

4. Put the doughnuts on two floured baking sheets so that there is plenty of room between them. Cover with a kitchen towel, and let rise in a warm place until they are slightly puffed up and delicate, about 45 minutes.

5. About 15 minutes before the doughnuts are done rising, put the oil in a heavy-bottomed pot or Dutch oven over medium heat, and heat it to 375°F. Meanwhile, line some cooling racks, baking sheets, or plates with paper towels.

6. Carefully add the doughnuts to the oil, a few at a time. When the bottoms are deep golden, 45 seconds to 1 minute, use a slotted spoon to flip them; cook until they're deep golden all over. Add the doughnut holes, if you're making them; they cook faster, only about half a minute. Transfer the doughnuts to the prepared plates or racks, and repeat with the rest of the dough, adjusting the heat as needed to keep the oil at a steady 375°F. Glaze or fill the doughnuts as desired, and serve as soon as possible.

Classic Glazed Doughnuts

Whisk together **2 cups confectioners' sugar, ¼ cup milk,** and **1 teaspoon vanilla** until smooth. When **the doughnuts** are cool enough to handle, dip the tops into the glaze; if you like, flip and dip again so both sides are covered. Put on racks to let the glaze harden.

Boston Cream Doughnuts

For the glaze, whisk together **1¾ cups confectioners' sugar, ¼ cup unsweetened cocoa powder,** the **¼ cup milk,** and **1 teaspoon vanilla** until smooth. For the filling, combine **⅔ cup granulated sugar, 2 tablespoons all-purpose flour, 2 tablespoons cornstarch,** and **a pinch of salt** in a small saucepan. Over medium heat, whisk in **2 large eggs** and **2 cups heavy cream.** Continue cooking, whisking almost constantly, until the mixture just begins to boil and thicken, about 10 minutes. Adjust the heat so the mixture bubbles gently; cook until it coats the back of a spoon (when you draw your finger through this coating, the resulting line should hold its shape). Stir in **2 tablespoons softened unsalted butter** and **2 teaspoons vanilla.** Strain through a fine-mesh sieve, and cool to room temperature before using. Dip the tops of the doughnuts into the glaze, let it harden on a rack, then fill doughnuts with the pastry cream.

Jelly Doughnuts

When **the doughnuts** are cool enough to handle (but still warm), roll them around in a **shallow bowl of granulated sugar** to coat. Inject with **your favorite jelly.**

PÂTE À CHOUX

Gougères—baked cream puff pastries with cheese—belong to the remarkable category of dishes that are incredibly impressive and also require very little work. The secret to gougères—and other types of cream puffs, profiteroles, éclairs, even churros—is pâte à choux (paht-ah-SHOO), a dough that's both endlessly useful and shockingly fast and uncomplicated to make.

All of these confections, which seem like the exclusive domain of French pastry chefs with floppy white hats, start with this magical dough, which contains only four ingredients and comes together almost without thought: you vigorously beat butter, water, and flour over heat, then stir in eggs one at a time (this actually requires some elbow grease, though you can use an electric mixer) until the batter is smooth. Start to finish, the process takes about 3 minutes, and if you do the stirring by hand, you'll save yourself a trip to the gym.

A piping bag (an inexpensive investment that lasts forever) is the easiest way to form the dough into whatever shape you choose, but you can always use a plastic freezer bag with one corner snipped off, or two spoons. Any imperfections that occur with a plastic bag or spoons can be repaired by dipping your finger into water and smoothing out the rough spots.

When baked, the dough puffs up to at least double its size (hence "cream puff," the American term for a profiterole), leaving a hole in the middle that's begging to be filled. I've included recipes for the most likely candidates—pastry cream and whipped cream, each with flavoring options—as well as one for the world's easiest chocolate sauce.

But this is just the beginning; because pâte à choux contains no sugar, a savory filling is as natural a choice as a sweet one. So you could use prosciutto, pesto, or something like a spinach-artichoke dip, as well as ice cream, fruit jam, or honeyed mascarpone. Mix some cheese into the dough before baking, and you've got gougères; pipe strips of the dough into hot oil, and you've got churros. The possibilities are nearly endless. Just don't tell your guests how easy it was.

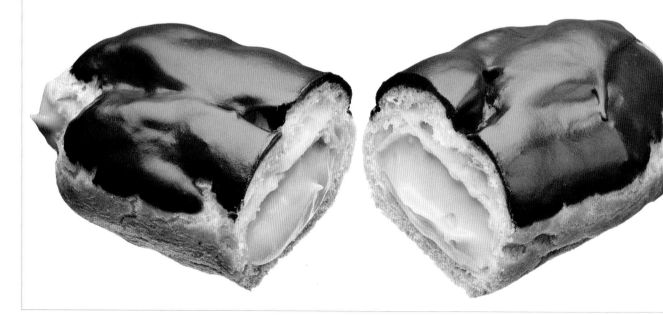

Basic Cream Puff Pastries

MAKES: 2 to 4 dozen pastries, depending on size

½   cup (1 stick) unsalted butter, plus more for greasing

Salt

1   cup all-purpose flour

4   large eggs

1. Heat the oven to 400°F and grease a baking sheet with a little butter. Put the butter and a pinch of salt in a saucepan over high heat; add 1 cup water and bring to a boil. Turn the heat to low and add all the flour at once; stir constantly with a wooden spoon until the mixture pulls away from the pan and forms a ball, about 30 seconds. Remove the pan from the heat and beat in the eggs one at a time (use an electric mixer, if you like), and beat until the mixture is smooth. (At this point, you can cover the dough and refrigerate it for up to two days.)

2. Scoop the dough into a pastry bag with a plain ½-inch tip, or a plastic freezer bag with a corner cut off. Pipe the pastry into rounds onto the baking sheet, or just use two spoons to form your desired shape. Cream puffs should be about 1 inch wide and a little over 1 inch tall; éclairs should be 3- to 4-inch fingers, about 1 inch wide.

3. Bake until the pastries are golden brown, nicely puffed up, and sound hollow when you tap on them, about 30 minutes for cream puffs and 40 minutes for éclairs. Use a skewer to prick one or two holes in each one to allow the steam to escape; transfer to a rack and let cool to room temperature.

4. To fill the pastries using a pastry bag, poke a hole into the bottom of the pastry and pipe the filling into it, or cut off the top caps of each pastry, spoon in the filling, and close it up like a sandwich. (Éclairs can be slit open and filled, too.) Serve as is, or drizzle with chocolate sauce.

PASTRY CREAM
MAKES: 2½ cups

⅔   cup sugar

2   tablespoons all-purpose flour

2   tablespoons cornstarch

   Salt

2   large eggs

2   cups heavy cream, half-and-half, or whole milk

2   tablespoons unsalted butter, softened

2   teaspoons vanilla extract

1. Combine the sugar, flour, cornstarch, and a pinch of salt in a small saucepan. In a separate bowl, mix the eggs and cream. Over medium heat, whisk the egg mixture into the sugar mixture; whisk occasionally at first to get rid of lumps, then pretty much constantly until the mixture starts to boil and thickens, about 10 minutes.

2. Adjust the heat so the mixture bubbles gently. The mixture is ready when it coats the back of a spoon; when you draw your finger through this coating, the resulting line should hold its shape. Stir in the butter and vanilla, and strain the mixture through a fine-mesh strainer. Let cool to room temperature before using.

VARIATIONS:

CHOCOLATE PASTRY CREAM: Add 2 ounces chopped semisweet chocolate to the mixture as it cooks.

COFFEE PASTRY CREAM: Add 1 tablespoon instant espresso or 2 shots freshly brewed espresso to the mixture as it cooks.

BOOZY PASTRY CREAM: Skip the vanilla. Add 2 tablespoons Scotch, bourbon, rum, or port to the finished mixture while it's still hot.

WHIPPED CREAM
MAKES: 2 cups

With a whisk or an electric mixer, beat **1 cup heavy cream** (and up to **¼ cup sugar,** if you like) to nearly stiff peaks, making sure not to overbeat. Use plain, or fold in any of the following:

- **Vanilla seeds** scraped from ½ pod, or **1 teaspoon extract**
- **Spices** (a pinch of ground cinnamon, cardamom, nutmeg, or cloves)
- **Citrus zest** (½ teaspoon grated)
- **Alcohol** (1 to 2 tablespoons bourbon, Grand Marnier, amaretto, framboise, Kahlúa, or whatever you like)
- **Ginger** (½ teaspoon finely grated or minced fresh ginger)
- **Maple syrup** (1 tablespoon, in place of some of the sugar)
- **Herbs** (1 tablespoon minced fresh mint or basil)

EASIEST CHOCOLATE SAUCE
MAKES: 1½ cups

In a small saucepan or in the microwave, melt together **1 cup milk** and **4 ounces chopped semisweet chocolate.** Remove from the heat and add another **4 ounces of chocolate;** stir until the chocolate is melted and the mixture is thickened and slightly cooled.

FRUIT DESSERTS
+12 WAYS

In late summer, some berries, peaches, plums, and cherries are still around, and fall fruits like figs, grapes, and especially apples and pears are at their peak of both flavor and supply. While this bounty may whisper "pie" to you, I urge you to reconsider.

If I'm going to sweeten, embellish, and cook fresh fruit—in other words, make it into a dessert—I want every additional ingredient to pull its weight. To me, pie crust contributes little aside from heft and calories. But a streusel topping of butter, oats, nuts, and cinnamon never fails to whet my appetite. Neither does a little sweetened cream or fresh cheese drizzled over the fruit and broiled to make a gratin, or a pancake-style batter poured over it to create the eggy baked French dessert known as a clafoutis. Sometimes I dispense with any topping at all and just gently poach some fruit in a little sweetened liquid—water or wine, infused with spices or herbs or nothing at all—for a dessert that's killer on its own or with a scoop of vanilla ice cream on top.

The ideas in these recipes are well suited to improvisation, especially when it comes to the fruit: feel free to use raspberries instead of blackberries, or nectarines instead of mangos. In fact, almost any fruit can sub for any other as long as you bear in mind that different fruits cook at different rates. Very soft berries and ripe stone fruits require almost no cooking time before they become tender and release their juices, but apples and pears take a little longer to soften, whether you're roasting, baking, broiling, or poaching them. I like my crisps on the juicy side; if you prefer a less liquid filling, add a tablespoon or two of flour or (even better) cornstarch to the fruit. The crisps and gratins serve 6 to 8, the clafoutis serve 4 to 6, and the poached fruit serves 4.

CRISP	GRATIN

Corn and Blueberry

Heat the oven to 375°F. Toss **5 cups fresh blueberries** and **1 cup fresh corn kernels** with the **juice of ½ lemon, 2 tablespoons granulated sugar,** and **2 teaspoons cornstarch.** Spread in a greased 8- or 9-inch square pan. Combine ⅔ cup packed brown sugar, 5 tablespoons cold butter, ½ cup rolled oats, ½ cup all-purpose flour, ½ cup chopped pecans, ½ teaspoon ground cinnamon, and a dash of salt in a food processor; pulse a few times. Crumble over the fruit and bake until the topping is browned, 40 to 45 minutes.

Blackberry Gratin with Sour Cream

Heat the broiler. Toss **6 cups fresh blackberries** with **2 teaspoons each sugar and cornstarch.** Sauté in **1 tablespoon butter** over medium heat until tender and beginning to thicken, about 5 minutes. Spread in a greased 9 by 13-inch pan. Whisk together **1 cup sour cream, ¼ cup milk, ¼ cup sugar, 1 tablespoon cornstarch,** and **½ teaspoon vanilla.** Drizzle over the berries and broil 4 to 6 inches from the flame until lightly browned, 3 to 5 minutes. Let sit for 5 minutes before serving.

Strawberry Crisp with Pine-Nut Topping

Substitute **6 cups quartered fresh strawberries** for the blueberries and corn. Substitute **pine nuts** for the pecans, and add **½ teaspoon almond extract** to the topping if you like.

Sweet Peach and Tomato Crisp with Coconut-Cashew Topping

Substitute **4 cups sliced peaches** and **2 cups sliced tomatoes** for the blueberries and corn, **¼ cup each shredded coconut and chopped cashews** for pecans, and **¼ teaspoon ground ginger** for half the cinnamon.

Honeyed Plum

Substitute **6 cups sliced ripe plums** for the berries. Substitute **honey** for the sugar in **the sour-cream mixture.**

Apple and Walnuts

Substitute **6 cups sliced apples** (peeled or not) for the berries; sauté in two batches (in **1 tablespoon butter** per batch) over medium heat for 10 minutes each. Substitute **honey** for the sugar and **cinnamon** for the vanilla in **the sour-cream** mixture, and sprinkle the apples with **¼ cup walnuts** before drizzling on the apples.

Cherry Pistachio

Heat the oven to 350°F. Combine **¾ cup heavy cream, ¾ cup milk, ½ cup sugar, 3 large eggs, ⅓ cup all-purpose flour,** and **½ teaspoon almond extract** in a blender; blend until smooth. Put **1 pound fresh cherries** (pitted or not) in a buttered and floured 8- or 9-inch pan. Pour the batter over the cherries and scatter **¼ cup pistachios** on top. Bake until nicely browned on top and a knife inserted into the middle comes out clean, about 40 minutes.

Butter-Vanilla Pears

Combine **2½ cups sugar,** 5 cups water, **4 tablespoons (½ stick) butter,** and **a vanilla bean** split in half in a saucepan and bring to a boil. Peel **4 pears** and core them by digging into the bottom end with a melon baller, spoon, or paring knife, leaving the fruit whole. Add the pears to the pan and simmer over medium-low heat, turning occasionally, until tender, 10 to 20 minutes. Cool, then transfer the pears to serving plates. Simmer the liquid until reduced by half; drizzle over the pears.

Peach Clafoutis with Star Anise

Substitute **3 ground star anise** (a coffee grinder works), **½ teaspoon vanilla,** and **a pinch of cayenne** for the almond extract. Substitute **quartered ripe peaches** for the cherries, and skip the pistachios.

Mango Coconut

Substitute **½ teaspoon each vanilla and ground cinnamon** for the almond extract, and use **coconut milk** instead of milk. Substitute **cubed fresh mango** for the cherries, and skip the pistachios.

Pineapple in White Wine with Rosemary and Black Pepper

Substitute **a not-too-dry white wine** (like Riesling) for half the water, and **1 fresh rosemary sprig** and **¼ teaspoon black pepper** for the vanilla. Skip the butter. Substitute **1 pineapple, cut into chunks,** for the pears.

Apricots in Spiced Red Wine

Substitute **fruity red wine** (like pinot noir) for half the water. Substitute **5 slices of fresh ginger** and **1 teaspoon ground cardamom** for the vanilla, and skip the butter. Substitute **10 to 12 halved fresh pitted apricots** for the pears.

KNAFEH À LA CRÈME

I had been cooking for only a few years when a friend gave me *A Book of Middle Eastern Food*, by Claudia Roden. In my cooking life, there has been no more important influence than that book.

Born in Cairo to a family of Syrian Jews, educated in Paris, and a longtime resident of London, Roden has written extensively about the foods of North Africa, Spain, the Mediterranean, and the Middle East. Her *Book of Jewish Food* is the most comprehensive work on the subject, and unlike many books on the topic, it gives equal weight to the cooking of Sephardic and Ashkenazi Jews.

Knafeh à la Crème

SERVES: 12

FOR THE SYRUP

2¼ cups sugar

2 tablespoons lemon juice

2 tablespoons orange-blossom water

FOR THE CREAM FILLING

¾ cup rice flour

5 cups milk

4 tablespoons sugar

1½ tablespoons orange-blossom water

⅔ cup heavy cream

FOR THE PASTRY

1 pound knafeh pastry, or shredded phyllo

1 cup (2 sticks) unsalted butter, melted

⅔ cup pistachios, coarsely chopped.

1. Make the syrup: Boil the sugar, 1¼ cups water, and the lemon juice for 10 to 15 minutes, then add the orange-blossom water. Let it cool, then chill in the refrigerator.

2. Make the filling: Mix the rice flour with enough of the cold milk to make a smooth paste. Bring the rest of the milk to a boil. Add the rice-flour paste to the boiling milk, stirring vigorously with a wooden spoon. Leave on very low heat and continue to stir constantly until the mixture thickens, being careful not to let it burn. Add the sugar and orange-blossom water and stir well. Refrigerate until cool before adding the cream and mixing well.

3. Make the pastry: Put the knafeh pastry in a large bowl. Pull out and separate the strands as much as possible with your fingers so they do not stick together. Pour the melted butter over it and work it in very thoroughly with your fingers, pulling out and separating the strands and turning them over so they do not stick together and are entirely coated with butter.

4. Heat the oven to 350°F. Spread half the pastry on the bottom of a 12-inch pie pan. Spread the cream filling over it evenly and cover with the rest of the pastry. Press down and flatten with the palm of your hand. Bake for about 45 minutes, then raise the temperature to 425°F and bake 15 minutes longer, or until the pastry colors slightly.

5. While the knafeh is still hot, run a sharp knife around the edges of the pie to loosen the sides and turn out onto a large serving dish. Pour the cold syrup all over the hot knafeh, and sprinkle the top with chopped pistachios. (You could also pour half the syrup before serving and pass the rest around for guests to help themselves to more.) Serve immediately.

This beautiful pie of knafeh (essentially, shredded phyllo) filled with a cream thickened with rice flour and scented with orange-blossom water, is as exotic now as Roden's first round of recipes was to me forty years ago.

ICE POPS
+12 WAYS

The summertime appeal of ice pops is easy to understand. They're sweet, colorful, lickable, and a manageably small snack in an age of gargantuan portions. They recall a simpler time, before the era of artisanal-gelato shops. And they're cold.

Too bad the ice pops you buy at the supermarket tend to be sickeningly sweet and neon bright, thanks to an abundance of high-fructose corn syrup and artificial colors. Thankfully, this is something you can easily remedy, because it's child's play to make ice pops at home, as long as you have a blender or a food processor (and for some recipes, not even that); some ice-pop molds, either purchased or jerry-rigged; and a freezer.

You might be surprised at what you can freeze—and what tastes good frozen. The suggestions here represent just a few possibilities and, I think, interesting ones. Some are recreations of childhood treats, though without the unpronounceable ingredients. Others, like the entire savory quadrant, were inspired by flavor profiles I've come to appreciate as an adult. The boozy ones, similarly, are intended for a grown-up palate and have enough alcohol in them to serve as an aperitif (try the Mojito, page 291) or afternoon attitude adjuster.

If you don't have, and don't want to buy, plastic molds, just pour the mix into 4 to 6 paper cups and stick them in the freezer. After an hour or so, insert a wooden stick into each cup—the mixture will have solidified enough that the stick should stay upright—and continue to freeze until totally solid.
To remove the pops from their molds, run them under cool running water for a few seconds to loosen them. Then unmold and lick to your heart's content. These recipes make eight ice pops.

FRUITY	SAVORY

Strawberry Basil

Purée **2 cups hulled and quartered strawberries, 3 tablespoons sugar, 2 teaspoons lemon juice, 2 tablespoons fresh basil leaves,** and water as needed to get the machine going.

Avocado Cilantro

Purée **2 ripe avocados, ¼ cup lime juice, ½ cup fresh cilantro leaves, 1½ cups water,** and **salt** and **pepper.**

Peach Ginger

Purée **2 cups chopped fresh peaches** (peeled or not), **3 tablespoons sugar, 2 teaspoons lemon juice, ½ pinch of grated fresh ginger,** and water as needed.

Cherry Vanilla

Purée **2 cups pitted fresh cherries, 3 tablespoons sugar, 2 teaspoons lemon juice, 2 teaspoons vanilla,** and water as needed.

Tomato Cucumber

Purée **1 pound ripe tomatoes, ½ small seeded cucumber, 2 tablespoons olive oil, 1 tablespoon sherry vinegar, 1 garlic clove, ½ cup water,** and **plenty of salt** and **pepper.**

Coconut Curry

Purée **2 cups coconut milk, 1 inch peeled fresh ginger, 1 tablespoon curry powder, 1 small hot fresh chile, 2 tablespoons lime juice,** and **salt** and **pepper.**

CREAMY	BOOZY

Orange Cream

Whisk together **⅔ cup milk, 1⅓ cups orange juice, 3 tablespoons sugar,** and **½ teaspoon vanilla** until the sugar dissolves.

Grapefruit Campari

Cook **¼ cup sugar** and ¼ cup water over medium-low heat until the sugar dissolves. Combine with **1½ cups grapefruit juice** and **½ cup Campari.**

Chocolate Chili

Cook **2 cups milk, 6 ounces chopped bittersweet choc- olate, 3 tablespoons sugar, 1 tablespoon cocoa powder,** and **¼ teaspoon chili powder** over medium-low heat, stirring, until smooth. Stir in **½ teaspoon vanilla.** Cool slightly before freezing.

Banana Peanut

Purée **2 medium bananas, 1 cup milk, ¼ cup sugar, ¼ cup peanut butter,** and **½ teaspoon vanilla.** Sprinkle **1 teaspoon chopped roasted peanuts** into each ice-pop mold before adding the banana mixture.

Fennel Pernod

Make **the sugar syrup** as above. Purée with **2 cups coarsely chopped fennel** and **½ cup Pernod or other anise liqueur.**

Mojito

Make **the sugar syrup** as above. Purée with **⅓ cup rum, ½ cup fresh mint leaves, ⅓ cup lime juice,** and 1 cup water.

WHOLE WHEAT BREAD +3 WAYS

Those of us who cook believe that you have to cook to eat well; baking bread is different. With so many relatively decent loaves readily available in stores, bread baking can be regarded as more of a hobby than a necessity. The result, of course, will be eaten and enjoyed—and bakers know the rewards of blowing people's minds with a good loaf. But baking is not mandatory.

As with any practice, baking skills improve over time. But the odd thing about bread making is that any epiphanies you have along the way are only temporarily gratifying. You always make progress, but then your standard rises; and in the end, baking provides that oddly addictive combination of satisfaction and frustration. So recently I've challenged myself to make 100 percent whole-grain bread, and to make it delicious.

The results of that challenge are the recipes here, developed through plenty of trial and error, and inspiration from some of the best bread bakers I know (Charles Van Over, Jim Lahey, and Trine Hahnemann). While my quest to make the perfect whole-grain loaf is ongoing, I find these three versions—a crusty baguette, dense, chewy, sourdough rye, and olive-oil-rich focaccia—to be incredibly satisfying. For now.

Not Quite Whole-Grain Baguettes

MAKES: 3 loaves

100 grams rye or whole wheat flour (about ¾ cup)

400 grams all-purpose flour (a scant 3 cups), plus more for handling

10 grams kosher salt (about 2½ teaspoons)

6 grams instant yeast (about 2 teaspoons)

1. Combine the dry ingredients in the bowl of a food processor. With the machine running, add water until a ball forms, about 30 seconds. (Start with 1½ cups water; you may need a little more or less.) Then process for an additional 30 to 45 seconds. Put the dough ball in a bowl, cover with plastic wrap, and let sit until risen, 2 to 3 hours.

2. Cut the dough into 3 pieces, and using an absolute minimum of flour to prevent sticking, form each into a rough log. (You could also make one large boule, or a ciabatta-shaped loaf.) Cover with a towel and let sit about 20 minutes. Then shape into long baguettes; support their shape by letting them rise in baguette pans or a lightly floured piece of canvas. Heat the oven to 465°F. (If you have a pizza stone, leave it on the rack you'll be baking the loaves on.)

3. The loaves will be slightly puffed and ready to bake in 30 minutes or so. Slash or cut the top of the loaves. Slide into the oven on a peel or in baguette pans. Bake, lowering the heat if necessary to prevent browning, until the loaves read 210°F internally (not more), 20 to 30 minutes. Cool on a rack.

Whole Wheat Focaccia

MAKES: 1 loaf

400 grams whole wheat flour, plus more for dusting (3 cups)	3 tablespoons plus 1 teaspoon olive oil
6 grams instant yeast (about 2 teaspoons)	Kosher salt, for sprinkling
	Freshly ground black pepper
8 grams kosher salt (2 teaspoons)	1 tablespoon chopped fresh rosemary

1. Combine the flour, yeast, and salt in a food processor. Turn the machine on and add 1 cup warm water (or more as needed) and 1 tablespoon of the oil through the feed tube. Process until the dough becomes a barely sticky, easy-to-handle ball, about 30 seconds. If it's too dry, add more water a tablespoon at a time and process for another 10 seconds. If it's too wet (unlikely), add more flour 1 tablespoon at a time. Shape the dough into a ball and roll in a bowl with the teaspoon of oil. Cover and let rise until it almost doubles in size, from 1½ to 2 hours.

2. Grease a large baking sheet with another tablespoon of oil. Press the dough onto the sheet, spreading it ¼ to ½ inch thick; dimple the top with your fingertips and sprinkle with salt, pepper, and rosemary; drizzle with the remaining tablespoon of olive oil. Cover with a towel and let the dough sit until it puffs nicely, 60 minutes.

3. Heat the oven to 500°F. Bake until golden and springy to the touch, 10 to 15 minutes. Let cool on the baking sheet before cutting.

Sourdough Rye

MAKES: 2 loaves

FOR THE SOURDOUGH STARTER	2 cups rye flour
2⅔ cups rye flour	2 cups whole wheat or white flour
Pinch of instant yeast (no more than 1/16 teaspoon)	1 tablespoon kosher salt
FOR THE DOUGH	1½ cups cracked rye or rye flour
Sourdough starter	

1. Make the starter: In a tall, narrow, nonmetal widemouth jar or straight-sided pitcher, mix ⅔ cup rye flour with ½ cup water, along with the instant yeast. Cover and let sit for about 24 hours, then add another ⅔ cup flour and ½ cup water (no more yeast). Repeat twice more, at 24-hour intervals. Then, 24 hours after the fourth addition, you have your starter. (From now on, keep the starter in the refrigerator; you don't need to proceed with the recipe for a day or two if you don't want to. Before using the starter, set aside a ladleful—½ to ¾ cup—in a container and stir in ½ cup rye flour and a scant ½ cup water. Mix well, cover, and refrigerate for future use. This starter will keep for a couple of weeks. If you don't use it during that time and you wish to keep it alive, add ½ cup each flour and water every week or so and stir.)

2. Make the dough: Combine the remaining starter in a big bowl with the rye flour, the whole wheat or white flour, and 2¼ cups water. Mix well, cover with plastic wrap, and let sit overnight, up to 12 hours.

3. The next morning, the dough should be bubbly and lovely. Add the salt, the cracked rye, and 1 cup water—it will be more the consistency of a thick batter than a traditional dough.

4. Pour and scrape the dough into two 8 by 4-inch nonstick loaf pans. The batter should come to within 1 inch of the top, no higher. Cover (an improvised dome is better than plastic wrap; the dough will stick to whatever it touches) and let rest until it reaches the rim of the pans, 2 to 3 hours, usually.

5. Heat the oven to 325°F and bake the loaves until a skewer comes out almost clean, about 1½ hours or a little longer; the internal temperature will measure between 190°F and 200°F.

6. Remove the loaves from the pans and cool on a rack. Wrap in plastic and let sit for a day before slicing, if you can manage that; the texture is definitely better the next day.